ST. MARY PARISH LIBRARY

3 3446 00644 8399

D1762242

748.2075 Felt, Tom. 2009
FEL
Encyclopedia BOOK
of Cobalt

ENCYCLOPEDIA OF Cobalt Glass

IDENTIFICATION & VALUES

Tom Felt
and
Gene & Bernadette Girard

COLLECTOR BOOKS
A Division of Schroeder Publishing Co., Inc.

Front cover, clockwise from top left: Cambridge Glass Company compote, 7" high x 7" diameter, $150.00 – 160.00. United States Glass Company footed cheese and cracker with domed cover, 5⅝" high x 10" diameter, $60.00 – 70.00 set. H. C. Fry Glass Company candle holder, 4" high x 4" diameter base, $200.00 – 250.00 pair. Imperial Glass Corporation triple-light heart candlestick, 6¼" high x 8½" wide x 4⅝" diameter base, $75.00 – 85.00 each. Dunbar Glass Corporation three horizontal ribbed vase with Rockwell decoration, 8" high x 5" diameter top, $50.00 – 60.00.

Back cover: Hazel-Atlas Glass Company Newport. Left to right: (1) Footed sherbet, 2⅞" high x 3⅝" diameter, $12.00 – 15.00; (2) sherbet plate, 5⅞" diameter, $5.00 – 6.00; (3) oval platter, 11¾" x 9¼", $35.00 – 40.00; (4) high footed salt and pepper, 4¼" high, pair $35.00 – 40.00; (5) handled cream soup, 2¼" high x 4⅝" diameter, $15.00 – 20.00; (6) luncheon plate, 8½" diameter, $10.00 – 15.00; (7) cup, 2¾" high x 3¼" diameter, $10.00 – 12.00; (8) saucer, 5⅝" diameter, $4.00 – 5.00; (9) round platter, 11" diameter, $35.00 – 40.00; (10) creamer, 4¼" high x 2⅞" diameter, $12.00 – 15.00; (11) footed sugar, 4" high x 2⅞" diameter, $12.00 – 15.00; (12) cereal bowl, 2" high x 5½" diameter, $35.00 – 40.00. Louie Glass Company pitcher, 8¾" high x 6¼" diameter, $50.00 – 60.00.

Cover design by Beth Summers
Book design by Beth Ray
Photography by Bob O'Grady

COLLECTOR BOOKS
P.O. Box 3009
Paducah, Kentucky 42002 – 3009

www.collectorbooks.com

Copyright © 2009 Tom Felt & Gene and Bernadette Girard

All rights reserved. No part of this book may be reproduced, stored in any retrieval system, or transmitted in any form, or by any means including but not limited to electronic, mechanical, photocopy, recording, or otherwise, without the written consent of the authors and publisher.

The current values in this book should be used only as a guide. They are not intended to set prices, which vary from one section of the country to another. Auction prices as well as dealer prices vary greatly and are affected by condition as well as demand. Neither the authors nor the publisher assumes responsibility for any losses that might be incurred as a result of consulting this guide.

Searching for a Publisher?

We are always looking for people knowledgeable within their fields. If you feel that there is a real need for a book on your collectible subject and have a large comprehensive collection, contact Collector Books.

Proudly printed and bound in the United States of America

CONTENTS

Introduction…4
History of Cobalt…6
Identifying Cobalt Glass…7
Pricing…8
Acknowledgments…8
Candlesticks…9
Console Sets…45
Bowls…70
Compotes…86
Candy and Nut Dishes…102
Table Settings…110
Cake Stands…120
Cheese and Cracker & Chip and Dip Sets…122
Center Handle Servers…124
Trays and Platters…127
Relish, Celery, and Pickle Dishes…130
Mayonnaise Sets…133
Gravy Bowls…134
Salt and Pepper Shakers & Salt Dips…135
Sugar Bowls…137
Cookie and Sweet Meat Jars…138
Kitchen Items…139
Cups and Saucers…142
Mugs…158
Glasses and Tumblers…159
Pitchers…160
Decanters…167
Bar Items…185
Cocktail Shakers…195
Smoking Items…205
Perfumes…209
Bottles…210
Children's Dishes…211
Kerosene and Oil Lamps…215
Miscellaneous Items…221
Baskets…223
Vases…224
Appendix: Company Information…267
Reference and Bibliography…297
Index…299

INTRODUCTION

Most glass manufacturers produced cobalt glass at one time or another during their existence. Early American pressed glass and blown wares from the nineteenth century included limited cobalt items. Few of these are included in this book as they are scarce and usually expensive. Elegant Art Glass or Off Hand Art Glass in cobalt are represented by Durand Art Glass and the Imperial Glass Corporation, both of whom produced free hand glass, circa 1923 to 1931. Most of the cobalt glass in this book is from two categories. The first is the machine made glassware usually referred to as "Depression Glass" from the mid 1920s to World War II. The second is the hand finished glass, or so called "Elegant Depression Glass," from approximately the same time frame.

Cobalt glass has become popular again in the past twenty years. Many of these items are reissues by companies that produced them earlier, reissued from old molds by different or new companies, and new or reproduction molds, both domestic and imported. Some of these newer items have been included in this book, both because they are attractive and to help distinguish old from new. An appendix at the end of the book lists all of the manufacturers represented and, where possible, we have included dates for their production of cobalt glass.

The book is divided into sections by the type of item included. Companies are alphabetical in each chapter and items shown for each company are in roughly chronological order. Unattributed items appear at the end of each section, with those that can be assigned to a particular country appearing before those whose nation of origin is unknown.

Bowls and candlesticks may be found in their respective sections or in the one devoted to console sets. Identical items are not duplicated in both sections. Footed bowls and compotes are separated by size. Items in this category under eight inches in diameter will be found in compotes, and items over eight inches in diameter in bowls or console sets. Descriptions of items follow a standard format: company name, line number if known, dimensions, and pattern name. An original company name is given without quotation marks, while a name given by collectors or researchers appears in quotation marks, with the originator of the name also indicated when known. We have also included color names whenever a company used terminology other than cobalt. Royal blue, Ritz blue, and regal blue were among some of the more popular names utilized by companies.

Because most of the photographs in this book are nearly the same size, dimensions have been included for all items. At least one and often two or three dimensions have been taken from the actual examples in the photograph. Dimensions in the catalogs often vary from catalog to catalog and may be different from the actual item. A candlestick or bowl listed as ten inches will often measure plus or minus one-half inch. Measurements from one actual example to another can easily vary plus or minus one-fourth inch or more, particularly in the case of bowls and other pieces with hand finished rims.

We have tried to include a representative sampling of cobalt glass and to make this book as comprehensive as possible, but clearly it is not a complete encyclopedia of every piece ever made. That would require a volume ten to fifty times the size of this one! We have utilized many resources in compiling this work and encourage the reader to consult the reference and bibliography section for further information.

Introduction

Rare Stiegel Blue

THUS runs the headline of the James McCreery advertisement from which this illustration was taken. It first appeared in that smart weekly, the *New Yorker*. There is color in the copy that is somehow transferred to the black and white reproduction. It runs:

"Deep as Sapphire, the exquisite blue that Baron Stiegel created while America was still young—the blue that makes you catch your breath when you see the few priceless specimens in the American Wing at the Metropolitan—lives again in this charming decorative stemware. A blue that is at once the essence of things old and precious—modern and smart. The fashion significance of blue glass is proved by its use at such exclusive restaurants as the Ritz, the Embassy Club, the Crillon. A pleasant discovery to find it at McCreery's priced at $10 the dozen."

Good, colorful copy.

Plate 1. Trade journal report on the popularity of Stiegel blue (a name used by some companies for cobalt) from the *Crockery & Glass Journal*, May 1928.

HISTORY OF COBALT

Cobalt glass has been around for thousands of years. Glass containing cobalt has been discovered from the Babylonian-Assyrian period, the Mycenaean era, and the Roman Empire. A specimen of glass containing cobalt was found in Tut-Ankh-Amen's tomb from circa 1321 BC. These earliest examples of glass containing cobalt were probably the result of ancient glass workers acquiring ingredients with cobalt in it by chance. Sometime between 1100 AD and 1400 AD cobalt was used to color the glass in church windows.

Commercially, cobalt was not used as a glass colorant until the late 1800s. True cobalt blue is a dark navy blue. Many people call the lighter more delicate blues made with copper compounds cobalt blue because of the higher price it commands on the market place. Small quantities of cobalt were produced by American glass companies in the late 1800s to mid 1920s. Most of the American cobalt glass in this book is from the mid 1920s to World War II. Several companies, including the Hazel-Atlas Glass Company, the L. E. Smith Glass Company, and the Macbeth-Evans Glass Company, produced the machine molded cobalt glass during the 1930s that can be considered true depression glass. Often this glass had patterns or designs molded in the glass that disguised the imperfections. Both the machine made and hand finished elegant glass are included in this book and collectors will have to determine the merit of each.

The consumer demand for darker hues in glassware reached its peak during this period. Often pieces found in cobalt blue will be found in ruby, ebony, amethyst, and dark green, all colors prominent in this time period. World War II curtailed the production of these colors because the materials used as colorants were required for the war effort. After World War II consumer demand reverted to crystal and lighter colored glass and most glass companies followed this trend. A lot of the cobalt glass produced after World War II was molded and not hand finished as the glass from the finer companies of the 1920s and 1930s had been.

England and many European countries also made cobalt glass. Ludwig Moser and Sohne and other contemporaries from Bohemia produced high quality cobalt blown and molded hand made glass from the 1880s into the 1930s, which is often cut and decorated with gold and paint. The most commonly found cobalt imports are from Germany, Czechoslovakia, and Austria from the period of 1918 to the 1930s. Most of these imports are blown with rough ground tops and sometimes bases, decorated with gold or silver. These imports were competitive with the American glass companies and attempts were made by the glass companies to have tariffs imposed without much success. These imports, other than the high quality glass made by companies like Moser, do not command the prices for cobalt glass today, even when compared to the machine made cobalt glass by American companies. These imports, often of better color, design, and workmanship, may find their place with collectors as American Depression and hand finished glass becomes scarcer and more expensive.

IDENTIFYING COBALT GLASS

COLOR

The cobalt colored glass made by American manufacturers varies in depth of color, tint, and brilliance. Most of the 1920 – 1940 glass companies made very dark cobalt blues that are difficult to differentiate. These companies used between one and three ounces of cobalt oxide per one hundred pounds of batch. Other metals or compounds that have effect on the appearance of cobalt glass are copper or copper oxides, potassium, and lead or lead oxides.

Copper oxide most often imparts a blue color that is on the green side to the glass. When used with cobalt as a colorant it has a tendency to block the red or purple tinge that cobalt produces. Much of the cobalt glass made by the Cambridge Glass Company (as royal blue) shows this red to purple color. Not surprisingly, Cambridge's 1933 formulae for royal blue does not include copper oxide. This does not guarantee that all Cambridge royal blue will exhibit this red or purple color. Glass companies continually experimented with their colors and changed batch formula to decrease cost, improve handling, alter the color, or modify other properties. The best way to observe any difference in the color of glass is in direct sunlight.

Potassium in the glass batch increases the brilliancy or reflective qualities and the smoothness of the glass. A. H. Heisey and Company's cobalt (Stiegel blue) contains more than double the amount of potash or potassium oxide in the batch than was used by other companies. As a result, Heisey's Stiegel blue glass stands out in its brilliancy.

Lead or lead oxide in the batch increases the refractive index of the glass. Refraction refers to the way light waves are bent and reflected from the interior of the glass. The H. C. Fry Glass Company and Cambridge Glass Company included lead oxide in their cobalt batches.

Of the hand made glass companies, H. C. Fry and Central Glass Works produced blue glass with very little cobalt oxide and relied on copper oxide to produce blue. These blues are much lighter in color and the depth of the blue. Fry glass can be distinguished from Central by its brilliancy, smoothness and higher refractive index.

Comparing an unknown piece of glass with identified pieces in direct sunlight will often help in narrowing the field of companies who might have produced it. The most noticeable difference will be in color and brilliancy.

PATTERN

Pattern refers to the design molded in the glass when it is produced. Most machine-made glass has a pattern or design. Examples of these would be the Hazel-Atlas Glass Company's Royal Lace and Moderntone. Many of the hand finished glass companies also offered molded designs in the glass. The Cambridge Glass Company's #3400 line has four spires on the sides, the Paden City Glass Manufacturing Company's #412 and # 890 "Crow's Foot" patterns have a line of little bumps that end in a fleur de lis at the edge, and so on. The problem with identification by pattern is due to the practice of one company copying the design of another with small differences introduced, in response to the success of the competitor's pattern in the marketplace. The small differences were made to avoid patent infringement laws. Attention to detail is extremely important in differentiating between two patterns with similar design motifs.

SHAPE

Identifying glass that does not have a pattern or design associated with a company's line can sometimes be accomplished by shape. Glass was pressed or blown in a mold to give it the basic shape. The still hot pliable glass was then removed from the mold and manipulated by hand to give it a final shape. As an example, the same mold for a bowl could be used to produce a bowl with a flattened, rolled, flared, cupped, ruffled, or crimped rim. Similarly, molds for vases were often used to make cocktail shakers or pitchers by hand finishing the tops or applying a handle in the case of a pitcher. Thus it is important to look at the lower portion of these items where hand finishing does not usually alter the basic shape. If an item such as a bowl, compote, vase, or candlestick has a stem, this is often a clue to its identity. Stems are most often molded with little alteration by hand finishing.

Identifying Cobalt Glass

Much of the satisfaction in collecting glass comes from the challenge of identifying the company that made an item and when it was produced. If you are in the business of buying or selling glass, identification is important in determining value. On the internet, identification is important as many collectors limit their purchases to one or several companies and limit their search to just those companies.

PRICING

Prices are given as a range for the item(s), as pictured. Pairs of items such as candlesticks are usually more desirable, hence one half of the lower price for a pair should be considered as the value for a single one. Most items in sets, other than candlesticks, are given an individual price range. The range will vary depending on the value of an item, with more expensive pieces having a larger range.

The prices have been determined based on dealers' prices at glass shows and shops, auctions, internet listings, and personal buying experience. In some cases the ranges differ from other published sources; when this occurs it is because they reflect the prices for which these item are selling for in the current marketplace. Prices have changed in the past ten years due to the influence of internet auctions, in particular. Desirable, high quality, scarce, or rare items have increased in value due to bidder competition. Other items, which were regionally scarce but now are abundant, have decreased. The Hazel-Atlas Glass Company's Royal Lace line in cobalt is a prime example. Ten years ago the going price for a dinner plate was $45.00 – 50.00. Currently you can buy a cobalt Royal Lace dinner plate in excellent condition for 50% of the old value, including shipping.

All prices are for complete items in excellent condition. Chips, cracks, stains, scratches, and other damage decrease an item's value. Scratches and wear on the bottom are expected and will not affect value. The value of very old (nineteenth century) and very rare pieces are less affected by minor imperfections but more commonplace items may be virtually un-salable if damaged.

Attractive and well executed etchings and cuttings add to the value of an item. Simple and/or poorly executed etchings and cuttings add little and may even detract from the value. Gold, silver, and platinum decorations are very attractive on cobalt glass, and will add value if in good condition. Worn or peeled decorations will detract from the value of an item.

In no way are price ranges in this book meant to set prices or influence the market. They are a guide for collectors and dealers who might want a starting point. The final price will remain an issue to be determined by the buyer and the seller.

ACKNOWLEDGMENTS

We are grateful to everyone who has helped us during the course of preparing this book for publication. Special thanks to Bob Carlson, Sheldon & Helen Chazin, Kelly Conway, Don Crabb, Jason Lalli, Rosalyn Lalli, Louis Lopilato-Cartagena, David McInturff, Dean Six, Kathy & Larry Thompson. We were also aided in ways large and small by the staffs of the Chrysler Museum of Art, Norfolk, Virginia, the Fostoria Glass Society of America, Moundsville, West Virginia, the Museum of American Glass in West Virginia, Weston, West Virginia, the National Heisey Glass Museum, Newark, Ohio, the Rakow Research Library of the Corning Museum of Glass, Corning, New York, and the Wheaton Arts Museum of American Glass, Millville, New Jersey.

CANDLESTICKS

Plate 2. A. A. Importing Company #OG1648 Diana the Huntress candlesticks. 10½" high x 4¾" diameter base. Circa 1977 – 1979. Pair $35.00 – 40.00.

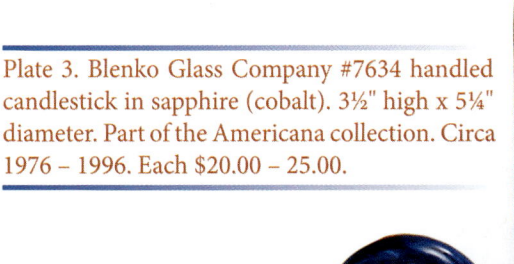

Plate 3. Blenko Glass Company #7634 handled candlestick in sapphire (cobalt). 3½" high x 5¼" diameter. Part of the Americana collection. Circa 1976 – 1996. Each $20.00 – 25.00.

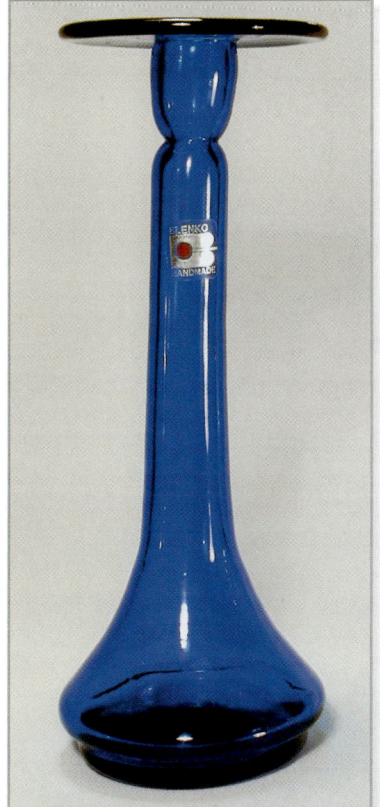

Plate 4. Blenko Glass Company #8810S blown candlestick in sapphire. 9½" high x 3¼" base. Also made as #8810M (11⅜" high) and #8810L (15" high). Circa 1988 only. Each $25.00 – 30.00. (Photograph courtesy of Richard Stoer.)

Candlesticks

Plate 5. Boston and Sandwich Glass Company wafer joined two part candlestick. 9⅛" high x 4" hexagonal base. Circa 1875 – 1887. Each $300.00 – 350.00.

Plate 6. Cambridge Glass Company twist stem candlesticks in cobalt blue 1 or 2. 8½" high x 4½" diameter base. Probably cobalt blue 1, since this is a lighter blue than most cobalt blue 2 items. Circa 1924 – 1926. Pair $65.00 – 75.00.

Plate 7. Cambridge Glass Company #109 Dolphin candlesticks in cobalt blue 2. 9½" high x 5" diameter base. Circa 1925 – 1926. Pair $350.00 – 450.00.

Candlesticks

Plate 8. Cambridge Glass Company #2862 candlesticks in Ritz blue. 6½" high x 3½" diameter base. Unknown silver decoration similar to Rockwell Silver Company decoration. Circa 1929 – 1931. Pair $90.00 – 100.00.

Plate 9. Cambridge Glass Company blown candle/vase with unknown gold encrusted acid etching. 9½" high x 3¼" diameter base. Circa early 1930s. Pair $100.00 – 120.00.

Plate 10. Cambridge Glass Company #225 ball stem candlesticks in royal blue. 9⅜" high x 4⅝" diameter base. Circa 1931. Pair $140.00 – 150.00.

Candlesticks

Plate 11. Cambridge Glass Company #3500/74 Gadroon candlesticks in royal blue. 4½" high x 4⅝" diameter base. Circa 1933 – 1940s. Reissued by the Fenton Art Glass Company in 1989, but only in colors other than cobalt and marked with the Fenton logo. Pair $70.00 – 90.00.

Plate 12. Cambridge Glass Company #3500/31 Gadroon candlesticks in royal blue. 6" high x 4⅝" diameter base. Circa 1933 – 1940. This is an early version of the candlestick. It was later redesigned to have rams' heads on the candle socket, as on the #3500/74. Reissued by the Imperial Glass Corporation circa 1970 – 1972 in cobalt with the Aurora Jewels carnival finish, marked IG on the base. Pair $100.00 – 110.00.

Plate 13. Cambridge Glass Company #1273 candlesticks in royal blue with Wheeling Decorating Company gold encrusted acid Minton style etching. 9½" high x 4⅛" base. Circa 1933. Pair $175.00 – 200.00.

Candlesticks

Plate 14. Cambridge Glass Company #1402/80 Tally-Ho candlestick in royal blue with Cambridge's gold decoration #D/1007. Circa 1933. Each $65.00 – 75.00.

Plate 15. Cambridge Glass Company #627 candlesticks in royal blue. 4" high x 4⅞" diameter base. Circa 1933 – 1942. Pair $80.00 – 90.00.

Plate 16. Cambridge Glass Company #628 candlesticks in royal blue. 3¼" high x 4⅝" diameter base. Circa 1933 – 1942. Pair $60.00 – 70.00.

Candlesticks

Plate 17. Cambridge Glass Company #3500/108 Gadroon candlesticks in royal blue. 2⅝" high x 4" diameter base. Circa 1939 – 1941. Pair $45.00 – 55.00.

Plate 18. Cambridge Glass Company #1338 three-light candlestick in royal blue. Usually called Caprice, although originally issued as part of the Gadroon pattern and used with other lines. Circa late 1930s – 1942. Each $175.00 – 225.00.

Plate 19. Central Glass Works #2000 trumpet shaped candlesticks in royal blue, with unknown gold line decoration. 9" high x 4½" diameter base. Circa 1924 – 1930s. Pair $90.00 – 100.00.

Candlesticks

Plate 20. Central Glass Works #2000 trumpet shaped candlesticks in royal blue. 7" high x 3⅞" diameter base. These in combination with a flared bowl made up a console set called "Zaricor" by Hazel Marie Weatherman. Circa 1924 – 1930s. Pair $60.00 – 70.00.

Plate 21. Co-operative Flint Glass Company #279 candlesticks. Called "Sawtooth" by collectors. 6¾" high x 3¼" diameter base. This candlestick was originally introduced circa 1902 and remained in production until at least 1928. This shade of blue differs enough from the cobalt brought out by the company in 1924 to identify it as a color from much earlier, probably when the candlestick was first issued. Pair $35.00 – 40.00.

Plate 22. Co-operative Flint Glass Company #449 candlesticks. 9" high x 4¼" diameter base. Also made in 7½" height with a 3⅜" diameter base (as #448) and in 10" height with a 4⅝" diameter base (as #450). Circa 1924 – 1934. Pair $140.00 – 150.00.

Candlesticks

Plate 23. Co-operative Flint Glass Company #503 candlesticks. 5⅝" high x 4¾" diameter base. Designed for 1½" diameter candles. With unknown gold encrusted acid etching decoration. Circa 1924 – 1934. Pair $60.00 – 70.00.

Plate 24. Co-operative Flint Glass Company #503 candlestick. 5⅝" high x 4¾" diameter base. Designed for 1½" diameter candle. The crystal insert, which is 1" at the top, tapering to ¾", made it possible to use a standard taper candle. Circa 1924 – 1934. Each $30.00 – 35.00. (Photograph courtesy of Robert Carlson.)

Plate 25. Co-operative Flint Glass Company #322 Ray candlesticks. 7⅜" high x 3⅜" hexagon base. Also made in a 9⅛" height with a 4⅛" diagonal base as part of the Ray or Douglass patterns. Circa 1924 – 1934. Pair $65.00 – 75.00.

Candlesticks

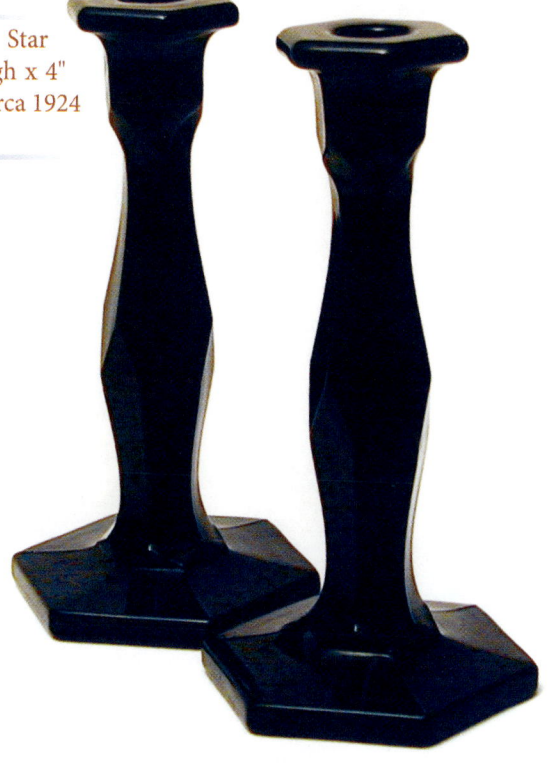

Plate 26. Co-operative Flint Glass Company Star candlesticks, unknown pattern number. 8¼" high x 4" hexagon base. Also made in 5" and 7" heights. Circa 1924 – 1934. Pair $90.00 – 100.00.

Plate 27. Dalzell Viking hexagonal candlesticks. 7½" high x 3½" hexagon base. Made for the Metropolitan Museum of Art and marked MMA on the bottom. Circa 1988 – 1998. Reproduction of a candlestick originally made by the New England Glass Company, circa 1850 – 1870. Previously reproduced for the MMA by the Imperial Glass Corporation, circa 1979 – 1984. Pair $40.00 – 50.00.

Plate 28. Dalzell Viking #1937 Dolphin candlesticks. 4" high x 3¼" hexagon base. Made from the Westmoreland Glass Company #1049 small dolphin mold. Circa 1988 – 1998. Pair $30.00 – 40.00.

Candlesticks

Plate 29. Dalzell Viking #1938 Dolphin candlesticks. 9¼" high x 3¾" hexagon base. Made from the Westmoreland Glass Company #1049 large dolphin mold. Circa 1990 – 1998. Pair $40.00 – 50.00.

Plate 30. Dalzell Viking #970 candlestick. 3⅞" high x 4¼" diameter base. Made from the New Martinsville Glass Manufacturing Company/Viking Glass Company #970 mold. Circa 1993 – 1998. Each $15.00 – 20.00.

Plate 31. Dalzell Viking #8566 squirrel tail candlestick. 6½" high x 3½" x 4" rectangular base. Reissue of the New Martinsville Glass Manufacturing Company/Viking Glass Company #415 Flame candlestick. Circa 1994. Each $15.00 – 20.00.

Candlesticks

Plate 32. Diamond Glass-Ware Company candlesticks. Called "Mae West" by collectors. 8" high x 4¾" diameter base. Heavy silver deposit of bird and branches with flowers by Rockwell Silver Company, Meriden, Connecticut. Marked on the bottom rim "R S Co. Sterling" and stamped on bottom with Rockwell shield and number 232. Circa 1923 – 1925. Pair $60.00 – 70.00.

Plate 33. Diamond Glass-Ware Company trumpet shaped candlestick, with silver decoration consisting of baskets of flowers and medallions by unknown decorator. The same decoration is on a console set by the U. S. Glass Company (plate 177 on page 68). 9" high x 4⅜" diameter base. Circa 1928 – 1931. Each $20.00 – 25.00.

Plate 34. Diamond Glass-Ware Company #99 candle holder with gold edging and branch with leaves by unknown decorator. 3⅛" high x 4" square base. See plate 125 on page 50 for a Diamond #99 console set. Circa 1930 – 1931. Each $25.00 – 35.00.

Candlesticks

Plate 35. Duncan and Miller Glass Company #28 candlesticks. 3¾" high x 4¼" diameter base. Also made in 5¾" height. Circa 1931 – 1937. Pair $100.00 – 120.00.

Plate 36. Duncan and Miller Glass Company #111 Terrace candlestick. 3" high x 4" diameter base. Circa 1935 – 1937. Each $75.00 – 80.00.

Plate 37. Duncan and Miller Glass Company #113 Radiance candle holder. 3⅞" high x 4¼" base. Circa 1937. Each $30.00 – 35.00. (Photograph courtesy of Richard Stoer.)

Candlesticks

Plate 38. Farber Shlevin, Inc. 8" high four-light candle holder and two 6" high two-light candle holders, marked "Diana Chrome, Farber Shlevin, Inc., Brooklyn, New York." Unattributed glass. Set $120.00 – 130.00.

Plate 39. Fenton Art Glass Company #1611 candle holders in royal blue. This line was originally introduced in 1930 as Agua Caliente. Later the name was changed to Georgian. 4⅛" high x 4⅜" diameter base. Circa 1930 – 1935. Pair $100.00 – 125.00.

Plate 40. Fenton Art Glass Company #S5474 dolphin candlesticks. 6¾" high x 3⅝" hexagon base. These are a reproduction of a Boston and Sandwich Glass Company candlestick, originally produced circa 1855 – 1870 in two pieces, with the candle socket attached to the base with a wafer. Made for the Sandwich Glass Museum and marked SGM on the bottom along with the Fenton F in a circle logo. Circa 1995 – 1998. The Pairpoint Glass Company also reproduced these candlesticks for the Sandwich Museum as #137, circa 1980s – 1994 and 1998 to the present. Pair $70.00 – 75.00.

Candlesticks

Plate 41. Fostoria Glass Company #4113 blown candlesticks in regal blue. 5⅝" high x 3¼" diameter base. Circa 1933 – 1938. Pair $120.00 – 130.00.

Plate 42. Fostoria Glass Company #2496 Baroque trindle candlestick in regal blue. 5⅞" high x 5" diameter base. Patented 1933 by designer George Sakier (D91,687). Circa 1935 – 1937. Each $150.00 – 175.00.

Plate 43. H. C. Fry Glass Company #3101 candlesticks in royal blue. 2⅞" high x 4¾" diameter base. Circa 1928 – 1933. Pair $50.00 – 60.00.

Candlesticks

Plate 44. Hazel-Atlas Glass Company #K976 mold blown candlestick in Ritz blue. 7¼" high x 3½" diameter base. Circa 1930s. Each $10.00 – 15.00. (Photograph courtesy of Richard Stoer.)

Plate 45. A. H. Heisey & Company #301 Old Williamsburg two-light candelabrum in Stiegel blue and crystal. 10¼" high x 5¼" hexagon base. Circa 1933 – 1941. Each $1,200.00 – 1,300.00.

Plate 46. A. H. Heisey & Company #1404 Old Sandwich candlestick in Stiegel blue. 6" high x 4¼" round scalloped base. Circa 1933 – 1937. Usually marked with the Diamond H in the center of the base underneath. Each $250.00 – 275.00.

Candlesticks

Plate 47. A. H. Heisey & Company #1405 Ipswich footed centerpiece and vase in Stiegel blue and crystal. Made in two parts: 7½" high x 3⅜" square based vase with 3" high x 2½" base candle holder. Total height 9¾". Circa 1933 – 1941. Each $550.00 – 600.00.

Plate 48. A. H. Heisey & Company #142 three-light candlestick in Stiegel blue. Named "Cascade" by researchers. 7¼" high x 7¾" wide x 5⅜" diameter base. Circa 1933 – 1941. Each $500.00 – market.

Plate 49. A. H. Heisey & Company #110 candlestick in Stiegel blue. Named "Sandwich Dolphin" by researchers. 10" high x 4¼" square base. This is a reproduction of a Boston and Sandwich Glass Company candlestick from the 1800s, for which Heisey had the original wooden model. Circa 1933 – 1935. Each $750.00 – market.

Candlesticks

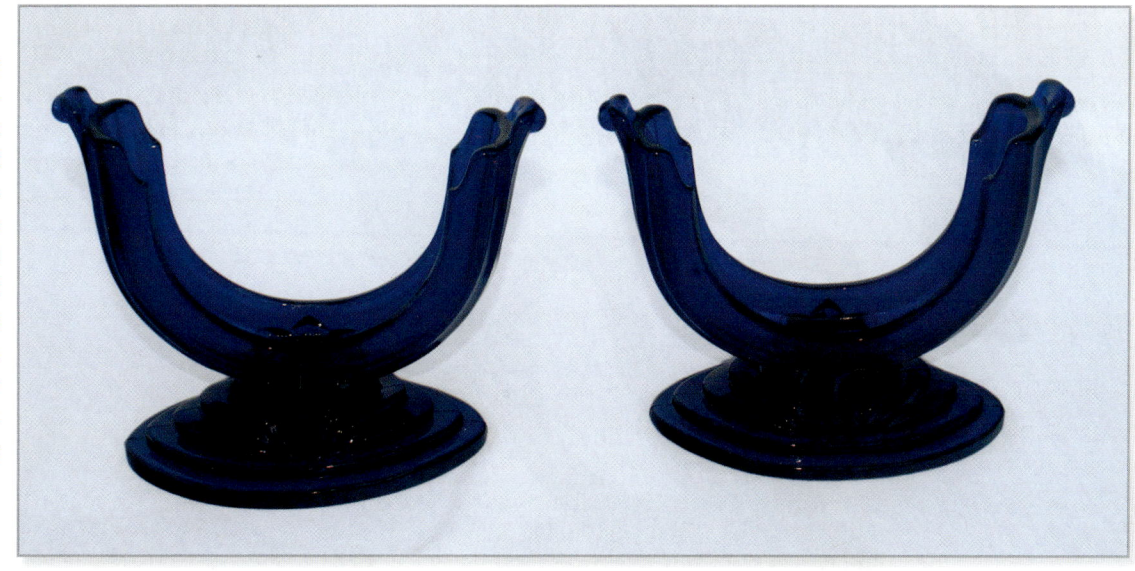

Plate 50. A. H. Heisey & Company #141 U-shaped candlesticks in Stiegel blue. Named "Edna" by researchers. 6" high x 6¾" wide with 3" high x 5½" oval base. Intended to hold a U-shaped candle that burns from both ends. Circa 1933 – 1936. Pair $1,200.00 – market. (Photograph courtesy of Kathy & Larry Thompson.)

Plate 51. A. H. Heisey & Company #1428 Warwick horn of plenty or cornucopia candlesticks in Stiegel blue. 2⅜" high x 3" long oval base. Circa 1935 – 1941. Sometimes marked with the Diamond H in the center of the base, underneath. Pair $250.00 – 350.00.

Plate 52. Imperial Glass Corporation #635 candlestick in Ritz blue. Called "Premium" by collectors. 8½" high x 4⅛" diameter base. Circa 1932. Each $50.00 – 60.00.

Candlesticks

Plate 53. Imperial Glass Corporation #753 triple-light heart candlestick in Ritz blue. 6¼" high x 8½" wide x 4⅝" diameter base. Circa 1932 – 1943. Each $75.00 – 85.00.

Plate 54. Imperial Glass Corporation #728 candle holder in Ritz blue. 3⅛" high x 3" diameter base. Named "Munsell" by Hazel Marie Weatherman. Circa 1932 – 1933. Each $40.00 – 50.00.

Plate 55. Imperial Glass Corporation #71790 handled candle holders in sapphire blue. 5⅜" high x 3¾" square base. Reproduction of a rare Boston and Sandwich Glass Company lacy-style candlestick. Made in two parts, but joined together using an adhesive, rather than a wafer, as would have been the case with the originals. Made for the Smithsonian Institution and marked "SI" (difficult to make out, since it is worked into the design near the handle). Circa 1976 – 1982. Pair $60.00 – 80.00.

Candlesticks

Plate 56. Imperial Glass Corporation #643 Hobnail candle holder, issued as #15783 in ultra blue. 2" high x 4½" diameter. Circa 1977 – 1979. Marked IG on the inside bottom. Each $15.00 – 20.00. (Photograph courtesy of Richard Stoer.)

Plate 57. Imperial Glass Corporation #71762 dolphin candle holders in ultra blue. 10¾" high x 4" square base. These candle holders are reproductions of candlesticks originally made by the Boston and Sandwich Glass Company in the 1800s and were made for the Metropolitan Museum of Art, marked "MMA" on the bottom. Circa 1980 – 1983. Pair $45.00 – 50.00.

Plate 58. Indiana Glass Company #14 handled candlestick. 2½" high x 4¼" octagon base. This candlestick was originally introduced in the 1950s (or earlier), but this color appears to have been a special order in the 1990s for the Upper Deck, Ltd., a wholesale catalog company that specializes in antique reproductions. Pair $25.00 – 30.00.

Candlesticks

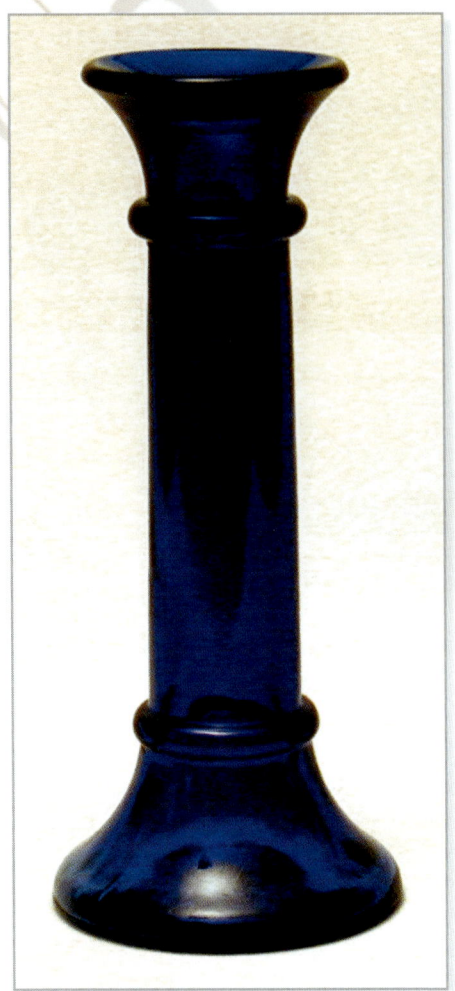

Plate 59. Indiana Glass Company #6222 Gothic candlestick/bud vase. 7" high x 3" diameter base. Circa 1997 – present. Each $4.00 – 5.00.

Plate 60. McKee Glass Company #200 candlesticks in Ritz blue. 3" high x 4½" octagon base. Circa 1930s. Pair $20.00 – 25.00.

Plate 61. McKee Glass Company Early American Rock Crystal three-lite candelabra (McKee catalog description) in Ritz blue. 6" high x 4½" diameter base. Circa 1930s. Each $300.00 – 350.00.

Candlesticks

Plate 62. Morgantown Glass Works #7643 Jacobi candlesticks in Ritz blue and crystal. Known as "Golf Ball" stem to collectors. 4" high x 3¼" diameter base. Circa 1930s. Pair $300.00 – 350.00.

Plate 63. Mosser Glass #315 candlestick. 5" high x 4⅜" diameter round base. This is made from a Beaumont Company mould (see plate 109, page 45), but modified so that the reissue has a round base, rather than scalloped as on the original. Began production in 2003. Each $18.00 – 20.00.

Plate 64. New Martinsville Glass Manufacturing Company #37/2 Georgian single candlesticks in Ritz blue. Georgian is the company's name for this pattern, now known as "Moondrops" to collectors. 5" high x 4⅝" diameter base. Circa 1932 – 1942. Pair $90.00 – 100.00.

Candlesticks

Plate 65. New Martinsville Glass Manufacturing Company #37 Georgian crimped or ruffled top candle holders in Ritz blue. Known as "Moondrops" to collectors. 2" high x 5" diameter top. Also made cupped and flared. See New Martinsville console sets for the flared version (plate 152, page 59). Circa 1932 – 1942. Pair $65.00 – 75.00.

Plate 66. New Martinsville Glass Manufacturing Company #34 candle holder in Ritz blue. Called "Addie" by William Heacock in honor of Addie Miller, the pioneer of New Martinsville research. 3⅛" high x 3¾" diameter base. These candle holders have eight points on the top rim, which is not consistent with the remainder of Line #34 having twelve points. Production from circa 1932 into the mid 1930s. Each $25.00 – 30.00.

Plate 67. New Martinsville Glass Manufacturing Company #35 candle holders in Ritz blue. Called "Fancy Squares" by collectors. 2½" high x 4" diameter base. The tableware in this line had two lobes on the corners. Some of the accessory items and these candle holders had four. It is possible these are line #36, which did have four lobes on the corners. Circa 1932. Pair $65.00 – 75.00.

Candlesticks

Plate 68. New Martinsville Glass Manufacturing Company #18 two-way candlestick in Ritz blue. 5⅝" high x 6" diameter base. Advertised by New Martinsville in December 1935 as Crystal Eagle and later shown in catalogs as part of the Radiance pattern. Circa 1935 – 1942. Each $75.00 – 85.00.

Plate 69. New Martinsville Glass Manufacturing Company #45 or #4500 Janice one-light candlesticks in Ritz blue. Designated #4554/31 Janice by New Martinsville. 5⅜" high x 5⅛" diameter base. These candlesticks were reissued by Dalzell Viking from 1993 to 1998 in cobalt. They are included here as New Martinsville products because of the quality of the glass and finish, the flat base, the silver deposit decoration, which is more typical of the 1930s than the 1990s, and also the undated catalog page reprinted in Hazel Marie Weatherman's *Colored Glassware of the Depression Era 2* which included the #4554 candlesticks with a large number of items made in cobalt. Advertised in January 1940, production in Ritz blue most likely began in late 1939 and ended prior to 1942. Pair $90.00 – 100.00.

Plate 70. New Martinsville Glass Manufacturing Company (Viking Glass Company) candleblocks in crystal with swan necks in blue. Made from the #451 candlestick. It is difficult to date these pieces. The same candleblocks with crystal swan necks were sold exclusively by Montgomery Ward in the spring-summer 1945 catalog. This was a few years after Ritz blue had been discontinued by New Martinsville. If they were made as a special order (like the Montgomery Ward crystal ones), they might date later, after the company had reorganized as the Viking Glass Company, since other swan-neck items in cobalt blue were advertised in December 1949. (See plate 798, page 295.) Note that each candleblock should have a pair of swan necks; both of these have had one swan broken off. Pair, in perfect condition, $25.00 – 30.00.

Candlesticks

Plate 71. Paden City Glass Manufacturing Company #115 candlesticks in royal blue. 9" high x 4½" hexagon base. Both have a grey notch cutting around the base, up the stem, and around the top rim. This style candlestick was also made in a 7" height. Circa 1930s. Pair $125.00 – 135.00.

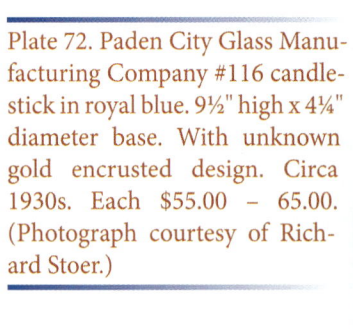

Plate 72. Paden City Glass Manufacturing Company #116 candlestick in royal blue. 9½" high x 4¼" diameter base. With unknown gold encrusted design. Circa 1930s. Each $55.00 – 65.00. (Photograph courtesy of Richard Stoer.)

Plate 73. Paden City Glass Manufacturing Company #191-½ candlesticks in royal blue. Named "Party Line" by Hazel Marie Weatherman. 4⅛" high x 3¾" diameter base. The #191 candlestick is the same except that the steps or ripples go all the way to the bottom, leaving no room for decoration. Circa 1930s. Pair $60.00 – 70.00.

Candlesticks

Plate 74. Paden City Glass Manufacturing Company #412 "keyhole" candlesticks in royal blue. Named "Crow's Foot Square" by Jerry Barnett. 5⅛" high x 4⅝" square base. Marked "sterling" silver decoration by unknown decorator (named "Pod Flower" by William Walker). Circa 1930s. Pair $60.00 – 70.00.

Plate 75. Paden City Glass Manufacturing Company #412 "keyhole" candlesticks in royal blue. Named "Crow's Foot Square" by Jerry Barnett. 5⅛" high x 4⅝" square base. With hand painted gold line decoration, by unknown decorator. Matching decoration is on #412 candy dish (plate 297, page 108). Circa 1930s. Pair $60.00 – 70.00.

Plate 76. Paden City Glass Manufacturing Company's #890 candlesticks in royal blue. Called "Crow's Foot Round" by Jerry Barnett. 6¾" high x 5" diameter base. Marked "sterling" silver decoration by unknown decorator (named "Pod Flower" by William Walker). Circa mid-1930s. Pair $150.00 – 160.00.

33

Candlesticks

Plate 77. Paden City Glass Manufacturing Company #220 candlesticks in royal blue with platinum line trim by an unknown decorator. Named "Largo" by Jerry Barnett. 4⅞" high x 4¾" diameter base. Circa 1937. Pair $85.00 – 95.00.

Plate 78. Pairpoint Corporation #1600 blown candlestick with a polished pontil. 10⅝" high x 4⅛" diameter base. Circa 1930s. Each $300.00 – 350.00.

Plate 79. Pairpoint Corporation #B1627 controlled bubble ball stem candlestick. 9" high x 3⅛" diameter base. Circa 1930s. Each $300.00 – 350.00.

Candlesticks

Plate 80. Pairpoint Corporation controlled bubble candlestick. 4" high x 4" diameter base. Circa 1930s. Each $160.00 – 175.00. (Photograph courtesy of Richard Stoer.)

Plate 81. Pairpoint Glass Company #202 Princess Feather candlesticks. 3⅝" high x 3⅝" diameter base. Reissue of the Westmoreland Glass Company's #201 mold, but with a domed base, unlike the original Westmoreland version that had a flat base. Circa 1990 to the present. Pair (current catalog price) $40.00.

Plate 82. Plum Glass Company #3 Doric Border candlestick. 4⅜" high x 4⅜" diameter base. Circa 1989 – 1990s. Reissued from a Westmoreland Glass Company mold and usually marked with the Westmoreland WG logo with the letters PG next to it. Each $10.00 – 12.50. (Photograph courtesy of Richard Stoer.)

Candlesticks

Plate 83. Seneca Glass Company candlesticks. 8⅜" high x 3¼" diameter base. Silver decoration by Rockwell Silver Company, Meriden, Connecticut. Marked on the rim of the base, "R S Co." Circa 1930. Pair $60.00 – 70.00.

Plate 84. L. E. Smith Glass Company #982 double candle holders. Called "Arrowhead" by collectors. 5⅜" high x 6⅝" spread x 6" round domed base. Sold as #982 console set with bowl in 1930s. Pair $40.00 – 50.00.

Plate 85. L. E. Smith Glass Company #1402 candle holders. 3" high x 4¼" diameter base. This was a Greensburg Glass Company mold acquired by L. E. Smith in 1920. Circa 1930s in blue. Pair $35.00 – 40.00.

Candlesticks

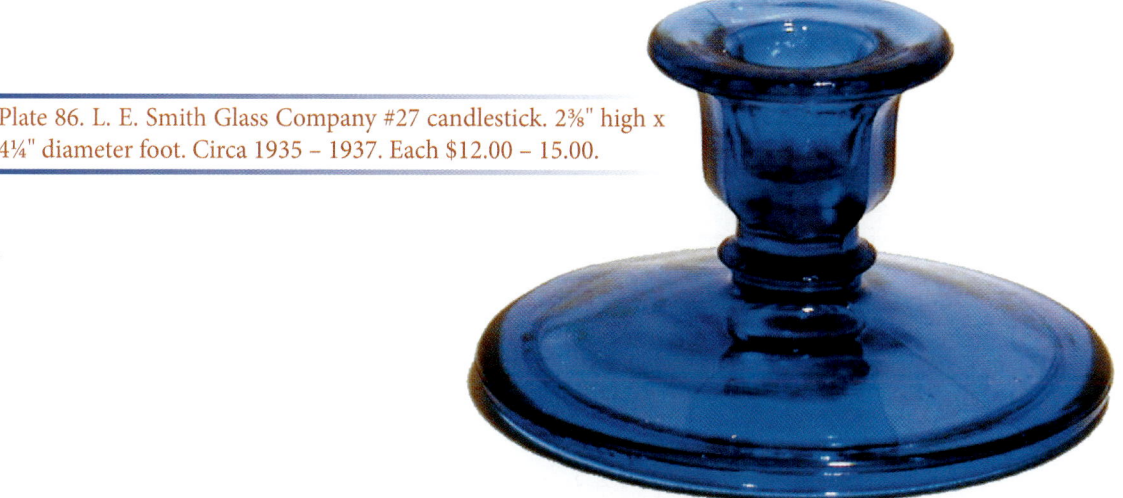

Plate 86. L. E. Smith Glass Company #27 candlestick. 2⅜" high x 4¼" diameter foot. Circa 1935 – 1937. Each $12.00 – 15.00.

Plate 87. L. E. Smith Glass Company #615 eight-piece table set. 3½" high x 12" diameter circle. Circa 1937. Set $85.00 – 100.00.

Plate 88. L. E. Smith Glass Company #5211 Moon and Star candle holder in sapphire blue. 9¼" high x 5" diameter scalloped base. Circa 1985 – 1987. L. G. Wright Glass Company made an almost identical candlestick, the only differences being very slight variances in the thickness of the stem and depth of the socket. Each $50.00 – 75.00.

Candlesticks

Plate 89. Summit Art Glass Company #1932/2 elephant candle holder bowl. 5¾" high x 8½" diameter. Made by Summit from the original Westmoreland Glass Company mold for Rosso Wholesaler Glass Dealers, Inc. Circa 1980s – 1990s. Bowl $40.00 – 50.00

Plate 90. United States Glass Company #300 candlesticks in royal blue. 8½" high x 4¼" diameter base. Unknown gold line decoration. Manufactured by Factory B (the old Bryce, McKee & Company plant in Pittsburgh). Circa 1923 – 1930s. Pair $90.00 – 100.00.

Plate 91. United States Glass Company #74 candlesticks with unknown silver basket of flowers with scroll decoration. 10¼" x 4¾" diameter base. Circa 1923 – 1935. Pair $140.00 – 150.00.

Candlesticks

Plate 92. United States Glass Company #76 candlestick with an unknown hand painted flowers and gold line decoration. 8½" high x 4¼" diameter base. Production was by both Factory G (one of the Glassport, Pennsylvania, plants) and Factory R (the Tiffin Glass Company plant). Circa 1923 – 1935. Each $40.00 – 50.00.

Plate 93. United States Glass Company #309 Queen Anne candlestick in royal blue. 8¼" high x 4⅜" diameter scalloped base. Circa 1924 – 1925. Each $100.00 – market.

Plate 94. Val Saint-Lambert Luxval candlesticks. 5" high x 4¾" long x 2⅛" wide base. Circa 1935. Pair $40.00 – 50.00.

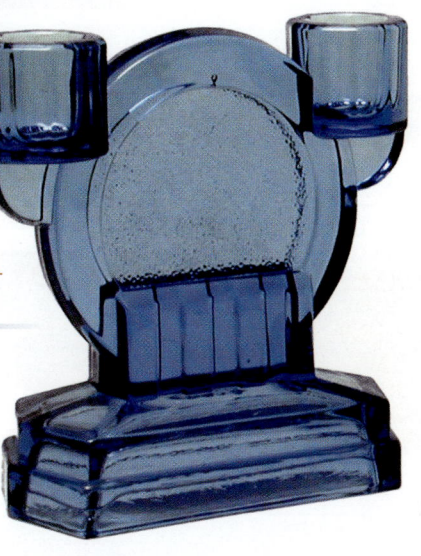

Candlesticks

Plate 95. Viking Glass Company #1827 Yesteryear candle holder. 2¾" high x 6" top diameter x 2½" diameter foot. Circa early 1970s. Each $20.00 – 25.00.

Plate 96. Viking Glass Company Spiral candlestick. 6¼" high x 3⅝" square base. This is a reissue of the Westmoreland Glass Company #1933 Spiral candlestick. Circa 1985 – 1986. Each $20.00 – 25.00.

Plate 97. Westmoreland Specialty Company #235 candlesticks. 2" high x 4⅜" long (including handle). Made by Westmoreland in opal, circa 1900 – 1918. Although cobalt is not a documented color for Westmoreland in the early 1900s, it seems likely that this pair dates to the same time period. Pair $40.00 – 50.00.

Candlesticks

Plate 98. L. G. Wright Glass Company #22-15 Daisy and Button miniature stove candleholder. 3" high x 2" square top. With satin finish. Circa early 1960s. Each $24.00 – 28.00.

Plate 99. Czechoslovakian candlestick with an unknown thin silver lines and dot decoration. 8¼" high x 4⅛" diameter. Marked Czech. Circa 1920 – 1930s. Each $15.00 – 20.00.

Plate 100. Czechoslovakian candlestick with unknown silver bird and lines decoration. 10¼" high x 4⅛" diameter base. Marked Czech. Circa 1920 – 1930s. Each $15.00 – 20.00.

Candlesticks

Plate 101. European candlesticks. 8½" high x 3½" diameter base. Pair $40.00 – 50.00.

Plate 102. European candlesticks. 10⅛" high x 4⅝" diameter base. Pair $50.00 – 60.00.

Plate 103. European candlesticks. 3½" high x 4⅛" diameter base. Unknown silver dots and line decoration. Pair $30.00 – 40.00.

Candlesticks

Plate 104. German candlesticks. 8⅜" x 3⅝" diameter base. Marked Germany. Circa 1920 – 1930s. Pair $40.00 – 50.00.

Plate 105. Unattributed candlesticks. 11½" high x 5⅜" diameter domed base. Blown quality workmanship with pontil as broken. Pair $400.00 – 500.00.

Plate 106. Unattributed "luster" candlestick. 12" high x 6" diameter top x 5" diameter base. The facets and the top of the candlestick have been cut and polished. Each $600.00 – 700.00.

Candlesticks

Plate 107. Toy candlesticks. Left to right: (1) Unattributed handled candle holder. 2" high x 2½" diameter base. Lacy style. Circa early 1900s. Each $20.00 – 25.00. (2) Westmoreland Glass Company #1013 three-light candlestick. 4½" high x 2⅜" diameter hexagon base. Circa 1980 – 1989. Each $40.00 – 50.00. (3 and 5) Summit Art Glass Company handled candle holders, #3 with Shirley Temple decal. 1⅞" high x 2¾" diameter octagon base. Reissue of the Westmoreland Glass Company #1211 birthday candlestick, made 1985 for Rosso Wholesaler Glass Dealers, Inc. and also offered in Summit's own catalogs. Each $20.00 – 25.00. (4) Imperial Glass Corporation #13794 Old Williamsburg miniature candlestick. 3½" high x 2" hexagon base. Reissue of the A. H. Heisey & Company #33 candlestick, known as "Skirted Panel" to collectors. Produced in a limited edition for the Heisey Collectors of America, circa 1981 – 1982. Marked ALIG on the bottom rim. Each $35.00 – 45.00. (6) Mosser Glass #154 candlestick. 4⅛" high x 2¼" diameter hexagon base. Circa 1988 – 2001. Each $10.00 – 15.00. (7) Taiwan handled candle holder. 2" high x 2½" diameter base. Circa 1980s. Each $8.00 – 10.00. (8) Meisenthal #2153 toy candlestick. 4" high x 2⅝" diameter base. Circa 1889 – 1907. Each $35.00 – 40.00.

Plate 108. Unattributed reproduction toy candlesticks. Left: 3" high. Right: 1⅝" high. These toys were mistakenly identified as McKee and Brothers and Boston and Sandwich Glass Company, respectively, in a book by one of the co-authors, *The Glass Candlestick Book*, volume 2. They are now known to be contemporary reproductions. Circa 1990s. 4½" size, pair $8.00 – 10.00. 1⅝" size, pair $5.00 – 8.00.

CONSOLE SETS

Plate 109. Beaumont Company #115 lobed or scalloped bowl with keyhole candle holders. Bowl: 3⅝" high x 11½" diameter. Candle holders: 5⅜" high x 4½" diameter scalloped base. The scalloped base and small nibs protruding on the keyholes distinguish these candle holders from similar keyhole candle holders by the Paden City Glass Manufacturing Company and Cambridge Glass Company. Probably made circa 1930. There is a reproduction or reissue of this candlestick made by Mosser Glass that can be distinguished by the flatter round base and lesser quality of workmanship. (See plate 63, page 29.) Bowl $35.00 – 45.00. Candlesticks, pair $35.00 – 45.00.

Plate 110. Cambridge Glass Company #441 footed, flared panel optic bowl with #437 candlesticks in cobalt blue #2. Bowl: 4⅛" high x 9¾" diameter. Candlesticks: 9½" high x 4⅜" diameter base. With unknown gold encrusted acid etching. Circa 1925 – 1926. Bowl $75.00 – 85.00. Candlesticks, pair $90.00 – 100.00.

Console Sets

Plate 111. Cambridge Glass Company #3400/4 four footed flared bowl with #437 candlestick in Ritz blue. Bowl: 4" high x 11½" diameter. Candlestick: 9½" high x 4⅜" diameter foot. Circa 1929 – 1931. Bowl $75.00 – 85.00. Candlestick, each $70.00 – 80.00.

Plate 112. Cambridge Glass Company #842 decagon bowl with #627 candlesticks. Bowl: 3⅜" high x 12" diameter. Candlesticks: 4" high x 4¾" diameter base. The bowl and one candlestick are Ritz blue, produced circa 1929 – 1931. The second candlestick is royal blue, produced circa 1931 – 1940s. Bowl $65.00 – 75.00. Candlesticks, each $15.00 – 17.50 (Ritz blue), $17.50 – 20.00 (royal blue).

Plate 113. Cambridge Glass Company #3400/45 four footed crimped or ruffled bowl with #646 or #3400/646 keyhole candlesticks in royal blue. Bowl: 5⅜" high x 12⅜" diameter. Candlestick: 5" high x 4⅝" diameter decagon base. Circa 1931 – 1940s. Shown with Cambridge's #1111 9" Heron flower frog. Bowl $85.00 – 95.00. Candlesticks, pair $100.00 – 120.00. Frog $135.00 – 145.00.

Console Sets

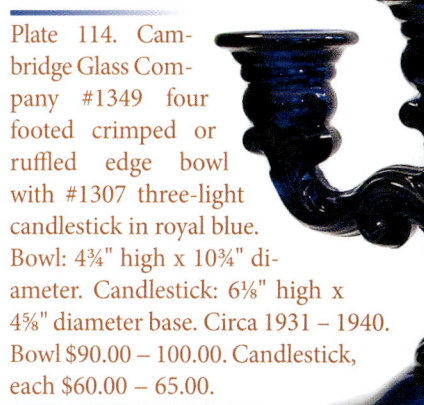

Plate 114. Cambridge Glass Company #1349 four footed crimped or ruffled edge bowl with #1307 three-light candlestick in royal blue. Bowl: 4¾" high x 10¾" diameter. Candlestick: 6⅛" high x 4⅝" diameter base. Circa 1931 – 1940. Bowl $90.00 – 100.00. Candlestick, each $60.00 – 65.00.

Plate 115. Cambridge Glass Company #7801 low footed cupped bowl or compote with #437 candlesticks in royal blue. Bowl: 5½" high x 8" diameter. Candlesticks: 9⅜" high x 4⅜" diameter foot. Both have #708 gold encrusted acid etching by Cambridge. Circa 1931 – 1940s. Compote $75.00 – 85.00. Candlesticks, pair $100.00 – 120.00.

Plate 116. Central Glass Works rolled edge bowl with #2000 trumpet shaped candlesticks in royal blue. Bowl (probably #2000, as it is from the same mold as the straight, flared and rolled edge bowl): 3½" high x 8⅜" diameter. Candlesticks: 7" high x 3⅞" diameter base. Both with gold encrusted acid etching, believed to be a scaled down version of the #905 St. Regis pattern by Honesdale Decorating Company, Honesdale, Pennsylvania. This console set was named "Zaricor" by Hazel Marie Weatherman. Circa 1930s. Bowl $35.00 – 40.00. Candlesticks, pair $70.00 – 80.00.

Console Sets

Plate 117. Central Glass Works flared footed bowl with #2000 trumpet shaped candlesticks in royal blue. Bowl (probably #2000): 5" high x 9¾" diameter. Candlesticks: 9" high x 4½" diameter. Both with unknown gold encrusted acid etching. Circa 1930s. Bowl $45.00 – 55.00. Candlesticks, pair $90.00 – 100.00.

Plate 118. Central Glass Works flared footed bowl with #2000 trumpet shaped candlesticks in royal blue. Bowl (probably #2000): 5" high x 10" diameter. Candlesticks: 7" high x 3⅞" diameter base. Unknown decorator of gold line and fleur de lis design. This bowl is not pictured on a catalog showing other #2000 pieces, but the foot, stem, and base are the same. Circa 1930s. Bowl $45.00 – 55.00. Candlesticks, pair $70.00 – 80.00.

Plate 119. Central Glass Works flared bowl with #2000 trumpet shaped candlesticks in royal blue. Bowl (probably #2000): 3⅞" high x 9¾" diameter. Candlesticks: 9¼" high x 4⅜" diameter base. Both with unknown white gold encrusted acid etched decoration. Circa 1930s. Bowl $35.00 – 45.00. Candlesticks, pair $90.00 – 100.00.

Console Sets

Plate 120. Diamond Glass-Ware Company flared bowl with 9" high trumpet shaped candlesticks. Bowl: 3¼" high x 10" diameter. Candlesticks: 9" high x 4⅜" diameter base. Unknown silver decoration consisting of a woman's head in silhouette, baskets of flowers, and a garland of flowers and leaves. This decoration was named "Silhouette" by Tim Schmidt in his book, *Central Glass Works* (Schiffer Publishing, 2004). It is now known to be Victoria by the National Silver Deposit Ware Company, New York, N.Y. This set most likely had a black base or stand for the bowl, which is missing. Circa 1928 – 1931. Bowl $35.00 – 45.00. Candlesticks, pair $90.00 – 100.00.

Plate 121. Diamond Glass-Ware Company cupped bowl with candlesticks (named "Mae West" by collectors). Bowl: 3⅞" high x 8" diameter. Candlesticks: 8" high x 4¾" diameter. The set is decorated with a heavy silver deposit marked "RS Co. Sterling" on the base of the candlesticks. There is a shield with "Rockwell" written in it stamped on the bottom of the bowl and candlesticks with a number 2244-8 in gold lettered on the bottom of both candlesticks. These marks were used by the Rockwell Silver Company, Meriden, Connecticut. Produced circa 1928 – 1931. Bowl $125.00 – 135.00. Candlesticks, pair $140.00 – 150.00.

Plate 122. Diamond Glass-Ware Company cupped bowl with candlestick/shelf supports. Bowl: 4" high x 8¼" diameter. Candlesticks: 8" high x 5" diameter base. The set has unknown silver decoration marked "sterling silver." Produced circa 1928 – 1931. Bowl $90.00 – 100.00. Candlesticks: $150.00 – 160.00.

Console Sets

Plate 123. Diamond Glass-Ware Company Victory flat top bowl with candle holders. Bowl: 2⅞" high x 12" diameter. Candle holders: 3⅛" high x 4½" diameter base. Named Victory in a 1929 advertisement. Victory included the full line of tableware for which Diamond is probably best known. The bowl is seen here displayed on a base that is a slightly lighter blue, probably not made by Diamond. Produced circa 1928 – 1931. Bowl $90.00 – 100.00. Candle holders, pair $100.00 – 110.00.

Plate 124. Diamond Glass-Ware company flared bowl with trumpet shaped candlesticks. Bowl: 3½" high x 9⅞" diameter. Candlesticks: 9" high x 4⅜" diameter base. The set has unknown silver deposit of alternating grape clusters and grape leaf decoration. Produced circa 1928 – 1931. Bowl $75.00 – 85.00. Candlesticks, pair $100.00 – 110.00.

Plate 125. Diamond Glass-Ware Company #99 bowl with candlesticks. Bowl: 3⅜" high x 11⅜" diameter across center points. Candlesticks: 3" high x 4" square base. The set has Diamond's Jack and the Beanstalk decoration in gold. This set was advertised in September 1930. The set was probably produced earlier and continued until Diamond's demise in June 1931. Bowl $35.00 – 45.00. Candlesticks $45.00 – 55.00.

Console Sets

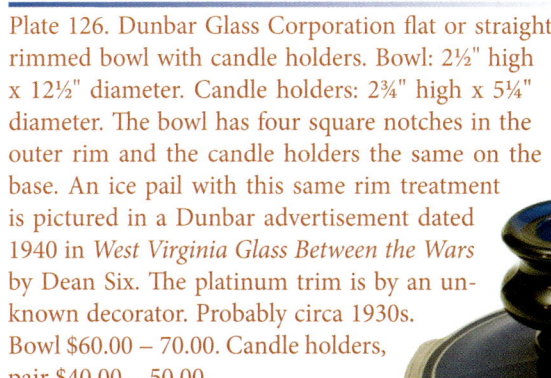

Plate 126. Dunbar Glass Corporation flat or straight rimmed bowl with candle holders. Bowl: 2½" high x 12½" diameter. Candle holders: 2¾" high x 5¼" diameter. The bowl has four square notches in the outer rim and the candle holders the same on the base. An ice pail with this same rim treatment is pictured in a Dunbar advertisement dated 1940 in *West Virginia Glass Between the Wars* by Dean Six. The platinum trim is by an unknown decorator. Probably circa 1930s. Bowl $60.00 – 70.00. Candle holders, pair $40.00 – 50.00.

Plate 127. Duncan and Miller Glass Company #50 oval flared bowl with #28 candlesticks. Bowl: 3¼" high x 12⅜" long. Candlesticks: 5¾" high x 4½" diameter base. Both marked "Sterling" silver overlay of dogwood by unknown decorator. Circa 1931 – 1937. Bowl $150.00 – 160.00. Candlesticks, pair $160.00 – 170.00.

Plate 128. Duncan and Miller Glass Company #16 flared oval bowl with candlesticks. Bowl: 5¼" high x 14" long. Candlesticks: 6" high x 4¾" diameter base. Both with unknown platinum trim. Circa 1931 – 1937. Bowl $165.00 – 175.00. Candlesticks, pair $150.00 – 160.00.

Console Sets

Plate 129. Duncan and Miller Glass Company #12 three-footed bowl with #12 candlestick. Bowl: 4¼" high x 10" diameter. Candlestick: 6" high x 4¾" diameter base. Circa 1931 – 1937. Bowl $65.00 – 75.00. Candlestick, each $55.00 – 65.00.

Plate 130. Fenton Art Glass Company #1502 diamond optic rolled rim bowl with diamond optic candle holders in royal blue. Bowl: 2¼" high x 12" diameter. Candle holders: 2¾" high x 4½" diameter. This candlestick was made circa 1927 – 1937, but production in royal blue is a little hazy. *Fenton Glass, the Second Twenty-Five Years* by William Heacock indicates 1928, while *Fenton Art Glass, 1907 – 1939* by Margaret and Kenn Whitmyer states that shakers in this pattern were made in royal blue circa 1937. Bowl $65.00 – 75.00. Candle holders, pair $50.00 – 60.00.

Plate 131. Fenton Art Glass Company #950 oval cornucopia-shaped footed bowl with cornucopia-shaped candle holders in royal blue. Bowl: 3½" high x 12" long. Candle holders: 5½" high. This version of the cornucopia with flat tops on the bowl and the candle holders is the rarer of the two #950 sets. It is believed that the flat version was made in the first year of production, then the rims of the bowl and candlesticks were bent up and down, with the latter style remaining in production for six or seven years. The flat version was produced circa 1932. Bowl $75.00 – 85.00. Candle holders, pair $90.00 – 100.00.

Console Sets

Plate 132. Fenton Art Glass Company #950 oval cornucopia-shaped footed bowl with cornucopia-shaped candle holders in royal blue. Bowl: 5½" high x 11" long. Candle holders: 5½" high. This version has the rims bent up and down on opposing sides of the bowl and candle holders. Produced circa 1933 – 1939. Bowl $65.00 – 75.00. Candle holders, pair $65.00 – 75.00.

Plate 133. Fenton Art Glass Company #1093 flared, open edge bowl with flat rim, three-footed candle holders in royal blue. Known as "Basket Weave" to collectors. Bowl: 2¼" high x 8¼" diameter. Candle holders: 1¾" high x 5" diameter flat rim. Produced circa 1935 – 1936. Bowl $30.00 – 40.00. Candle holders, pair $40.00 – 50.00.

Plate 134. Fenton Art Glass Company #1092 crimped open edge bowl with three-footed candle holders in royal blue. Known as "Basket Weave" to collectors. Bowl: 2½" high x 9" diameter. Candle holders: 2¼" high x 5" diameter. Originally produced in carnival glass circa 1911. Royal blue production circa 1935 – 1936. Bowl $45.00 – 55.00. Candle holders, pair $60.00 – 70.00.

53

Console Sets

Plate 135. Fenton Art Glass Company #1790 three-footed bowl with three-footed candle holders in royal blue. Known as "Leaf Tiers" to collectors. Bowl: 4" high x 10" diameter. Candle holders: 2" high x 5½" diameter. This bowl and candle holders have simulated bark on the legs and leaves on the outside. They were originally made in carnival glass circa 1914. Produced in royal blue circa 1935. Bowl $115.00 – 125.00. Candle holders, pair $200.00 – 225.00.

Plate 136. Fenton Art Glass Company #1234 six-lobed bowl with six-lobed, three leg candle holders in royal blue. Bowl: 3" high x 9" diameter. Candle holders: 1¾" high x 4⅜" diameter. Advertised by S. S. Kresge Company, Detroit, Michigan, in the mid-1930s. Circa 1935 – 1936. Bowl $25.00 – 35.00. Candle holders, pair $20.00 – 30.00.

Plate 137. Fenton Art Glass Company #848 eight-point flared bowl with three leg candle holders in royal blue. Bowl: 3⅜" high x 9" diameter. Candle holders: 1¾" high x 4⅜" diameter. This is called flower bowl by collectors. Advertised by F. W. Woolworth Company in the mid-1930s. Produced circa 1936. Bowl $25.00 – 35.00. Candle holders, pair $20.00 – 30.00.

Console Sets

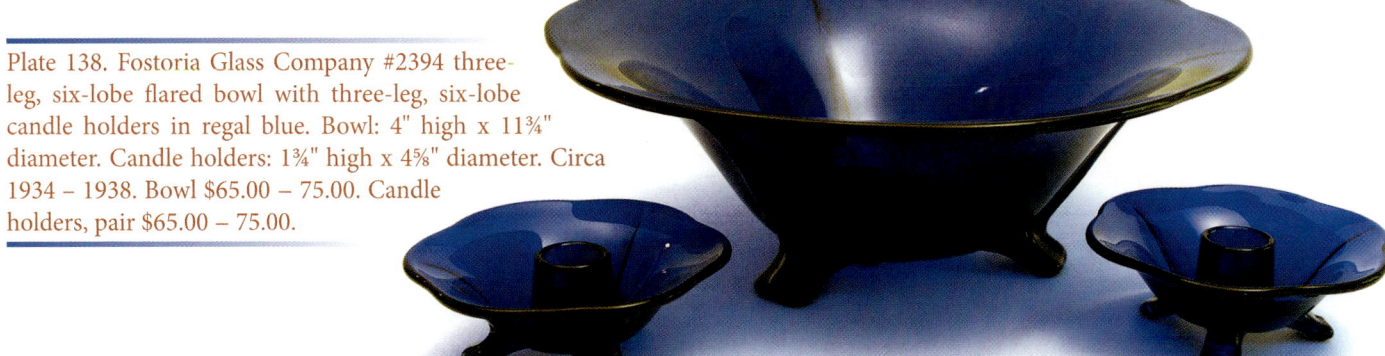

Plate 138. Fostoria Glass Company #2394 three-leg, six-lobe flared bowl with three-leg, six-lobe candle holders in regal blue. Bowl: 4" high x 11¾" diameter. Candle holders: 1¾" high x 4⅝" diameter. Circa 1934 – 1938. Bowl $65.00 – 75.00. Candle holders, pair $65.00 – 75.00.

Plate 139. Fostoria Glass Company #4024 crystal footed, eight-lobed bowl with candle holders in regal blue. Bowl: 4" high x 10" diameter. Candle holders: 5⅝" high x 2⅞" base. Circa 1934 – 1942. Bowl $90.00 – 100.00. Candle holders $90.00 – 100.00.

Plate 140. H. C. Fry Glass Company swirl connector, nine-lobe footed flared bowl with eight-lobe base with swirl connector to base and swirl connector candle holders in royal blue and crystal. Bowl: 6¼" high x 11¾" diameter. Candle holders: 4" high x 4" diameter base. Circa 1929 – 1933. Bowl $200.00 – 250.00. Candle holders, pair $200.00 – 250.00.

Console Sets

Plate 141. Hazel-Atlas Glass Company Royal Lace three-leg straight or flared bowl with three-leg straight or flared candle holders in Ritz blue. Bowl: 4½" high x 10" diameter. Candle holders: 2¼" high x 5" diameter. Produced circa 1934 – 1941. Bowl $65.00 – 75.00. Candle holders, pair $100.00 – 125.00.

Plate 142. Hazel-Atlas Glass Company Royal Lace three-leg rolled bowl with three-leg rolled candle holders in Ritz blue. Bowl: 3½" high x 10¾" diameter. Candle holders: 1⅞" high x 5¼" diameter. Produced circa 1934 – 1941. Bowl $300.00 – 400.00. Candle holders, pair $400.00 – 500.00.

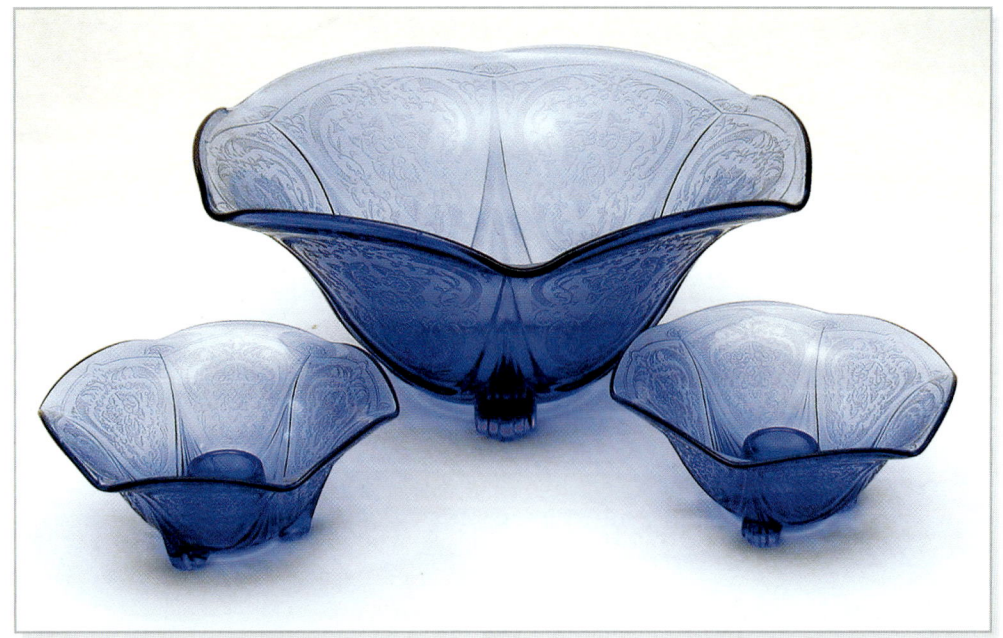

Plate 143. Hazel-Atlas Glass Company Royal Lace three-leg ruffled or crimped bowl with three-leg ruffled or crimped candle holders in Ritz blue. Bowl: 4⅜" high x 10" diameter. Candle holders: 2¼" high x 5" diameter. Produced circa 1934 – 1941. Bowl $250.00 – 350.00. Candle holders, pair $350.00 – 450.00.

Console Sets

Plate 144. A. H. Heisey and Company #1428 Warwick horn of plenty floral bowl with two-light candlesticks in Stiegel blue. Bowl: 4¼" high x 11" diameter. Candlesticks: 3⅜" high x 7⅜" spread. Circa 1933 – 1941. Bowl $450.00 – 550.00. Candlesticks, pair $450.00 – 500.00.

Plate 145. A. H. Heisey and Company #1401 Empress three dolphin footed flared floral bowl with #135 Empress candlesticks in Stiegel blue. Bowl: 4½" high x 10¾" diameter. Candlesticks: 6½" high x 4¾" diameter base. Circa 1933 – 1937. Bowl $500.00 – 700.00. Candlesticks, pair $600.00 – 800.00.

Plate 146. A. H. Heisey and Company #1433 footed, flared floral bowl with two-light candlesticks in Stiegel blue. Named "Thumbprint and Panel" by researchers. Bowl: 3½" high x 11" diameter. Candlesticks: 5¼" high x 6" spread. Circa 1934 – 1937. Bowl $250.00 – 300.00. Candlesticks, pair $250.00 – 300.00.

Console Sets

Plate 147. Imperial Glass Corporation #6567/28 interior-paneled, flared bowl with #635 candlesticks (known as "Premium" to collectors) in Ritz blue. Bowl: 3¼" high x 9" diameter. Candlesticks: 8½" high x 4⅛" base. Unknown marked "Sterling" silver lily of the valley decoration on set. Circa 1932. Bowl $65.00 – 75.00. Candlesticks, pair $90.00 – 100.00.

Plate 148. Imperial Glass Corporation #7286 octagon, four-footed, flat rim bowl with #39 candlesticks (known as "Pillar Flute" to collectors) in Ritz blue. Bowl: 2⅞" high x 8½" diameter. Candlesticks: 2½" high x 4¼" diameter base. Both have a marked "Sterling" silver decoration of dogwood believed to be by the Sterling Decorationg Company in Cincinnati, Ohio. Circa 1932. Bowl $40.00 – 50.00. Candlesticks, pair $40.00 – 50.00.

Plate 149. Imperial Glass Corporation #153 footed, flared bowl with two-light candlesticks in Ritz blue. Named "Newbound" by Hazel Marie Weatherman. Bowl: 3½" high x 10" diameter. Candlesticks: 3⅜" high x 4¼" spread. Circa 1933 – 1938. Bowl $40.00 – 50.00. Candlesticks, pair $25.00 – 35.00.

Console Sets

Plate 150. McKee Glass Company Early American Rock Crystal footed center bowl, for raw fruit or table decoration (McKee description) with two-light candelabra in Ritz blue. Bowl: 5½" high x 13¼" diameter. Candlesticks: 5" high x 4½" diameter base. Circa 1930s. Bowl $275.00 – 300.00. Candelabra, pair $275.00 – 300.00.

Plate 151. New Martinsville Glass Manufacturing Company #37 Georgian bowl with #37/3 triple-light candle holders in Ritz blue. Georgian is the company's original name for the pattern, now known as "Moondrops" to collectors. Bowl: 5" high x 13" long (wing to wing). Candle holders: 5⅛" high x 5⅛" diameter base. Advertised in a 1933 ad as #37/3 console set. Circa 1933 – 1942. Bowl $100.00 – 110.00. Candle holders, pair $175.00 – 185.00.

Plate 152. New Martinsville Glass Manufacture Company #37 Georgian three-footed bowl with flared candle holders in Ritz blue. Known as "Moondrops" to collectors. Bowl: 2⅝" high x 10" diameter. Candle holders: 2" high x 4¾" diameter. The "Moondrops" candle holders were made flared, crimped, and cupped. See plate 65, page 30, for a crimped version. New Martinsville refers to this as Georgian pattern in one advertisement, but this does not resemble the Georgian or Thumbprint patterns made by numerous other glass companies. Circa 1933 – 1942. Bowl $75.00 – 85.00. Candle holders, pair $70.00 – 80.00.

Console Sets

Plate 153. Paden City Glass Manufacturing Company #412 flat or straight rim bowl with "keyhole" candlesticks in royal blue. Named "Crow's Foot Square" by Jerry Barnett. Bowl: 3½" high x 11½" diameter. Candlesticks: 5¼" x 4⅝" square base. Circa 1930s. Bowl $65.00 – 75.00. Candlesticks, pair $50.00 – 60.00.

Plate 154. Paden City Glass Manufacturing Company #412 "keyhole" candlestick in royal blue (named "Crow's Foot Square by Jerry Barnett) with Cambridge Glass Company #993 four-leg bowl (marked with the Cambridge Triangle C). Candlestick: 5⅜" high x 4½" diameter base. Bowl: 3½" high x 12¾" diameter. The bowl and the candlestick both have a marked "Sterling" silver Evangeline decoration by the National Silver Deposit Ware Company, Inc., New York, New York. They were obtained at an estate auction in New York as a set. It is unknown if they were joined together by the purchaser, retailer, or the decorator, but obviously National obtained blanks from both Cambridge and Paden City for decorating. A reminder to the glass enthusiast not to make attributions solely based on decoration! Circa 1930s. Bowl $80.00 – 90.00. Candlestick, each $25.00 – 30.00.

Plate 155. Paden City Glass Manufacturing Company #412 rolled edge bowl with "mushroom" candle holder in royal blue. Named "Crow's Foot Square" by Jerry Barnett. Bowl: 2" high x 12" square. Candle holder: 2½" high x 5½" square. Circa 1930s. Bowl $100.00 – 125.00. Candle holder, each $45.00 – 55.00.

Console Sets

Plate 156. Paden City Glass Manufacturing Company #207 footed rolled rim console bowl with candlesticks in royal blue. This relatively rare set has not previously been named, so we decided to get into the name calling game and are calling it "Massy," meaning massive, which it is. Bowl: 4⅛" high x 12¼" diameter. Candlesticks: 10¾" high x 5⅜" diameter base. Bowl and candlesticks are decorated with the Paden City gold encrusted "Samarkand" etching (named by Jerry Barnett). Circa 1930s. Bowl: $175.00 – 200.00. Candlesticks, pair $175.00 – 200.00.

Plate 157. Paden City Glass Manufacturing Company #881 Gadroon flared bowl with candlesticks in royal blue. Also known as "Wotta Line" (name given by Hazel Marie Weatherman). Bowl: 4¼" high x 10¾" diameter. Candlestick: 5⅞" high x 5" diameter base. The bowl has Paden City's #533 "Irwin" acid etched decoration (named by William Walker). The candlesticks have the same etching, but gold encrusted. Circa 1932 – 1939. Bowl $90.00 – 100.00. Candlesticks, pair $100.00 – 110.00.

Plate 158. Paden City Glass Manufacturing Company #215 Glades footed, flat rim bowl with two-light candle holders in royal blue. Glades is the original manufacturer's name for this pattern. Hazel Marie Weatherman called it "Hotcha." Bowl: 4" high x 11½" diameter. Candle holders: 5" high x 4⅛" diameter base. Circa 1936 – 1939. Bowl $140.00 – 150.00. Candle holders, pair $140.00 – 150.00.

Console Sets

Plate 159. Seneca Glass Company #12 crystal footed rolled edge console bowl with #30 crystal footed mushroom shaped candlesticks. Bowl: 3½" high x 10½" diameter. Candlesticks: 3⅝" x 4¾" diameter. Pictured in a 1931 Seneca catalog. Bowl $175.00 – 200.00. Candlesticks, pair $175.00 – 200.00.

Plate 160. Seneca Glass Company footed rolled edge console bowl with candlesticks. Bowl: 3¼" high x 10¾" diameter. Candlesticks: 8⅜" high x 3⅛" diameter base. The pieces in the set have a silver (white gold) filled acid etch by an unknown decorator. This set (and the three following) are attributed to Seneca based on the bowls, which are identical to the line #12 bowl pictured in the 1931 Seneca catalog. (See plate 159 above.) The cobalt is a shade lighter than the #12 bowl and the #30 candlesticks. This could be a batch variation or a deliberate change of formula, since reference sources mention both cobalt blue (as new in 1931) and royal blue (new in 1932). It isn't known if these are separate colors or just different terminology for the same color. Bowl $140.00 – 150.00. Candlesticks, pair $140.00 – 150.00.

Plate 161. Seneca Glass Company footed rolled edge console bowl with candlesticks. Bowl: 3¾" high x 12½" diameter. Candlesticks: 11" high x 3¾" diameter base. Both have unknown gold encrusted acid etching. The etching is the same as the silver (white gold) etching on the other Seneca sets. Probably circa 1930 – 1931. Bowl $140.00 – 150.00. Candlesticks, pair $140.00 – 150.00.

Console Sets

Plate 162. Seneca Glass Company footed rolled edge console bowl with candlesticks. Bowl: 3⅝" high x 12¾" diameter. Candlesticks: 11¼" high x 4" diameter base. Both have heavy silver design characteristics of the Rockwell Silver Company. The decoration is not marked with a stamp, shield, or number. Probably circa 1930 – 1931. Bowl $150.00 – 175.00. Candlesticks, pair $150.00 – 175.00.

Plate 163. Seneca Glass Company footed rolled edge console bowl with candlesticks. Bowl: 3⅞" high x 12⅛" diameter. Candlesticks: 11¼" high x 4" diameter base. The set has an unknown silver (white gold) encrusted acid etching. Probably circa 1930 – 1931. Bowl $140.00 – 150.00. Candlesticks, pair $140.00 – 150.00.

Plate 164. L. E. Smith Glass Company #1022 three-footed console bowl with #600 "double shield" double candlesticks. Named "Mount Pleasant" by Hazel Marie Weatherman. Bowl: 3¼" high x 9" diameter. Candlesticks: 4½" high x 5 3/4: wide. This bowl and candlesticks in black are pictured together in a catalog page from F. W. Woolworth. Made in blue circa 1934 – 1936. Bowl $25.00 – 30.00. Candlesticks, pair $35.00 – 40.00.

Console Sets

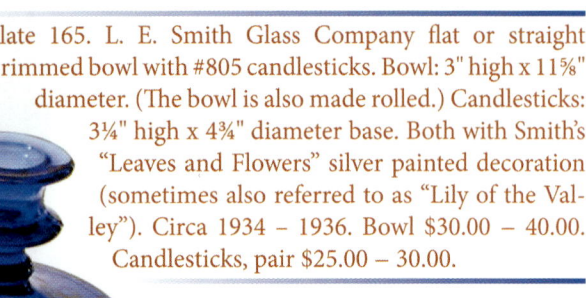

Plate 165. L. E. Smith Glass Company flat or straight rimmed bowl with #805 candlesticks. Bowl: 3" high x 11⅝" diameter. (The bowl is also made rolled.) Candlesticks: 3¼" high x 4¾" diameter base. Both with Smith's "Leaves and Flowers" silver painted decoration (sometimes also referred to as "Lily of the Valley"). Circa 1934 – 1936. Bowl $30.00 – 40.00. Candlesticks, pair $25.00 – 30.00.

Plate 166. L. E. Smith Glass Company #1 Modernistic bowl with candle holders. Named "Wig Wam" by Hazel Marie Weatherman. Bowl: 5½" high x 10" long. Candle holders: 3" high x 3¾" diameter base. The molds for this set were originally owned by the Co-operative Flint Glass Company, who produced this set in crystal and colors. However, this set can be confidently attributed to L. E. Smith, who acquired the molds around 1935, two years before Co-operative Flint went out of business. The color matches Smith's blue exactly and is lighter in shade than pieces made in cobalt by Co-operative Flint. Smith's factory records indicate this set was made circa 1936. (Note: Hazel Marie Weatherman's *Colored Glassware of the Depression Era 2* shows this bowl used with different style candlesticks on a catalog page that she dated 1930. It is now known that the date for that page is actually circa 1939.) Bowl $30.00 – 35.00. Candle holders, pair $30.00 – 35.00.

Plate 167. L. E. Smith Glass Company #4000 square footed bowl with square base candlesticks. Bowl: 4" high x 9" diameter. Candlesticks: 2½" high x 2¾" diameter. Circa 1936. Bowl $30.00 – 40.00. Candlesticks, pair $20.00 – 30.00.

Console Sets

Plate 168. United States Glass Company #8105 flat rim bowl with #300 candlesticks in royal blue. Bowl: 2½" high x 10¼" diameter. Candlesticks: 8½" high x 4¼" diameter base. Manufactured by Factory B (the old Bryce, McKee & Company plant in Pittsburgh). Unknown silver grape clusters and leaves decoration. Circa 1920s. Bowl $65.00 – 75.00. Candlesticks, pair $100.00 – 120.00.

Plate 169. United States Glass Company #8096 flared (almost flat) bowl with #79 candlesticks in royal blue satin with Gold Line decoration #1 by U. S. Glass. Bowl: 3" high x 9" diameter. Candlesticks: 6½" high x 4⅛" diameter base. These candlesticks were advertised with a different bowl in an English trade journal from 1926. (See plate 797, page 294.) Circa 1922 – 1935. Bowl $80.00 – 90.00. Candlesticks, pair $140.00 – 150.00.

Plate 170. United States Glass Company #15330 (or #330) flared, footed bowl with #15320 (or #320) candlesticks in royal blue satin with Gold Line decoration #1 by U. S. Glass. Bowl: 6" high x 9¼" diameter. Candlesticks: 10" high x 4" diameter base. Circa 1922 – 1936. Bowl $100.00 – 125.00. Candlesticks, pair $200.00 – 225.00.

Console Sets

Plate 171. United States Glass Company rimmed bowl (unidentified, so possibly made by another glass company) with #151 candlesticks. Bowl: 3" high x 10" diameter. Candlesticks: 8¾" high x 4¼" diameter base. The base of the bowl is similar in shape to the #179 console bowl, but the marie foot (small ridge around the bottom to hold the bowl for finishing) is smaller and the bowl terminates at a right angle above the marie foot. Unknown silver decoration of flowers (dogwood?) with vines or ribbons between. Circa 1922 – 1930s. Bowl $40.00 – 50.00. Candlesticks, pair $140.00 – 150.00.

Plate 172. United States Glass Company #15179 two-handled, footed flared bowl with two-handled candlesticks. Bowl: 6½" high x 9⅜" diameter. Candlesticks: 10" high x 5" diameter base. With unknown silver flower and leaf decoration. Circa 1922 – 1930. Bowl $140.00 – 150.00. Candlesticks, pair $165.00 – 175.00.

Plate 173. United States Glass Company #8105 rolled edge bowl with E15179 two-handled candlestick. Bowl: 3⅝" high x 9⅜" diameter. Candlestick: 10" high x 5" diameter base. With unknown gold encrusted acid etched decoration. Circa 1922 – 1930. Bowl $60.00 – 70.00. Candlestick, each $35.00 – 45.00.

Console Sets

Plate 174. United States Glass Company #15179 two-handled, footed flared bowl with two-handled candlesticks. Bowl: 6½" high x 9⅝" diameter. Candlesticks: 10" high x 5" diameter base. With unknown silver bird and tree branch decoration. Circa 1922 – 1930. Bowl $140.00 – 150.00. Candlesticks, pair $165.00 – 175.00.

Plate 175. United States Glass Company #15179 two-handled, footed flared bowl with two-handled candlesticks. Bowl: 6½" high x 9½" diameter. Candlesticks: 10" high x 5" diameter base. With unknown gold encrusted acid etched decoration. Circa 1922 – 1930. Bowl $140.00 – 150.00. Candlesticks, pair $165.00 – 175.00.

Plate 176. United Stated Glass Company #179 three-footed, flared bowl with #66 three-part mold, twist stem candlesticks. Bowl: 4¼" high x 10" diameter. Candlesticks: 8" high x 4" diameter base. Circa 1922 – 1937. Bowl $55.00 – 65.00. Candlesticks, pair $100.00 – 150.00.

Console Sets

Plate 177. United States Glass Company #8105 flared bowl with #76 candlesticks. Bowl: 4¼" high x 9½" diameter. Candlesticks: 8½" high x 4¼" diameter base. Production was by both Factory G (one of the Glassport, Pennsylvania, plants) and Factory R (the Tiffin Glass Company plant). Unknown silver decoration of a footed basket of flowers alternating with shields and a hanging basket joined by a garland. The same decoration appears on the Diamond Glass-Ware Company candlestick seen in plate 33, page 19. Circa 1923 – 1935. Bowl $65.00 – 75.00. Candlesticks, pair $75.00 – 85.00.

Plate 178. United States Glass Company #8105 flared bowl with #76 candlesticks. Bowl: 3⅞" high x 9¾" diameter. Candlesticks: 8¾" high x 4⅜" diameter base. Production was by both Factory G (one of the Glassport, Pennsylvania, plants) and Factory R (the Tiffin Glass Company plant). Unknown silver decoration of blossoms with leaves. Circa 1923 – 1935. Bowl $65.00 – 75.00. Candlesticks, pair $100.00 – 120.00.

Plate 179. United States Glass Company #15179 (#179) flat rim, footed bowl with #74 candlesticks. Bowl: 4⅝" high x 10¾" diameter. Candlesticks: 10¼" high x 4¾" diameter base. With unknown gold encrusted acid etched Minton-style decoration. This decoration is similar to the Tiffin Minton encrusted decoration offered as part of the Ritz-Carlton Assortment but is much larger. Circa 1923 – 1935. Bowl $100.00 – 125.00. Candlesticks, pair $100.00 – 125.00.

Console Sets

Plate 180. Czechoslovakian footed bowl with candlesticks. Bowl: 7" high x 6¾" diameter. Candlesticks: 8⅜" high x 3⅞" diameter. With an unknown silver leaves and line decoration. Stamped "Czecho-slovakia" on bottom. Circa 1920s – 1930s. Bowl $25.00 – 35.00. Candlesticks, pair $35.00 – 45.00.

Plate 181. Czechoslovakian high footed, flared bowl or compote with candlesticks. Bowl: 5½" high x 7⅝" diameter. Candlesticks: 8⅜" high x 3⅞" diameter base. With silver birds and leaves decoration. Stamped "Czecho-slovakia" on base. Circa 1920s – early 1930s. Bowl $25.00 – 35.00. Candlestick, pair $35.00 – 45.00.

BOWLS

Plate 182. Cambridge Glass Company #3400/5 four-footed, rolled edge console bowl in royal blue. 3" high x 11½" diameter. Circa 1933 – 1942. With Cambridge's #509 "Two Kids" flower frog (9¼" high). Bowl $110.00 – 120.00. Flower frog: $250.00 – 260.00.

Plate 183. Cambridge Glass Company. Left: E3400/1185 two-handled, flared bowl in royal blue. 4" high x 10" diameter. Circa 1933 – 1942. $70.00 – 80.00. Right: #3400/1180 two-handled, flared bowl in royal blue. 1¾" high x 5¼" diameter. Circa 1933 – 1942. Bowl $40.00 – 50.00.

Bowls

Plate 184. Cambridge Glass Company #39 Mount Vernon bowl in royal blue. 3" high x 10" diameter. Circa 1933 – 1942. Bowl $90.00 – 100.00.

Plate 185. Cambridge Glass Company #1351 three-footed, crimped bowl in royal blue. (Each foot consists of five beads.) 4" high x 10" diameter. Circa 1938 – 1942. With Cambridge's "Rose Lady" flower frog (8¾" high). Bowl $60.00 – 70.00. Flower frog: $125.00 – 135.00.

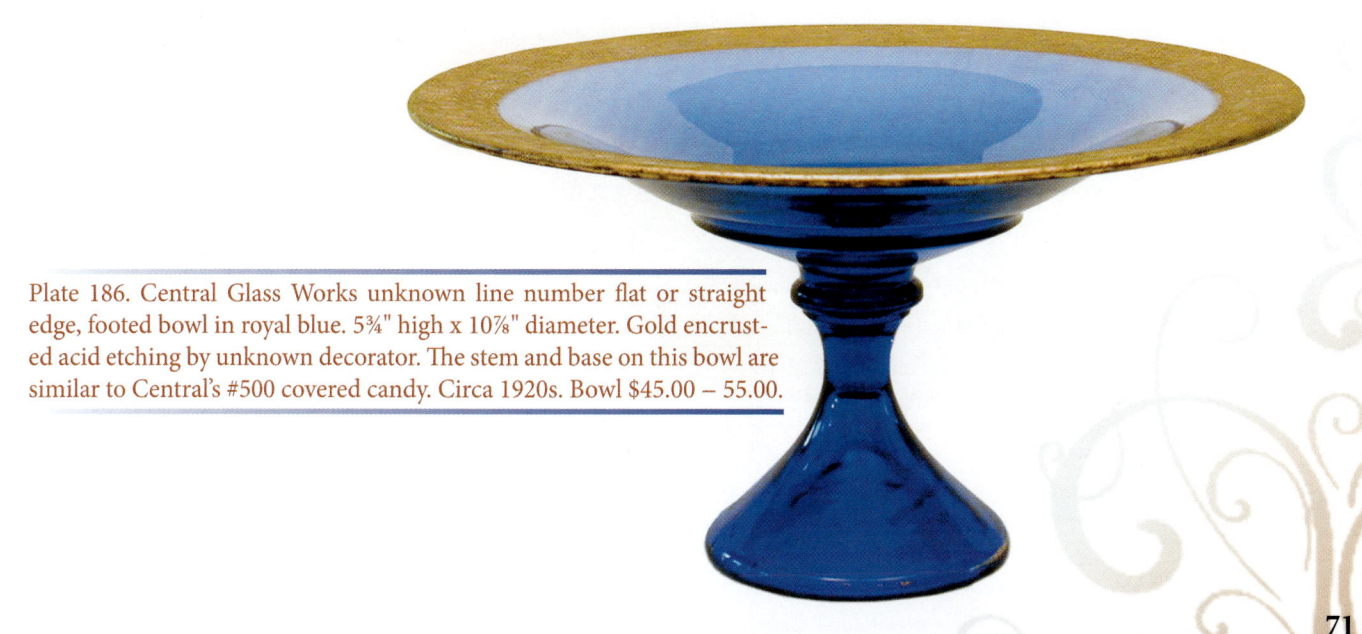

Plate 186. Central Glass Works unknown line number flat or straight edge, footed bowl in royal blue. 5¾" high x 10⅞" diameter. Gold encrusted acid etching by unknown decorator. The stem and base on this bowl are similar to Central's #500 covered candy. Circa 1920s. Bowl $45.00 – 55.00.

Bowls

Plate 187. Central Glass Works cupped or rolled edge bowl in royal blue. Probably line #2000, as it is from the same mold as the straight, flared, and rolled edge bowls in that pattern. 3½" high x 8⅜" diameter. With gold encrusted acid etching believed to be a scaled down version of the #905 St. Regis pattern by the Honesdale Decorating Company, Honesdale, Pennsylvania. Circa 1920s. Bowl $35.00 – 45.00.

Plate 188. Central Glass Works rolled edge bowl in royal blue. Probably line #2000. 3 1/16" high x 9¼" diameter. With gold encrusted acid etching believed to be a scaled down version of the #905 St. Regis pattern by the Honesdale Decorating Company, Honesdale, Pennsylvania. Circa 1920s. Bowl $35.00 – 45.00.

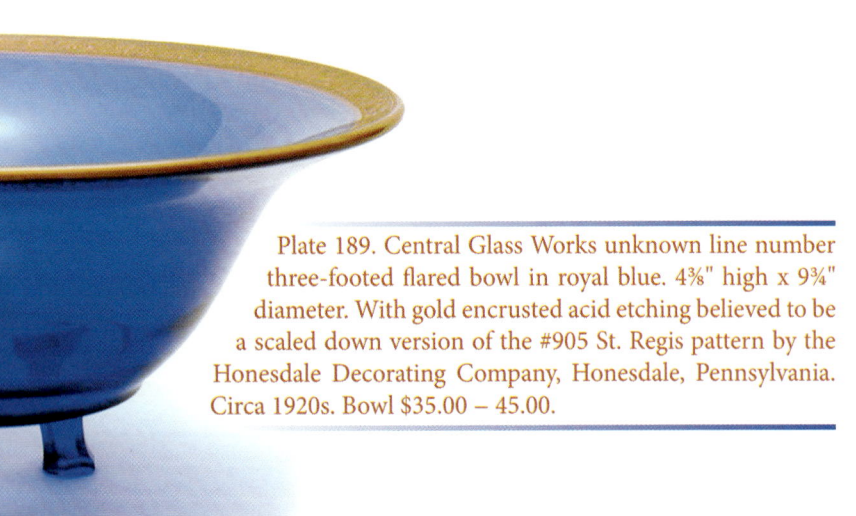

Plate 189. Central Glass Works unknown line number three-footed flared bowl in royal blue. 4⅜" high x 9¾" diameter. With gold encrusted acid etching believed to be a scaled down version of the #905 St. Regis pattern by the Honesdale Decorating Company, Honesdale, Pennsylvania. Circa 1920s. Bowl $35.00 – 45.00.

Bowls

Plate 190. Diamond Glass-Ware Company low cupped bowl. 2⅜" high x 10¼" diameter. Silver decoration called Victoria by The National Silver Deposit Ware Company, New York, N.Y. See plate 120, page 49, for a console set with the same decoration. Circa 1928 – 1931. Bowl $25.00 – 35.00.

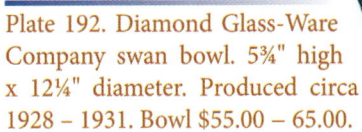

Plate 191. Diamond Glass-Ware Company low cupped bowl. 2¼" high x 10⅜" diameter. Silver deposit with the Rockwell Silver Company shield and #175-11 etched on the bottom. This Rockwell decoration was named "Kobi Basket" by Leslie Pina and Jerry Gallagher in their *Tiffin Glass, 1914 – 1940*. Circa 1928 – 1931. Bowl $90.00 – 100.00.

Plate 192. Diamond Glass-Ware Company swan bowl. 5¾" high x 12¼" diameter. Produced circa 1928 – 1931. Bowl $55.00 – 65.00.

Bowls

Plate 193. Diamond Glass-Ware Company six-lobed rim, three-footed bowl. 3¾" high x 12¼" diameter. The bowl is decorated with a silver deposit of branches and leaves and what look like dogwood flowers. The Fostoria Glass Company made a #2394 bowl identical to this except for the shape of the feet. (See plate 138, page 55.) This bowl in black glass is on display in the Museum of American Glass in West Virginia's collection as part of a console set with a pair of Diamond's #716 candlesticks. Circa 1930 – 1931. Bowl $70.00 – 80.00.

Plate 194. Duncan and Miller Glass Company #126 Venetian Line footed bowl. 6½" high x 10" diameter. Circa 1931 – 1937. Bowl $150.00 – 160.00.

Plate 195. Hazel-Atlas Glass Company bowls in Ritz blue: (1) 2¾" high x 6½" diameter. $35.00 – 40.00. (2) 3¼" high x 7½" diameter. $40.00 – 45.00. (3) 3¾" high x 8½" diameter. $45.00 – 50.00. (4) 4⅛" high x 9½" diameter. $50.00 – 55.00. (5) 4½" high x 10½" diameter. $85.00 – 95.00. (6) 5¼" high x 11½" diameter. $130.00 – 150.00. Circa 1936 – 1940.

Bowls

Plate 196. Hazel-Atlas Glass Company bowls in Ritz blue, showing the five sizes nested. See plate 195 for additional information.

Plate 197. Hazel-Atlas Glass Company Crisscross rolled edge bowl in Ritz blue. 4¼" high x 9⅝" diameter. Also made in 6⅝", 7⅝", 8⅝", and 10⅝" sizes. Circa 1938. Bowl $50.00 – 55.00.

Plate 198. A. H. Heisey and Company #1440 floral bowl in Stiegel blue. Called "Arch" by collectors. 3¾" high x 9¼" diameter. Circa 1934 – 1937. Bowl $400.00 – 500.00.

Bowls

Plate 199. Imperial Glass Corporation #7497B Lace Edge (or Laced Edge) flared bowl in Ritz blue. Also known as "Katy" to collectors. 3" high x 9" diameter. Circa 1936 – 1940. Bowl $35.00 – 45.00.

Plate 200. Imperial Glass Corporation #7497E Lace Edge (or Laced Edge) basket bowl in Ritz blue. Also known as "Katy" to collectors. 3⅞" high x 9" diameter. Circa 1936 – 1940. Bowl $35.00 – 45.00.

Plate 201. Imperial Glass Corporation #7286A four-footed, flared octagon bowl in Ritz blue with unknown Sterling Silver decoration. 3½" high x 8½" diameter. Circa 1930s. Bowl $35.00 – 45.00.

Bowls

Plate 202. Imperial Glass Corporation #727 octagon bowl in Ritz blue, with unknown Sterling Silver decoration. 1½" high x 9¾" diameter. With a base, this is part of the #7277F console set. Circa 1930s. Bowl $35.00 – 45.00.

Plate 203. H. Northwood and Company Regent small fruit bowl. Also known as "Leaf Medallion" to collectors. 2" high x 4¼" diameter x 2⅞" base. Circa 1904. Bowl $10.00 – 12.00.

Plate 204. Paden City Glass Manufacturing Company #412 flat rim bowl in royal blue. Named "Crow's Foot Square" by Jerry Barnett. 2¾" high x 11¾". Acid etched partially silver encrusted decoration, called "Cabbage Rose" by William Walker, which includes the flowers and leaves of the American Beauty decoration done by the Lotus Glass Company. Circa 1930s. Bowl $200.00 – 225.00.

Bowls

Plate 205. Paden City Glass Manufacturing Company #412 two-handled bowl in royal blue. Named "Crow's Foot Square" by Jerry Barnett. 3¼" high x 10", lobe to lobe. Circa 1930s. Bowl $50.00 – 60.00.

Plate 206. Paden City Glass Manufacturing Company #890 flared two-handled bowl in royal blue. Named "Crow's Foot Round" by Jerry Barnett. 3¼" high x 9½" diameter. Circa 1930s. Bowl $50.00 – 60.00.

Plate 207. Paden City Glass Manufacturing Company #890 three-leg, flat rim bowl in royal blue. Named "Crow's Foot Round" by Jerry Barnett. 3¾" high x 11¼" diameter. Circa 1930s. Bowl $80.00 – 90.00.

Bowls

Plate 208. Paden City Glass Manufacturing Company #991 two-handled bowl in royal blue. Named "Penny Line" by Hazel Marie Weatherman. 2" high x 8½" diameter. Advertised in 1932. Bowl $40.00 – 50.00.

Plate 209. Paden City Glass Manufacturing Company #881 Gadroon flared bowl in royal blue. Also known as "Wotta Line" (named by Hazel Marie Weatherman). 3¼" high x 9½" diameter. Advertised in 1932 by Paden City. Bowl $45.00 – 50.00.

Plate 210. Paden City Glass Manufacturing Company #895 two-handled bowl with gold trim on the rim in royal blue. Named "Lucy" by Jerry Barnett. 3¼" high x 9" diameter. This pattern was mentioned in the trade journals circa 1935. Bowl $45.00 – 50.00.

Bowls

Plate 211. Paden City Glass Manufacturing Company #895 flared, three-leg bowl in royal blue. Named "Lucy" by Jerry Barnett. 4¼" high x 10¾" diameter. With marked "Sterling" silver decoration by unknown decorator (named "Pod Flower" by William Walker). Circa 1935. Shown with Paden City's crystal seahorse flower frog. Bowl $65.00 – 75.00. Flower frog $100.00 – 125.00.

Plate 212. Paden City Glass Manufacturing Company #895 flared, three-leg bowl in royal blue. Named "Lucy" by Jerry Barnett. 4½" high x 10¾" diameter. Circa 1935. Bowl $55.00 – 65.00.

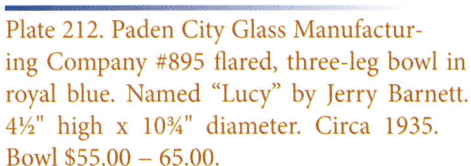

Plate 213. Paden City Glass Manufacturing Company #895 two-handled, flared bowl in royal blue. Named "Lucy" by Jerry Barnett. 3¼" high x 8¾" diameter. With marked "Sterling" silver decoration by unknown decorator (named "Pod Flower" by William Walker). Circa 1935. Bowl $35.00 – 45.00.

Bowls

Plate 214. Paden City Glass Manufacturing Company #215½ flat or straight rim, three-leg console bowl in royal blue. Named "Glenda" by Jerry Barnett. 3¼" high x 12½" diameter. This is a variation of the Paden City #215 Glades pattern (also known as "Hotcha," the name given to it by Hazel Marie Weatherman). The bowl has three spires originating at the legs and continuing up the sides of the bowl, which are not present on the #215 Glades pattern. Circa 1936 – 1939. Bowl $65.00 – 75.00.

Plate 215. Paden City Glass Manufacturing Company top hat bowl in royal blue. 4¾" high x 4" diameter base. With gold encrusted "Bridal Wreath" etching by an unknown decorator (named by William Walker and Paul Torsiello). Circa 1930s. Hat bowl $450.00 – 500.00.

Plate 216. L. E. Smith Glass Company. Left: #309 cupped three-leg bowl. Named "Mount Pleasant" by Hazel Marie Weatherman. 5½" high x 8¼" diameter. Shown in a catalog page as a special listing with F. W. Woolworth. Right: #309 "Mount Pleasant" flared and crimped, three-leg bowl. 5" high x 9¾" diameter. Circa 1930s. Each $30.00 – 35.00.

Bowls

Plate 217. L. E. Smith Glass Company #870 oval bowl. 4¾" high x 8" long. Circa 1930s. Bowl $35.00 – 45.00.

Plate 218. L. E. Smith Glass Company oval bowl or planter. 2¼" high x 6⅛" long. Circa 1930s. Bowl $30.00 – 35.00.

Plate 219. L. E. Smith Glass Company oval flared, footed bowl. 3" high x 8" wide. Advertised as part of an urn and bowl console set in "Mexican blue." (See plate 795, page 292.) Circa 1935. Bowl $20.00 – 25.00.

Bowls

Plate 220. L. E. Smith Glass Company #2400 two-handled fruit bowl. 4" high x 8⅜" diameter. Circa 1935 – 1936. Bowl $30.00 – 35.00.

Plate 221. United States Glass Company #15179 cupped bowl in royal blue satin with Gold Line decoration #1 by U.S. Glass. 5¾" high x 8" diameter. Circa 1920s. Bowl $65.00 – 75.00.

Plate 222. United States Glass Company #8105 flared bowl with unknown gold encrusted acid etching. 3¾" high x 10¼" diameter. Circa 1930s. Bowl $50.00 – 60.00.

Bowls

Plate 223. Czechoslovakian footed, ground top and base bowl with an unknown silver birds and flowers decoration. 4½" high x 9" diameter. Marked "Czecho-slovakia" on base. Circa 1920s – 1930s. Bowl $25.00 – 30.00.

Plate 224. Czechoslovakian flared ground top bowl with an unknown silver birds and leaves decoration. 4" high x 9" diameter. Marked "Czecho-slovakia" on base. Circa 1920s – 1930s. Bowl $25.00 – 30.00.

Plate 225. Czechoslovakian flared ground top bowl with an unknown silver diamonds and leaves decoration. 4" high x 9" diameter. Circa 1920s – 1930s. Bowl $25.00 – 30.00.

Bowls

Plate 226. Unattributed ten-lobed berry bowl set with unknown silver berries and leaves decoration. Large bowl: 3½" high x 10" diameter. Small bowls (six in the set, only two shown): 2¼" high x 5" diameter. This kind of "colonial" pattern was made by several glass companies. Circa early 1900s. Set $55.00 – 75.00.

Plate 227. Unattributed cut-to-clear under plate and flared bowl in cobalt cased crystal, cut and polished. Plate: 7¾". Bowl: 3¾" high x 7" diameter. Plate $30.00 – 40.00. Bowl $50.00 – 60.00.

COMPOTES

Plate 228. Cambridge Glass Company #1090 Decagon compote in Ritz blue. 7" high x 7" diameter. With Cambridge's #732 etching. Circa 1929 – 1931. Compote $150.00 – 160.00.

Plate 229. Cambridge Glass Company #3400/4 (#3135 stem) compote in royal blue with Lola silver deposit by Lotus Glass Company. 7" high x 7" diameter. Circa 1931 – 1942. Compote $275.00 – 300.00.

Plate 230. Cambridge Glass Company #1066 cupped bowl with crystal stem compote in royal blue. 4¼" high x 5¼" diameter. Circa 1931 – 1942. Compote $75.00 – 85.00.

Compotes

Plate 231. Cambridge Glass Company #3124 cupped compote in royal blue and crystal. 6" high x 5¼" diameter. Circa 1931 – 1942. Compote $100.00 – 125.00.

Plate 232. Cambridge Glass Company #3126 cupped compote in royal blue and crystal. 6⅛" high x 5½" diameter. Circa 1931 – 1942. Compote $100.00 – 125.00.

Plate 233. Cambridge Glass Company #3400/28 flat rim compote with "key hole" stem in royal blue and crystal. 5½" high x 7½" diameter. Circa 1931 – 1942. Compote $150.00 – 160.00.

87

Compotes

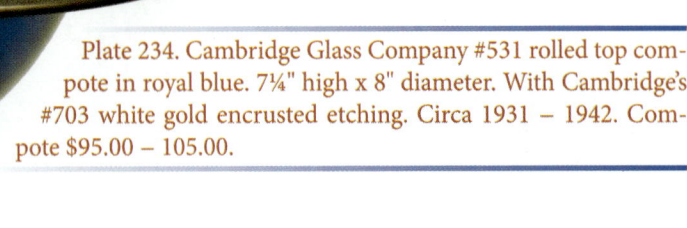

Plate 234. Cambridge Glass Company #531 rolled top compote in royal blue. 7¼" high x 8" diameter. With Cambridge's #703 white gold encrusted etching. Circa 1931 – 1942. Compote $95.00 – 105.00.

Plate 235. Cambridge Glass Company #11 Mount Vernon flat rim, footed compote in royal blue and crystal. 4" high x 7½" diameter. Circa 1931 – 1942. Compote $100.00 – 125.00.

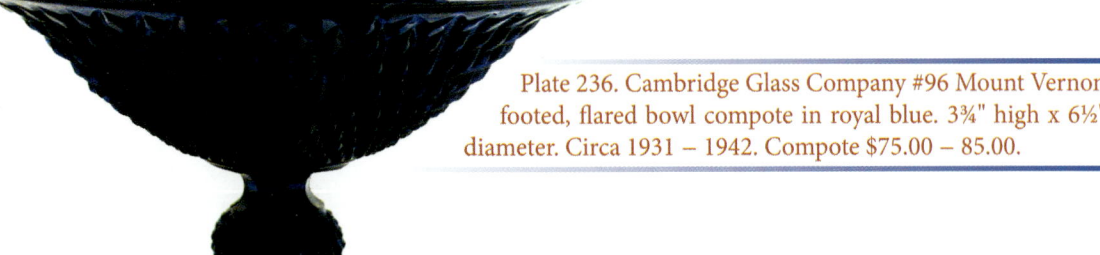

Plate 236. Cambridge Glass Company #96 Mount Vernon footed, flared bowl compote in royal blue. 3¾" high x 6½" diameter. Circa 1931 – 1942. Compote $75.00 – 85.00.

Compotes

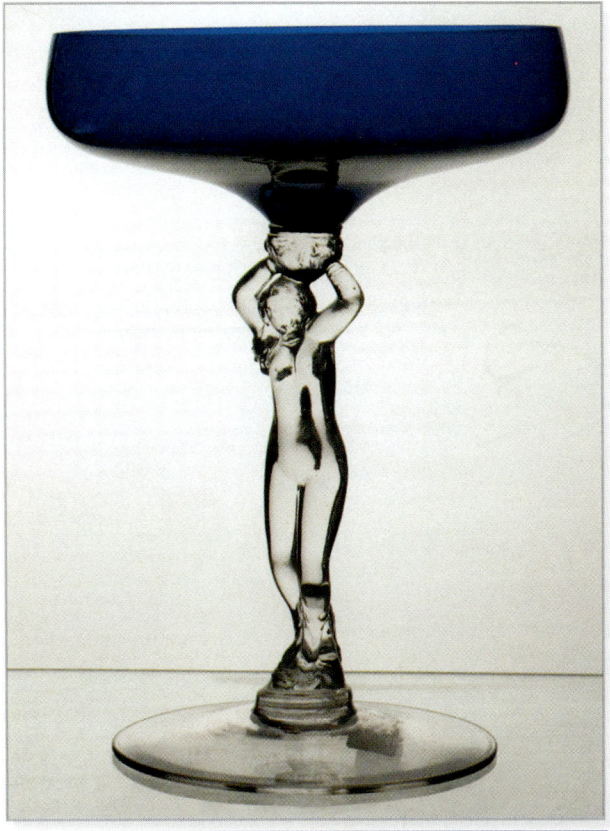

Plate 237. Cambridge Glass Company #3011 Statuesque Line cupped compote in royal blue and crystal. 7¼" high x 5⅜" diameter. Circa 1931 – 1942. Compote $600.00 – 650.00.

Plate 238. Cambridge Glass Company #3011 Statuesque Line compote with a #3400 cupped bowl in crystal and royal blue. 8" high x 6⅜" diameter. Circa 1931 – 1942. Compote $400.00 – 450.00.

Plate 239. Cambridge Glass Company #3011 Statuesque Line compote with a #3400 flared top bowl in crystal and royal blue. 8" high x 6¾" diameter. Circa 1931 – 1942. Compote $450.00 – 500.00.

Compotes

Plate 240. Cambridge Glass Company #3500 Gadroon cupped compote in royal blue and crystal. 6" high x 5¼" diameter. Circa 1933 – 1942. Compote $150.00 – 160.00.

Plate 241. Cambridge Glass Company #1402/61 Tally-Ho low footed, flat rim compote in royal blue. 2½" high x 5¾" diameter. Circa 1935 – 1942. Compote $75.00 – 85.00.

Plate 242. Cambridge Glass Company #1402/67 Tally-Ho cupped compote in royal blue. 5¼" high x 6½" diameter. Circa 1935 – 1942. Compote $70.00 – 80.00.

Compotes

Plate 243. Left: Central Glass Works flat or straight edge, high footed compote or bonbon in royal blue. 7" high x 7" diameter. Right: #2000 compote or bonbon in royal blue with gold encrusted acid etching decoration D-2049, "Hanging Garlands and Shields" by Wheeling Decorating Company. 5⅛" high x 6¾" diameter. Circa 1930s. Left compote $30.00 – 40.00. Right compote $50.00 – 60.00.

Plate 244. Central Glass Works flared high footed compote or bonbon in royal blue with gold encrusted acid etching believed to be a scaled down version of #905 Saint Regis by Honesdale Decorating Company, Honesdale, Pennsylvania. 6¾" high x 7" diameter. Circa 1930s. Compote $50.00 – 60.00.

Plate 245. Central Glass Works cupped or rolled in, low footed compote in royal blue with gold encrusted acid etching believed to be a scaled down version of #905 Saint Regis by Honesdale Decorating Company, Honesdale, Pennsylvania. 3⅞" high x 6" diameter. This compote has a stem treatment similar to the high footed bowl and the #500 covered candy. Circa 1930s. Compote $50.00 – 60.00.

Compotes

Plate 246. Co-operative Flint Glass Company #449 rolled edge, three part mold compote. 7" high x 6¾" diameter. Circa 1924 – 1934. Compote $60.00 – 70.00.

Plate 247. Diamond Glass-Ware Company Victory flared compote with gold edging. 5¾" high x 6¾" diameter. Advertised by Diamond in 1929. Compote $80.00 – 90.00.

Plate 248. Fostoria Glass Company #2327 flared compote in regal blue. 6¾" high x 7" diameter. Circa 1933 – 1940. Compote $75.00 – 85.00.

Compotes

Plate 249. H. C. Fry Glass Company crystal swirl stem, petal foot, flat rim compote in royal blue. 3½" high x 6⅞" diameter. Circa 1931 – 1933. Compote $100.00 – 125.00.

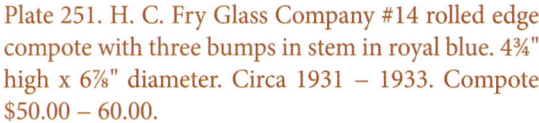

Plate 250. H. C. Fry Glass Company #2502 tall, flat rim compote in royal blue. 6" high x 6½" diameter. Circa 1931 – 1933. Compote $40.00 – 50.00.

Plate 251. H. C. Fry Glass Company #14 rolled edge compote with three bumps in stem in royal blue. 4¾" high x 6⅞" diameter. Circa 1931 – 1933. Compote $50.00 – 60.00.

Compotes

Plate 252. Hazel-Atlas Glass Company Florentine #1 compote in Ritz blue. Named "Poppy" by Hazel Marie Weatherman. 3⅜" high x 5" diameter. Circa 1935. Compote $55.00 – 65.00.

Plate 253. Imperial Glass Corporation #727 eight – pointed, tall stem, flared rim compote in Ritz blue. Named "Molly" or "Munsell" by Hazel Marie Weatherman. 6¾" high x 5½" diameter. Circa 1932 – 1940. Compote $30.00 – 40.00.

Plate 254. Morgantown Glass Works #7643 Golf Ball or Celeste cupped compote in Ritz blue. 5⅜" high x 6" diameter. Also sold with a cover. Circa 1929 – 1930s. Compote $270.00 – 300.00.

Compotes

Plate 255. Morgantown Glass Works? five crystal ball stem compote with cobalt foot and cupped bowl. 6½" high x 6½" diameter. The glass color, finish on lip of bowl, ball stem, and overall workmanship suggest a possible attribution to Morgantown in the 1930s. Compote $50.00 – 60.00.

Plate 256. Morgantown Glass Works? crystal tear-drop bubble stemmed compote. 6½" high x 6½" diameter. The tear-drop bubble stem was used by Morgantown and this compote shares the attributes that apply to Morgantown quality, color, and finish, leading to this possible identification. Compote $50.00 – 60.00.

Plate 257. Ludwig Moser & Sohne facet-cut glass compote with gold encrusted "Amazon Warrior" decoration. 6" high x 5" diameter. Signed "Moser." Circa 1918 – 1925. Compote $750.00 – 1,000.00.

Compotes

Plate 258. New Martinsville Glass Manufacturing Company #37 Georgian compote in Ritz blue. Georgian is the company's original name for this pattern, now known as "Moondrops" to collectors. 4" high x 5⅝" diameter. Circa 1933 – 1937. Compote $40.00 – 50.00.

Plate 259. H. Northwood and Company Regent jelly compote. Also known as "Leaf Medallion" to collectors. 4¾" high x 4¾" diameter. Circa 1904. Compote $75.00 – 85.00.

Plate 260. Paden City Glass Manufacturing Company #412 flared rim, stemmed compote in royal blue. Named "Crows Foot Square" by Jerry Barnett. 6⅜" high x 7" square. Circa 1930s. Compote $75.00 – 85.00.

Compotes

Plate 261. Paden City Glass Manufacturing Company #412 flared rim, stemmed compote in royal blue. Named "Crows Foot Square" by Jerry Barnett. 6½" high x 6⅞" square. With an acid etched partially silver encrusted decoration (named "Cabbage Rose" by William Walker) which includes the flowers and leaves of the American Beauty decoration done by the Lotus Glass Company. Circa 1930s. Compote $75.00 – 85.00.

Plate 262. Paden City Glass Manufacturing Company #412 flat rim, low-footed compote in royal blue. Named "Crows Foot Square" by Jerry Barnett. 3" high x 6¼" square. Circa 1930s. Compote $35.00 – 45.00.

Plate 263. Paden City Glass Manufacturing Company #412 rolled out rim, low-footed compote in royal blue. Named "Crows Foot Square" by Jerry Barnett. 3½" high x 6¼" square. With silver overlay, #65 Spring Time, by the Lotus Glass Company. Circa 1930s. Compote $100.00 – 125.00.

Compotes

Plate 264. Paden City Glass Manufacturing Company #412 flared rim, low-footed compote in royal blue. Named "Crows Foot Square" by Jerry Barnett. 3¾" high x 6½" square. With Sterling silver deposit Evangeline decoration by National Silver Company. Circa 1930s. Compote $75.00 – 85.00.

Plate 265. Paden City Glass Manufacturing Company #890 flared rim, tall stemmed compote in royal blue. Named "Crows Foot Round" by Jerry Barnett. 6½" high x 7" diameter. Circa 1930s. Compote $60.00 – 70.00.

Plate 266. Paden City Glass Manufacturing Company #895 flared rim, low footed compote in royal blue. Named "Lucy" by Jerry Barnett. 4" high x 6¾" diameter. Circa 1935 – 1939. Compote $45.00 – 55.00.

Compotes

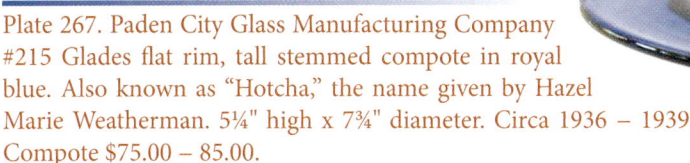

Plate 267. Paden City Glass Manufacturing Company #215 Glades flat rim, tall stemmed compote in royal blue. Also known as "Hotcha," the name given by Hazel Marie Weatherman. 5¼" high x 7¾" diameter. Circa 1936 – 1939. Compote $75.00 – 85.00.

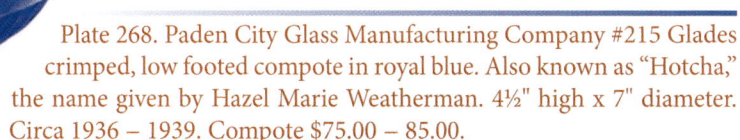

Plate 268. Paden City Glass Manufacturing Company #215 Glades crimped, low footed compote in royal blue. Also known as "Hotcha," the name given by Hazel Marie Weatherman. 4½" high x 7" diameter. Circa 1936 – 1939. Compote $75.00 – 85.00.

Plate 269. Pairpoint Corporation. Left to right: (1) #A299 footed compote (more likely a sherbet) with Pairpoint's Grapes engraving. 4" high x 4½" diameter. Compote $65.00 – 75.00. (2) #228 flat rim compote with Grapes engraving by Pairpoint. 4" high x 7⅞" diameter. Compote $250.00 – 300.00. (3) #228 flat rim compote with Grapes engraving by Pairpoint. 4" high x 7⅞" diameter. Compote $250.00 – 300.00. The three pieces are circa 1920s.

Compotes

Plate 270. Pairpoint Corporation #B372 controlled bubbles stem, flared rim compote. 8½" high x 7" diameter. Circa 1920s. Compote $350.00 – 400.00.

Plate 271. Pairpoint Corporation #B366 controlled bubbles stem, flat rim compote. 6⅛" high x 6½" diameter. Circa 1920s. Compote $250.00 – 300.00.

Plate 272. United States Glass Company #8177 tall stemmed, flat rim compote in royal blue satin with the Gold Line decoration #1 by U.S. Glass. 6½" high x 7" diameter. Circa 1930s. Compote $75.00 – 80.00.

Plate 273. Viking Glass Company #1600 Mount Vernon compote. 3⅞" high x 8" diameter. Made in the 1980s. Some of the pieces in this pattern resemble the Cambridge Mount Vernon pattern, but of poorer quality. See the candy dish (plate 283 on page 103) and decanter (plate 516 on page 183) for other examples. Compote $20.00 – 25.00.

Compotes

Plate 274. Czechoslovakian compote with unknown silver grape, vines, and grape leaves decoration. 5½" high x 7½" diameter. Circa 1920s – early 1930s. Compote $30.00 – 40.00.

Plate 275. Czechoslovakian compote with unknown silver fine line decoration. 2¾" high x 6¾" diameter. Circa 1920s – early 1930s. Compote $20.00 – 30.00.

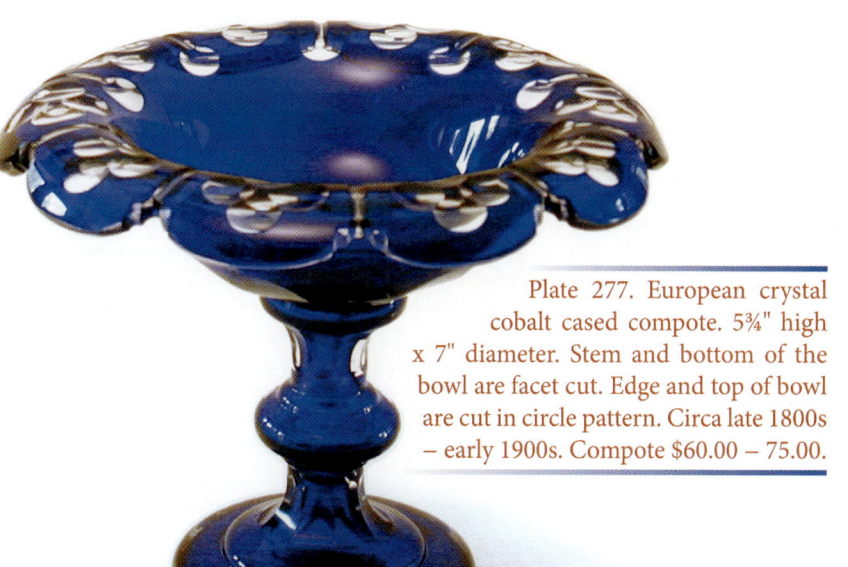

Plate 276. European (probably Czechoslovakian) tall compote with unknown silver decoration. 9" high x 6½" diameter. Circa early 1930s. Compote $30.00 – 40.00.

Plate 277. European crystal cobalt cased compote. 5¾" high x 7" diameter. Stem and bottom of the bowl are facet cut. Edge and top of bowl are cut in circle pattern. Circa late 1800s – early 1900s. Compote $60.00 – 75.00.

101

CANDY AND NUT DISHES

Plate 278. Cambridge Glass Company #3400/9 four-footed candy box and cover in royal blue. 4" high without lid (6¼" high with lid) x 7" diameter. Circa 1931 – 1940s. Candy box and cover $70.00 – 75.00.

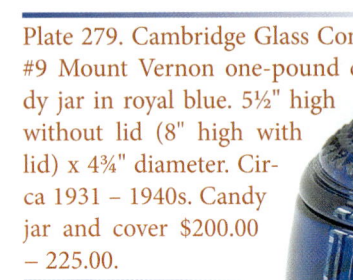

Plate 279. Cambridge Glass Company #9 Mount Vernon one-pound candy jar in royal blue. 5½" high without lid (8" high with lid) x 4¾" diameter. Circa 1931 – 1940s. Candy jar and cover $200.00 – 225.00.

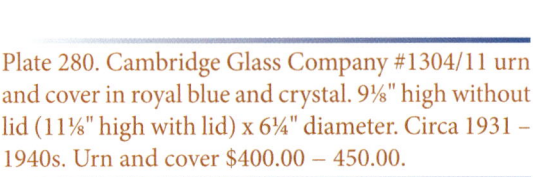

Plate 280. Cambridge Glass Company #1304/11 urn and cover in royal blue and crystal. 9⅛" high without lid (11⅛" high with lid) x 6¼" diameter. Circa 1931 – 1940s. Urn and cover $400.00 – 450.00.

Candy and Nut Dishes

Plate 281. Cambridge Glass Company #3500/41 Gadroon candy jar in royal blue. 7¼" high without lid (10" high with lid) x 4" diameter. Circa 1933 – 1940s. Candy jar and cover $300.00 – 400.00.

Plate 282. Cambridge Glass Company #3500/57 Gadroon three-compartment candy in royal blue. 1¼" high without lid (3¾" high with lid) x 8" across. Circa 1933 – 1940s. Candy and cover $75.00 – 85.00.

Plate 283. Dalzell Viking #1911 Mount Vernon footed bowl with cover. Offered as part of the Collectors Classic line. 6" high without lid (9¼" with lid) x 6" diameter. Circa 1993 – 1994. Bowl $20.00 – 30.00.

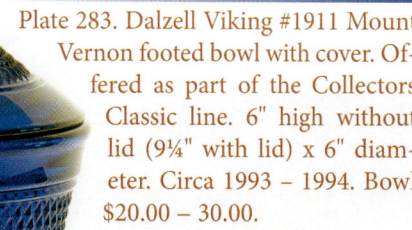

Candy and Nut Dishes

Plate 284. Fenton Art Glass Company #1532 Dolphin candy jar in royal blue. 5¾" high without lid (9" high with lid) x 4⅛" diameter. Circa 1929 – 1939. Candy jar and cover $90.00 – 100.00.

Plate 285. Fostoria Glass Company #2219 candy jar and cover in regal blue with unknown gold encrusted acid etching. 5¼" high without lid (7" high with lid) x 3¾" diameter. Circa 1933 – 1941. Candy jar and cover $70.00 – 75.00.

Plate 286. Fostoria Glass Company #4020 individual nut dish in regal blue. 2¾" high x 2" square base. Circa 1933 – 1942. Nut dish $45.00 – 50.00.

Plate 287. Hazel-Atlas Glass Company Royal Lace. Nut dish. 2⅛" high x 5⅛" diameter. Circa 1934 – 1941. $1,300.00 – 1,500.00.

Candy and Nut Dishes

Plate 288. Hazel-Atlas Glass Company bowl in Ritz blue in metal holder with handle. 1½" high x 4½" diameter. Circa 1936 – 1940s. Bowl $12.00 – 15.00.

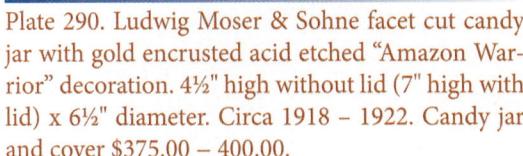

Plate 289. A. H. Heisey & Company #1430 candy jar in Stiegel blue. Known as "Aristocrat" to collectors. 7¼" high. Believed to be available with or without a cover. Circa 1933 – 1937. Candy jar without cover $300.00 – 325.00.

Plate 290. Ludwig Moser & Sohne facet cut candy jar with gold encrusted acid etched "Amazon Warrior" decoration. 4½" high without lid (7" high with lid) x 6½" diameter. Circa 1918 – 1922. Candy jar and cover $375.00 – 400.00.

105

Candy and Nut Dishes

Plate 291. Ludwig Moser & Sohne covered pokal form with gold decoration. 7⅝" high without lid (10½" high with lid) x 3½" diameter. Circa 1925. Covered pokal $275.00 – 300.00.

Plate 292. New Martinsville Glass Manufacturing Company #37 Georgian three-footed candy dish in Ritz blue. Georgian was the company's original name for the pattern, better known to collectors today as "Moondrops." 5½" high to top of finial x 4½" diameter. Circa 1933 – 1937. Candy dish $85.00 – 90.00.

Plate 293. Paden City Glass Manufacturing Company #881 Gadroon three-compartment candy dish in royal blue. Also known as "Hotcha," the name given by Hazel Marie Weatherman. 1⅞" high without lid (4" high with lid) x 6¾" diameter. Circa 1930s. Candy dish $40.00 – 50.00.

Candy and Nut Dishes

Plate 294. Paden City Glass Manufacturing Company #890 three-compartment candy dish in royal blue. Named "Crow's Foot Round" by Jerry Barnett. 1⅝" high with lid (4⅛" with lid) x 6¼" diameter. Circa 1930s. Candy dish without lid $10.00 – 15.00. Lid $50.00 – 60.00.

Plate 295. Paden City Glass Manufacturing Company #890 three-leg candy dish in royal blue. Named "Crow's Foot Round" by Jerry Barnett. 3⅜" high without lid (5¾" high with lid) x 6¼" diameter. Circa 1930s. Candy dish without lid $40.00 – 50.00. Lid $50.00 – 60.00.

Plate 296. Paden City Glass Manufacturing Company #412 three-compartment divided candy dish in royal blue. Named "Crow's Foot Square" by Jerry Barnett. 1⅝" high without lid (4" high with lid). With silver decoration by unknown decorator, named "Pod Flower" by William Walker. Circa 1930s. Candy dish $75.00 – 85.00.

Candy and Nut Dishes

Plate 297. Paden City Glass Manufacturing Company #412 three-compartment divided candy dish in royal blue. Named "Crow's Foot Square" by Jerry Barnett. 1⅝" high without lid (4" high with lid). With unknown gold line decoration. Circa 1930s. Candy dish $70.00 – 80.00.

Plate 298. Paden City Glass Manufacturing Company #503 (?) footed candy dish in royal blue. 6⅜" high without lid (9¾" high with lid). With Paden City's gold encrusted acid etching (named "Samarkand" by William Walker) and gray cutting of flowers, leaves, and vertical lines, by an unknown decorator. This candy dish is identical to the #503 pictured in the catalog with exception of a small ring below the finial. Circa 1930s. Candy dish $60.00 – 70.00.

Plate 299. L. E. Smith Glass Company #200 center handled nut or mint dish. Called "Mount Pleasant" by Hazel Marie Weatherman. 2¾" high x 6" diameter. Circa 1930s. Dish $25.00 – 30.00.

Candy and Nut Dishes

Plate 300. L. E. Smith Glass Company #50 three-leg bonbon dish. Usually collected as part of the "Mount Pleasant" pattern. 2" high x 6" diameter. Circa 1934 – 1936. Dish $12.00 – 15.00.

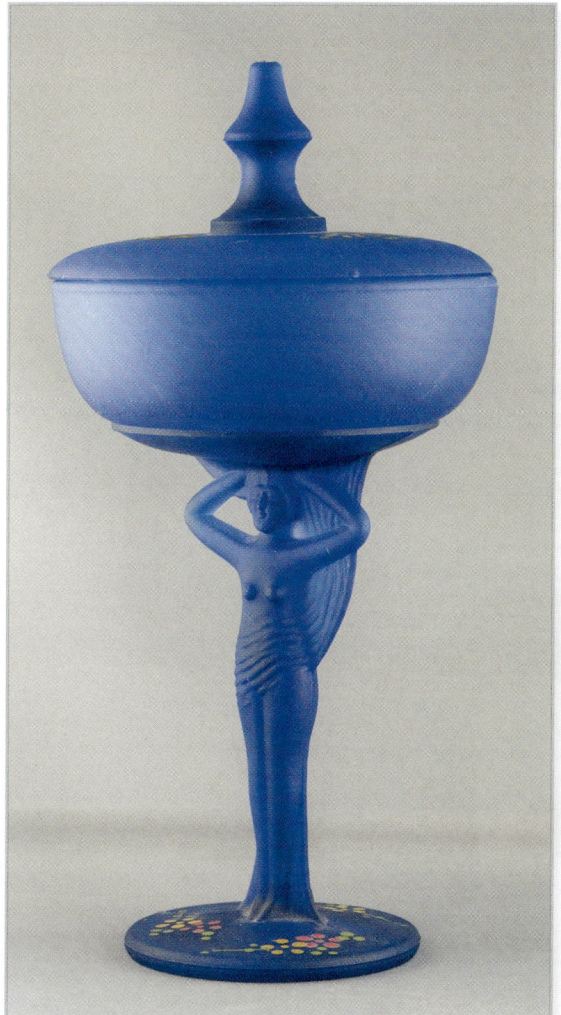

Plate 301. L. E. Smith Glass Company powder jar in blue satin with L. E. Smith hand-painted decoration. Named "Carrie" by collectors. 7⅜" high without lid (9½" high with lid) x 5" diameter. Also used as a candy jar. Circa 1937. Powder/candy jar $90.00 – 100.00.

Plate 302. L. E. Smith Glass Company #5204 Moon and Star candy box with cover. 7½" high x 6¼" diameter x 3¾" base. Circa 1988 – 1994. Candy box $65.00 – 75.00.

TABLE SETTINGS

Plate 303. Cambridge Glass Company #865 Decagon in Ritz blue. Circa 1929 – 1931. Left to right: (1) Luncheon plate. 8¼" point to point. $8.00 – 10.00. (2) Cup. 2½" high x 3¾" diameter. $8.00 – 10.00. (3) Saucer. 6" point to point. $4.00 – 5.00.

Plate 304. Cambridge Glass Company Mount Vernon in royal blue. Circa 1931 – 1940s.
Left to right: (1) #7 cup. 2¼" high x 3½" diameter. $15.00 – 18.00. (2) #7 saucer. 5¾" diameter. $15.00 – 18.00. (3) #40 dinner plate. 10½" diameter. $225.00 – 250.00. (4) #29 salt and pepper. 3⅜" high. Pair $80.00 – 85.00. (5) #1 9-ounce goblet. 5¾" high x 3⅛" diameter x 2⅜" square foot. $55.00 – 60.00. (6) #5 salad plate. 8½" diameter. $30.00 – 35.00. (7) #29 mustard. 2½ ounce. 3½" high x 2" diameter. $75.00 – 85.00. (8) #2 sherbet. 4" high x 4" diameter x 2¾" square foot. $20.00 – 25.00.

For additional pieces in Mount Vernon, see plate 184, page 71, plate 235 – 236, page 88, plate 279, page 102, plate 356, page 130, and plate 467, page 167.

Table Settings

Plate 305. Diamond Glass-Ware Company #99. Named "Charade" by Hazel Marie Weatherman. Circa 1930 – 1931.
Left to right: (1) Luncheon plate. 8" across. $20.00 – 25.00. (2) Cup. 2⅛" high x 2⅜" diameter. $15.00 – 20.00. (3) Saucer. 5½" square. $5.00 – 10.00.

Plate 306. Hazel-Atlas Glass Company Royal Lace. Circa 1934 – 1941.
Left to right: (1) Butter dish. 1⅝" high x 6½" diameter base. $300.00 – 350.00. With 2½" high cover $100.00 – 150.00. (2) Oval vegetable bowl. 2" high x 11" long x 7¾" wide. $55.00 – 65.00. (3) Footed sherbet. 3" high x 4⅛" diameter. $35.00 – 40.00. (4) 9-ounce tumbler. 4⅛" high. $35.00 – 40.00. (5) Handled cream soup. 4¾" diameter. $35.00 – 40.00. (6) Sherbet plate. 6" diameter. $12.00 – 15.00. (7) Dinner plate. 9⅞" diameter. $35.00 – 40.00. (8) Footed salt and pepper. 4⅛" high. Pair $250.00 – 300.00. (9) Sugar. 4⅛" high without lid. $35.00 – 40.00. With 4" diameter lid $145.00 – 150.00. (10) Creamer. 4⅛" high. $25.00 – 30.00. (11) Cup. 2⅝" high. $15.00 – 20.00. (12) Saucer. 5" diameter. $8.00 – 10.00. (13) Berry bowl. 5" diameter. $75.00 – 85.00.

Table Settings

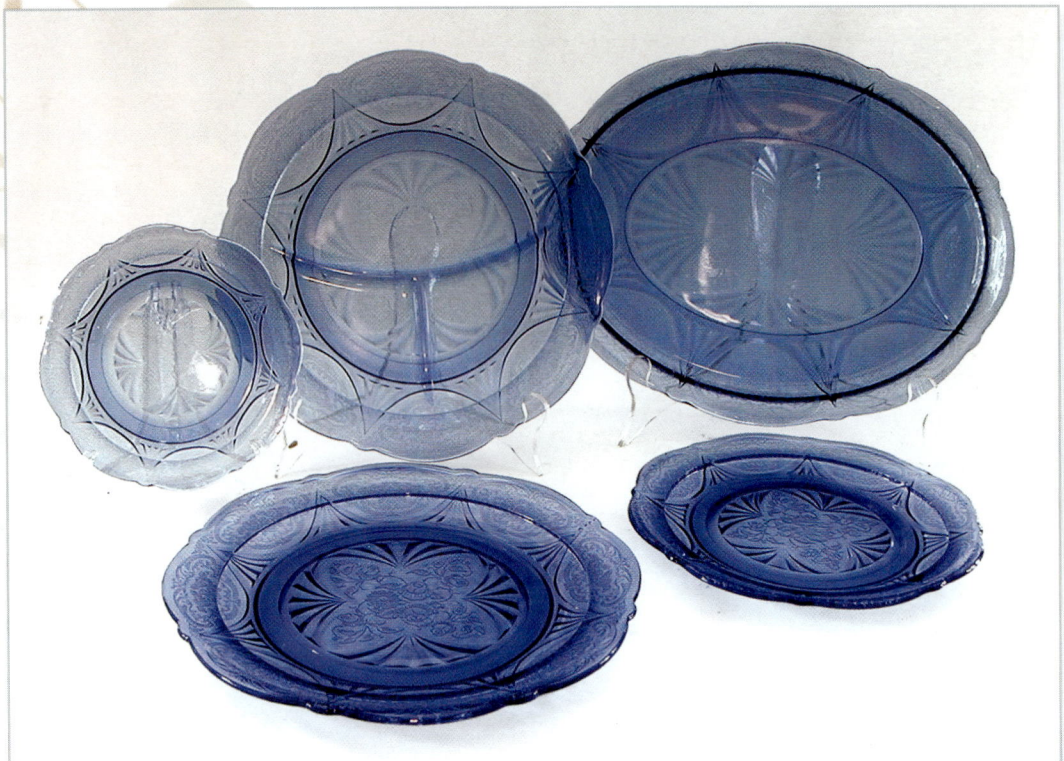

Plate 307. Hazel-Atlas Glass Company Royal Lace. Circa 1934 – 1941. Left to right: (1) Sherbet plate. 6" diameter. $12.00 – 15.00. (2) Dinner plate. 9⅞" diameter. $35.00 – 40.00. (3) Grill plate. 9⅞" diameter. $25.00 – 30.00. (4) Oval platter. 13" x 10". $55.00 – 60.00. (5) Luncheon plate. 8½" diameter. $30.00 – 35.00.

Plate 308. Hazel-Atlas Glass Company Royal Lace. Circa 1934 – 1941.
Left to right: (1) & (3) Individual berry bowls. 5" diameter. Each $75.00 – 80.00.
(2) Round berry. 10" diameter. $65.00 – 75.00.

Plate 309. Hazel-Atlas Glass Company Royal Lace. Circa 1934 – 1941.
Left to right: (1) Chrome plated metal footed sherbets. 3½" high x 4¼" diameter. These sherbets were offered in Butler Brothers' spring 1938 catalog in sets of six. (See plate 773, page 276.) Each $25.00 – 30.00. (2) Glass footed sherbet. 3" high x 4⅛" diameter. $35.00 – 40.00. (3) Sherbet plate. 6" diameter. $12.00 – 15.00.

For additional items in Royal Lace, see plate 141 – 143, page 56, plate 287, page 104, plate 381, page 138, plate 441, page 159, plate 451 – 452, page 162, plate 524, page 186, and plate 775, page 277.

Table Settings

Plate 310. Hazel-Atlas Glass Company Moderntone in Ritz blue. Butler Brothers' spring 1938 catalog offered an assortment of items in this pattern in "true blue," with prices ranging from 40 cents for the dozen (for 5" nappies) up to $1.44 a dozen (for the 9" vegetable bowls). See plate 774, page 277. Circa 1934 – 1942.
Left to right: (1) Sherbet. 3⅛" high. $12.00 – 14.00. (2) Sherbet plate. 5⅞" diameter. $4.00 – 5.00. (3) Oval platter. 12" across. $75.00 – 80.00. (4) 9-ounce tumbler. 4⅛" high. $25.00 – 30.00. (5) 5-ounce tumbler. 4" high. $50.00 – 55.00. (6) Oval platter. 11" across. $30.00 – 35.00. (7) Ruffled cream soup. 5" diameter. $55.00 – 65.00. (8) Luncheon plate. 7¾" diameter. $10.00 – 12.00. (9) Salt and pepper. 4½" high. Pair $40.00 – 45.00. (10) Cup. 2¼" high. $6.00 – 9.00. With saucer. 5½" diameter. $3.00 – 4.00. (11) Creamer. 3" high. $10.00 – 12.00. (12) Sugar. 3" high. $10.00 – 12.00 (without lid). $30.00 – 40.00 (with lid). (13) Salad plate. 6¾" diameter. $8.00 – 10.00.

Plate 311. Hazel-Atlas Glass Company Moderntone in Ritz blue. Circa 1934 – 1942.
Left to right: (1) Cream soup. 4¾" diameter. $16.00 – 18.00. (2) Ruffled cream soup. 5" diameter. $55.00 – 65.00.

Plate 312. Hazel-Atlas Glass Company Moderntone in Ritz blue. Circa 1934 – 1942.
Left to right: (1) Dinner plate. 8⅞" diameter. $14.00 – 16.00. (2) Custard. 2⅜" high x 3" diameter. $16.00 – 18.00. (3) Soup bowl. 7½" diameter. $90.00 – 100.00. (4) Luncheon plate. 7¾" diameter. $10.00 – 12.00. (5) Large berry bowl. 8¾" diameter. $35.00 – 40.00. (6) Berry bowl. 5" diameter. $25.00 – 30.00.

Table Settings

Plate 313. Hazel-Atlas Glass Company Moderntone in Ritz blue. Circa 1934 – 1942.
Left to right: (1) 9-ounce tumbler. 4⅛" high. $25.00 – 30.00. (2) 1½-ounce whiskey. 3½" high. $35.00 – 40.00. (3) 5-ounce tumbler. 4" high. $50.00 – 55.00.

For additional items in Moderntone, see plate 341, page 125, and plate 774, page 277.

Plate 314. Hazel-Atlas Glass Company "Ships," also known to collectors as "Sailboat" or "Sportsman Series." Circa 1936 – 1940.
Left to right: (1) Saucer with "Sailboat" decoration. 5½" diameter. $15.00 – 20.00. (2) Moderntone cup. 2¼" high. $6.00 – 8.00. (3) Plate with "Sailboat" decoration. 9" diameter. $30.00 – 35.00. (4) 5-ounce juice tumbler. 3¾" high. $12.00 – 15.00. (5) 10½-ounce ice tea tumbler. 4⅞" high. $12.00 – 15.00.

For additional items in the "Sportsman Series," see plate 442, page 159, plate 455 – 456, page 163, plate 545 – 546, pages 193 – 194, plate 555 – 559, pages 197 – 199, and plate 772 – 773, page 276.

Plate 315. Hazel-Atlas Glass Company Newport. Also known as "Hairpin." Circa 1936 – 1940.
Left to right: (1) Footed sherbet. 2⅞" high x 3⅝" diameter. $12.00 – 15.00. (2) Sherbet plate. 5⅞" diameter. $5.00 – 6.00. (3) Oval platter. 11¾" x 9¼". $35.00 – 40.00. (4) High footed salt and pepper. 4¼" high. Pair $35.00 – 40.00. (5) Handled cream soup. 2¼" high x 4⅝" diameter. $15.00 – 20.00. (6) Luncheon plate. 8½" diameter. $10.00 – 15.00. (7) Cup. 2¾" high x 3¼" diameter. $10.00 – 12.00. (8) Saucer. 5⅝" diameter. $4.00 – 5.00. (9) Round platter. 11" diameter. $35.00 – 40.00. (10) Creamer. 4¼" high x 2⅞" diameter. $12.00 – 15.00. (11) Footed sugar. 4" high x 2⅞" diameter. $12.00 – 15.00. (12) Cereal bowl. 2" high x 5½" diameter. $35.00 – 40.00.

Table Settings

Plate 316. New Martinsville Glass Manufacturing Company #34 "Addie" (named by William Heacock in honor of early researcher, Addie Miller) in Ritz blue. Also known to collectors as "Twelve Point." Circa 1932 – 1937.
Left to right: (1) Footed tumbler. 3⅝" high. $8.00 – 10.00. (2) Two-handled serving platter. 10½" diameter. $25.00 – 30.00. (3) Footed sherbet. 2⅛" high x 3⅝" diameter. $12.00 – 15.00. (4) Two-handled cream soup. 2⅝" high x 5" diameter. $15.00 – 20.00. (5) Luncheon plate. 8" diameter. $12.00 – 15.00. (6) Footed sugar. 3½" high. $12.00 – 15.00. (7) Footed creamer. 3¾" high. $12.00 – 15.00. (8) Cup. 2½" high x 3½" diameter. $8.00 – 10.00. (9) Saucer. 5½" diameter. $6.00 – 8.00.

For additional items in "Addie," see plate 66, page 30.

Plate 317. New Martinsville Glass Manufacturing Company #36 in Ritz blue. Circa 1932 – 1937.
Left to right: (1) Two-handle serving platter. 9½" square. $15.00 – 20.00. (2) Luncheon plate. 8" square. $10.00 – 12.00. (3) Sugar. 3⅝" high. $8.00 – 10.00. (4) Creamer. 3⅝" high. $8.00 – 10.00. (5) Cup. 3⅝" high. (Same as New Martinsville #35.) $8.00 – 10.00 (6) Saucer. 3⅜" square. $6.00 – 8.00.

Table Settings

Plate 318. New Martinsville Glass Manufacturing Company #37 Georgian in Ritz blue. This was the original name used by the company for the pattern better known to collectors as "Moondrops." Circa 1932 – 1940s.
Left to right: (1) Three-footed mayonnaise. 2¾" high x 5½" diameter. $55.00 – 60.00. (2) Ladle. 5" long. $15.00 – 20.00. (3) Sherbet plate (under mayonnaise). 6⅛" diameter. $6.00 – 8.00. (4) Dinner plate. 9½" diameter. $20.00 – 25.00. (5) Footed cup. 2¾" high x 3¾" diameter. $15.00 – 20.00. (6) Saucer. 5¾" diameter. $5.00 – 6.00.

For additional items in "Moondrops," see plate 64 – 65, page 29 – 30, plate 151 – 152, page 59, plate 258, page 96, plate 292, page 106, plate 359, page 131, plate 494 – 496, page 176, plate 565, page 201, plate 708, page 249, and plate 788, page 288.

Plate 319. New Martinsville Glass Manufacturing Company #38 in Ritz blue. Referred to as Hostmaster and Repeal in advertisements. Named "Mildred" by Hazel Marie Weatherman. Circa 1934 – 1940.
Left to right: (1) Oval sugar. 2½" high x 4" long x 3¼" wide. $25.00 – 30.00. (2) Oval creamer. 2¾" high x 4¾" long x 3" wide. $25.00 – 30.00. (3) Serving platter. 14" diameter. $60.00 – 70.00. (4) Plate. 8½" diameter. $15.00 – 20.00. (5) Cup. 2½" high x 3⅝" diameter. $12.00 – 15.00. (6) Saucer. 5⅞" diameter. $8.00 – 10.00.

For additional Hostmaster items, see plate 525, page 186.

Table Settings

Plate 320. Paden City Glass Manufacturing Company #220 "Crow's Foot Round" in royal blue (named by Jerry Barnett). Circa 1930s.
Left to right: (1) Round platter. 10¾" diameter. (Indentation in center indicates it probably is a cheese and cracker plate.) $30.00 – 35.00. (2) Dinner plate. 9" diameter. $20.00 – 25.00. (3) #412 oval platter. Named "Crow's Foot Square" by Jerry Barnett. 11" long x 8½" wide. (4) Cup. 2⅛" high x 3⅝" diameter. $10.00 – 12.00. (5) Saucer. 6½" diameter. $5.00 – 6.00.

For additional items in "Crow's Foot Round," see plate 76, page 33, plate 206 – 207, page 78, plate 265, page 98, plate 294 – 295, page 107, and plate 352, page 129.

Plate 321. Paden City Glass Manufacturing Company #890 in royal blue. Named "Largo" by Jerry Barnett and "Cantina" by Hazel Marie Weatherman. "Largo" has been adopted by collectors. Circa 1937 – 1939.
Left to right: (1) Handled plate with indentation (cheese and cracker). 10¾" diameter. $30.00 – 40.00. (2) Dinner plate. 9" diameter. $25.00 – 30.00. (3) Four-footed creamer. 3⅞" high x 2¾" diameter. $35.00 – 40.00. (4) Four-footed sugar. 3¾" high x 2⅞" diameter. $35.00 – 40.00. (5) Cup. 2⅛" high x 3½" diameter. $20.00 – 25.00. (6) Saucer. 6¼" diameter. $5.00 – 10.00.

For additional items in "Largo," see plate 77, page 34.

Table Settings

Plate 322. L. E. Smith Glass Company "Mount Pleasant" (named by Hazel Marie Weatherman). Also known as "Double Shield." Circa 1930 – 1936.
Left to right: (1) #505 footed sherbet. 3" high x 4¼" diameter. $8.00 – 10.00. (2) #50 ice tea glass. 6" high x 2⅝" diameter. $10.00 – 15.00. (3) #505 two-handled plate. 8½" diameter. $15.00 – 20.00. (4) #505 plate. 8" diameter. $10.00 – 12.00. (5) #505 salt and pepper. 4¼" high. Pair $40.00 – 45.00. (6) #505 creamer. 3" high x 3⅜" diameter. $12.00 – 15.00. (7) #505 sugar. 2¾" high x 3¾" diameter. $12.00 – 15.00. (8) #505 cup. 2¼" high x 3½" diameter. $10.00 – 12.00. (9) #505 saucer. 6¼" diameter. $4.00 – 6.00.

Plate 323. L. E. Smith Glass Company "Mount Pleasant" (named by Hazel Marie Weatherman). Also known as "Double Shield." Circa 1930 – 1936.
Left to right: (1) #525 three-leg triangle bowl. 2⅞" high x 5" diameter. $12.00 – 15.00. (2) #525 three-leg bowl. 3¼" high x 5¼" diameter. $12.00 – 15.00. (3) #525 three-leg cupped bowl. 3½" high x 4¾" diameter. $12.00 – 15.00.

Table Settings

Plate 324. L. E. Smith Glass Company "Mount Pleasant" (named by Hazel Marie Weatherman). Also known as "Double Shield." Circa 1930 – 1936.
Left to right: (1) #410 handled plate. 10½" square. $30.00 – 35.00. (2) #200 handled mayonnaise plate. 7" hexagon. $12.00 – 15.00. (3) #200 handled bowl. 2½" high x 6" hexagon. $12.00 – 15.00. (4) #410 handled bowl. 3¾" high x 8" square. $15.00 – 20.00.

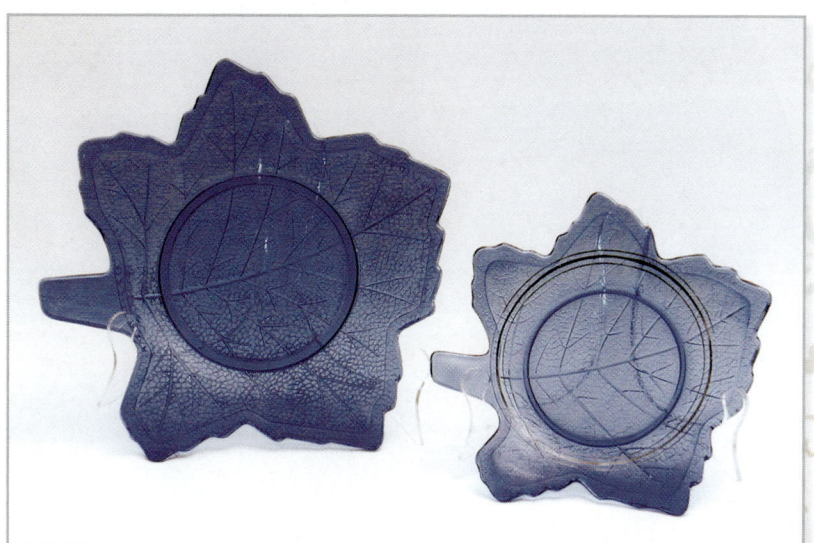

Plate 325. L. E. Smith Glass Company leaf plates, often considered part of the "Mount Pleasant" ("Double Shield") pattern. Circa 1936.
Left to right: (1) Leaf plate. 11¼" x 11½". $60.00 – 65.00. (2) Leaf plate. 8" x 8¼". $10.00 – 12.00.

For additional "Mount Pleasant" items, see plate 164, page 63, plate 216, page 81, and plate 299 – 300, page 108 – 109.

CAKE STANDS

Plate 326. Cambridge Glass Company #240 low footed cake stand in cobalt blue 2. 2" high x 9¾" diameter. With a gold encrusted acid etching by an unknown decorator. Circa 1925 – 1926. Cake stand $70.00 – 80.00.

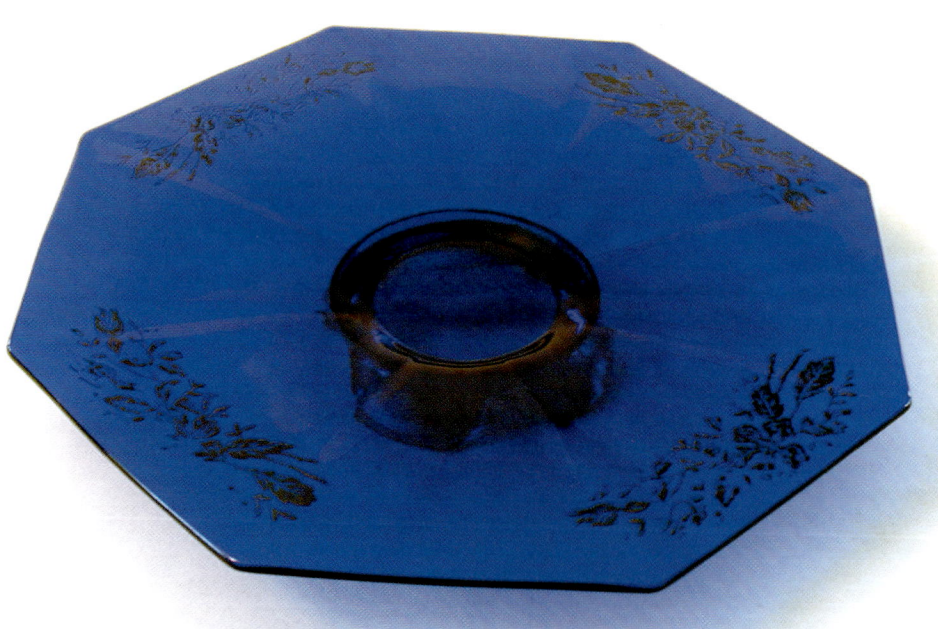

Plate 327. Imperial Glass Corporation #728 four-footed cake plate in Ritz blue with unknown sterling overlay. 1⅛" high x 10" octagon. Circa 1932 – 1940. Cake stand $50.00 – 60.00.

Cake Stands

Plate 328. Paden City Glass Manufacturing Company #412 stemmed cake stand in royal blue. Named "Crow's Foot Square" by Jerry Barnett. 4½" high x 8½" square. Circa 1930s. Cake stand $75.00 – 85.00.

Plate 329. Paden City Glass Manufacturing Company #895 low footed cake stand in royal blue. Named "Lucy" by Jerry Barnett. 2⅜" high x 12½" diameter. With silver decoration by an unknown decorator, named "Pod Flower" by William Walker. Circa 1935 – 1939. Cake stand $100.00 – 110.00.

Plate 330. United States Glass Company? footed cake stand. 1⅞" high x 10" diameter. Attribution to U. S. Glass is based on the foot. Circa 1930s. Cake stand $50.00 – 60.00.

CHEESE AND CRACKER SETS
&
CHIP AND DIP SETS

Plate 331. Cambridge Glass Company #135 stemmed cheese dish with cracker plate in cobalt blue #2. Cheese dish: 2⅝" high x 5⅜" diameter. Cracker plate: 10" diameter. With Cambridge's gold encrusted acid etching #708. Circa 1925 – 1926. Set $75.00 – 85.00.

Plate 332. Imperial Glass Corporation #727 octagon plate with cheese compote in Ritz blue. Plate: 11" point to point. Cheese compote: 3¼" high x 4½" diameter. With unknown sterling silver decoration of an urn and birds. Circa 1932 – 1940. Set $90.00 – 100.00.

Plate 333. Imperial Glass Corporation #1480 chip and dip. Known as "Fan Rib," made from an A. H. Heisey and Company mold. 13" diameter. See plate 776, page 279. Circa 1959 – 1962. Chip and dip $50.00 – 60.00.

Cheese and Crackers Sets & Chip and Dip Sets

Plate 334. Paden City Glass Manufacturing Company #412 footed cheese dish with cracker plate in royal blue. Named "Crow's Foot Square" by Jerry Barnett. Cheese dish: 2" high x 5¼" square. Cracker plate: 10" square. Silver overlay by unknown decorator. Circa 1930s. Set $65.00 – 75.00.

Plate 335. Paden City Glass Manufacturing Company #895 stemmed cheese dish with cracker plate in royal blue. Named "Lucy" by Jerry Barnett. Cheese dish: 2⅞" high x 5¼" diameter. Cracker plate: 10½" diameter. Plate with etched decoration by an unknown decorator, named "Pod Flower" by William Walker. Circa 1935 – 1939. Set $65.00 – 75.00.

Plate 336. United States Glass Company #15320 footed cheese and cracker with domed cover. 5⅝" high x 10" diameter. Circa 1930s. Set $60.00 – 70.00.

Plate 337. United States Glass Company #15320 footed cheese and cracker with domed cover. 5⅝" high x 10" diameter. With an unknown gold encrusted acid etching. Circa 1930s. Set $60.00 – 70.00.

CENTER HANDLE SERVERS

Plate 338. Cambridge Glass Company. Left to right: (1) #487 oval center handle server in royal blue with gold encrusted #708 acid etching by Cambridge. 10" wide x 12" long. Circa 1931 – 1940s. Server $65.00 – 75.00. (2) Cheese and cracker under plate in royal blue with the same #708 acid etching. (Missing the compote.) 8½" wide x 12" long. Cracker plate $90.00 – 100.00.

Plate 339. Central Glass Works #1435 pastry tray. 11" diameter. With gold encrusted acid etching believed to be scaled down version of #905 Saint Regis by the Honesdale Decorating Company, Honesdale, Pennsylvania. Circa 1930s. Server $45.00 – 55.00.

Plate 340. Fenton Art Glass Company #1639 center handle server in royal blue. Named "Elizabeth" by Margaret & Kenn Whitmyer in honor of Frank M. Fenton's wife. 9¼" square. Circa 1933 – 1939. Server $85.00 – 95.00.

Center Handle Servers

Plate 341. Hazel-Atlas Glass Company Moderntone center handled server. 10½" diameter. Made from the 10½" sandwich plate. Circa 1934 – 1942. Server $65.00 – 75.00.

Plate 342. Paden City Glass Manufacturing Company #412 center handled server in royal blue. Named "Crow's Foot Square" by Jerry Barnett. 10" square. With silver overlay by an unknown decorator. Circa 1930s. Server $45.00 – 55.00.

Plate 343. Paden City Glass Manufacturing Company #991 center handle server in royal blue. Named "Penny Line" by Hazel Marie Weatherman. 10½" diameter. Advertised in 1932. Server $45.00 – 55.00.

Center Handle Servers

Plate 344. Paden City Glass Manufacturing Company #895 center handled server in royal blue. Named "Lucy" by Jerry Barnett. 10¾" diameter. Mentioned in the trade journals in 1935. Server $45.00 – 55.00.

Plate 345. Paden City Glass Manufacturing Company #895 center handled server in royal blue. Named "Lucy" by Jerry Barnett. 10½" diameter. With silver overlay "Pod Flower" decoration by an unknown decorator (named by William Walker). Circa 1935 – 1939. Server $45.00 – 55.00.

Plate 346. L. E. Smith Glass Company #44 Colonial Lace center handle server. 4" high x 10¼" diameter. (Called Colonial Lace when reissued in the 1950s in milk glass.) Blue circa 1936. Made from a mold originally belonging to the Co-operative Flint Glass company. Server $75.00 – 85.00. (From the L. E. Smith Glass Company factory archives.)

TRAYS AND PLATTERS

Plate 347. Fostoria Glass Company #2440 Lafayette two-handled oval tray in regal blue. 8½" diameter. Circa 1934 – 1936. Tray $25.00 – 30.00.

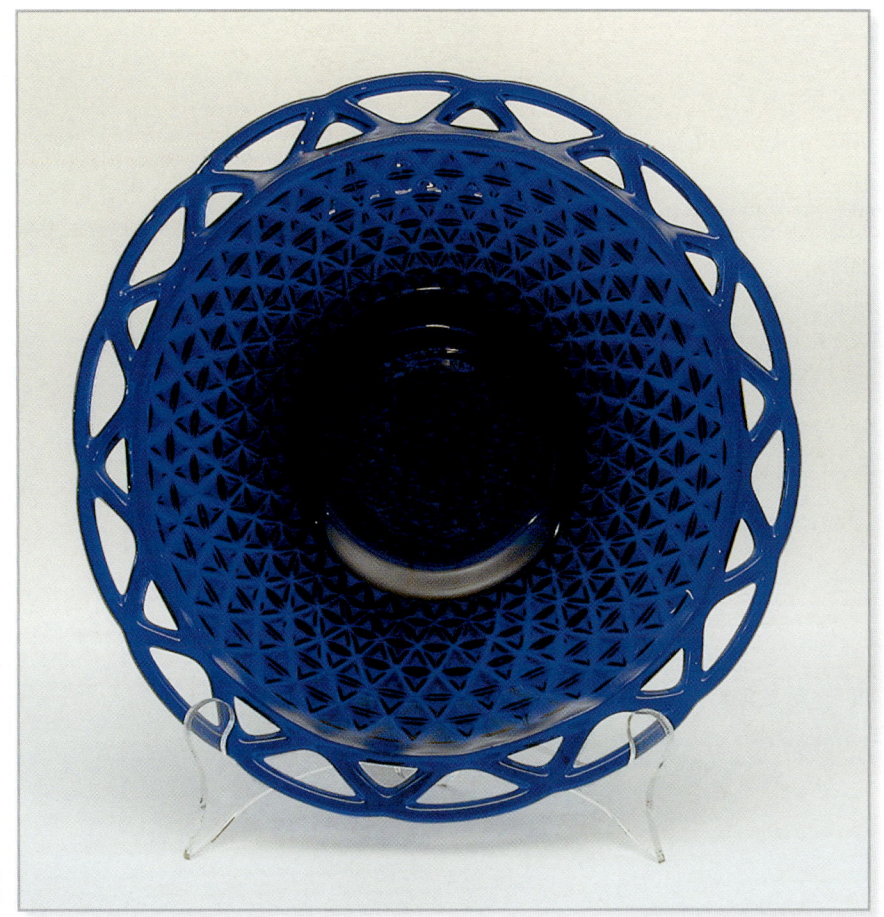

Plate 348. Imperial Glass Corporation #749 Lace Edge (or Laced Edge) plate in Ritz blue. 10½" diameter. Circa 1932 – 1940s. Plate $60.00 – 70.00.

Trays and Platters

Plate 349. New Martinsville Glass Manufacturing Company #35 tidbit tray in Ritz blue. Known as "Fancy Squares" to collectors. Made from 7¼" and 9" diameter plates. Circa 1933 – 1940s. Tidbit tray $65.00 – 75.00.

Plate 350. Paden City Glass Manufacturing Company #412 plate in royal blue. Named "Crow's Foot Square" by Jerry Barnett. 8½" square. With Paden City's "Orchid" acid etched decoration (named by Hazel Marie Weatherman). Circa 1930s. Plate (undecorated) $20.00 – 25.00. Plate with etching $150.00 – 160.00.

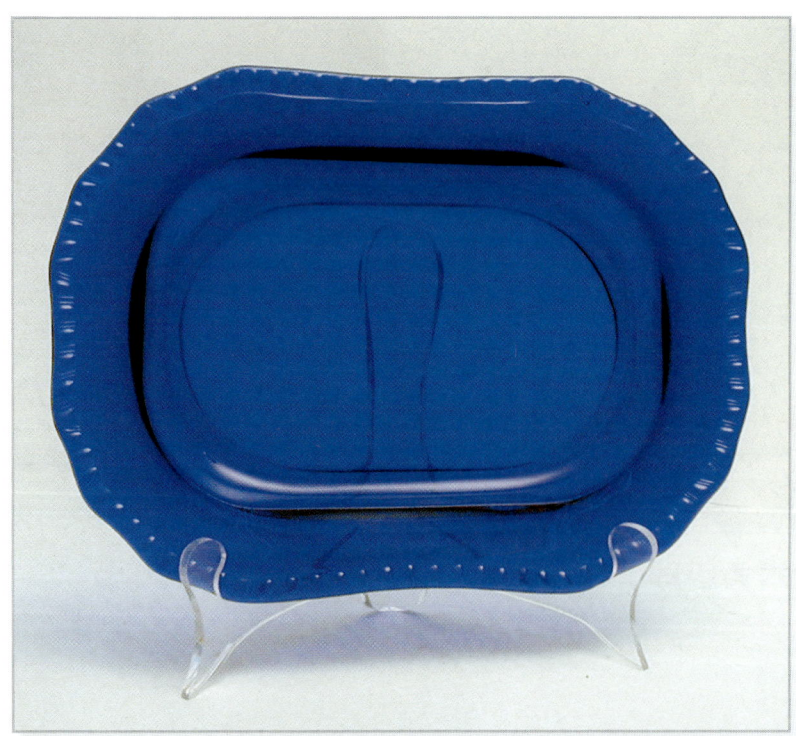

Plate 351. Paden City Glass Manufacturing Company #881 Gadroon serving tray in royal blue. Also known as "Wotta Line" (name given by Hazel Marie Weatherman). 10" x 7¼" rectangle. Circa 1930s. Tray $65.00 – 75.00.

Trays and Platters

Plate 352. Paden City Glass Manufacturing Company #890 two-handled serving platter in royal blue. Named "Crow's Foot Round" by Jerry Barnett. 11½" diameter. Silver overlay of flowers on rim and a star over an anchor in the center, marked "U. S. D. 1812, 1892 – 1942." U. S. D. 1812 is the National Society United Daughters of 1812. Established 1892, this platter commemorated their 50th year. Circa 1942. Platter $50.00 – 60.00.

Plate 353. Paden City Glass Manufacturing Company #895 two-handled serving platter in royal blue. Named "Lucy" by Jerry Barnett. 11¼" diameter. With unknown marked "Sterling" silver decoration, named "Pod Flower" by William Walker. Circa 1935 – 1939. Platter $50.00 – 60.00.

Plate 354. Pitman–Dreitzer and Company Newport serving platter. 13½" diameter. Pitman–Dreitzer was a manufacturer's representative and distributor. This pattern was probably made by the New Martinsville Glass Manufacturing Company, since most of Pitman–Dreitzer's advertisements from this time period featured New Martinsville glass. Circa 1935. Platter $25.00 – 30.00.

RELISH, CELERY, AND PICKLE DISHES

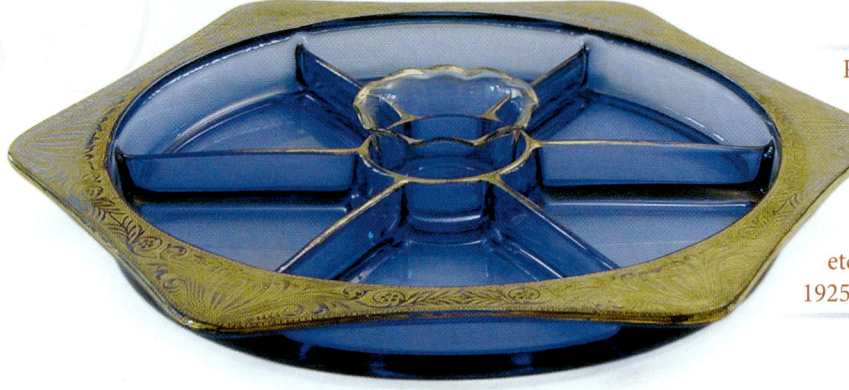

Plate 355. Cambridge Glass Company #389 six-compartment relish dish in cobalt blue #2. 1⅜" high x 11½" hexagon. With crimped dip bowl in center. 1½" high x 2¾" diameter. Gold encrusted acid etching by unknown decorator. Circa 1925 – 1926. Relish tray $75.00 – 85.00.

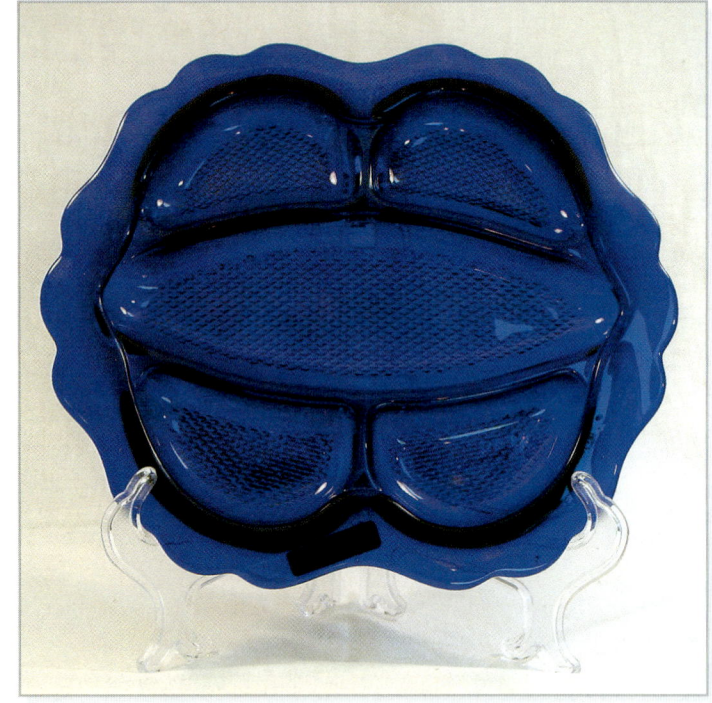

Plate 356. Cambridge Glass Company #104 Mount Vernon five-compartment celery and relish dish in royal blue. 1⅛" high x 12" long. Circa 1931 – 1940s. Relish dish $150.00 – 160.00.

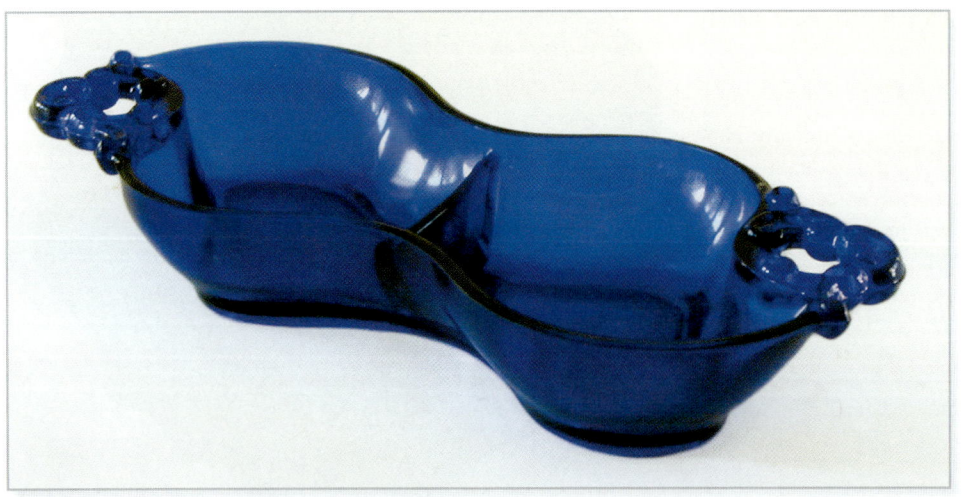

Plate 357. Cambridge Glass Company #3400/88 two-handled, two-compartment relish dish in royal blue. 1½" high x 8¾" long. Circa 1931 – 1940s. Relish dish $25.00 – 35.00.

Relish, Celery, and Pickle Dishes

Plate 358. Duncan and Miller Glass Company #111 Terrace tab-handled, five-compartment relish dish. 1⅜" high x 10½" diameter. Circa 1935 – 1937. Relish dish $190.00 – 200.00.

Plate 359. New Martinsville Glass Manufacturing Company #37 Georgian. This was the original name used by the company for the pattern better known today as "Moondrops" (name given by Hazel Marie Weatherman). Circa 1932 – 1940s. Left to right: (1) Boat-shaped celery. 1½" high x 11½" long x 4⅝" wide. $25.00 – 30.00. (2) Three-footed pickle dish. 3" high x 7½" wide. $30.00 – 35.00. (3) Three-footed, divided relish dish. 2" high x 8" diameter. $35.00 – 40.00.

Plate 360. Paden City Glass Manufacturing Company #215 Glades tab handled, four-compartment relish dish in royal blue. 1¼" high x 9" diameter. Circa 1936 – 1939. Relish dish $75.00 – 85.00.

131

Relish, Celery, and Pickle Dishes

Plate 361. L. E. Smith Glass Company #93 celery dish with sandblasted leaves and fruits. 1⅝" high x 10½" long. Circa 1936 – 1939. Celery dish $30.00 – 35.00. (From the L. E. Smith Glass Company factory archives.)

Plate 362. L. E. Smith Glass Company #93 two-part relish dish with sandblasted leaves and fruits. 1⅝" high x 10½" long. Circa 1936 – 1942. Relish dish $30.00 – 35.00. (From the L. E. Smith Glass Company factory archives.)

Plate 363. L. E. Smith Glass Company #65 handled, four-part relish dish. 6" wide x 15" long. Circa 1936. Relish dish $35.00 – 45.00. (From the L. E. Smith Glass Company factory archives.)

Plate 364. Unattributed chrome tray with five relish inserts. 11" wide x 18½" long. Could be anytime from circa 1930 – 1960. Relish dish $50.00 – 60.00.

MAYONNAISE SETS

Plate 365. Cambridge Glass Company #142/96 Tally-Ho footed twin salad dressing bowl in royal blue. 4¾" high x 6" diameter. Circa 1935 – 1940s. Bowl $75.00 – 85.00.

Plate 366. Paden City Glass Manufacturing Company #298 low-footed, rolled edge mayonnaise bowl with under plate in royal blue. Bowl: 4½" high x 6" diameter. Plate: 10¼" diameter. With Paden City's gold encrusted acid etching, named "Samarkand" by William Walker. Circa 1930s. Set $90.00 – 100.00.

Plate 367. Paden City Glass Manufacturing Company #895 three-leg, flared mayonnaise bowl with under plate in royal blue. Named "Lucy" by Jerry Barnett. Bowl: 3¾" high x 4¼" diameter. Plate: 6¼" diameter. Gold line trim by an unknown decorator. Circa 1936 – 1939. Set $45.00 – 55.00.

Plate 368. L. E. Smith Glass Company #635 footed mayonnaise bowl. 3" high x 4¼" square foot. Circa 1935 – 1936. Bowl $15.00 – 20.00.

GRAVY BOWLS

Plate 369. Paden City Glass Manufacturing Company #412 gravy bowl in royal blue. Named "Crow's Foot Square" by Jerry Barnett. 2½" high x 7⅜" long. Circa 1930s. Bowl $45.00 – 50.00.

Plate 370. Paden City Glass Manufacturing Company #895 low footed gravy bowl in royal blue. Named "Lucy" by Jerry Barnett. 4¼" high x 7½" long. Circa 1936 – 1939. Bowl $90.00 – 100.00.

SALT AND PEPPER SHAKERS & SALT DIPS

Plate 371. Boston and Sandwich Glass Company Christmas salt. 2½" high x 1¼" diameter. Marked on top, "Dana K. Alden Pat Dec. 25, 1877." Salt $110.00 – 120.00.

Plate 372. Cambridge Glass Company #3400 ball with crystal handled salt and pepper shakers in royal blue. 2" ball. Circa 1931 – 1940s. Pair $75.00 – 80.00.

Plate 373. Eales of Sheffield cobalt with silver salt and pepper shakers. 2½" high x 1" diameter. Box set $60.00 – 70.00.

Salt and Pepper Shakers & Salt Dips

Plate 374. Hazel-Atlas Glass Company. Circa 1936 – 1940s.
Left to right: (1) Fine ribbed marmalade with metal cover in Ritz blue. 3¾" high x 2¾" diameter. $25.00 – 30.00. (2) Ribbed salt and pepper shakers on metal tray. 2" high. Pair $25.00 – 30.00.

Plate 375. Unattributed horizontal ribbed salt and pepper shakers. 5½" high. Circa 1930. Pair $65.00 – 75.00.

Plate 376. Unattributed sterling silver with cobalt liner salts. 1¼" high x 3¼" long. Circa early 1900s. Each $30.00 – 40.00.

SUGAR BOWLS

Plate 377. Consolidated Lamp and Glass Company handled sugar jar with hand painted flowers. Known to collectors as "Open Heart Arches." 4¾" high to finial on top. Circa 1905. Sugar $150.00 – 175.00.

Plate 378. Unattributed crystal cased cobalt cut to clear handled sugar with silver base, cover, and spoon. 4¼" high. Circa 1890 – 1910. Sugar $90.00 – 100.00.

COOKIE AND SWEET MEAT JARS

Plate 379. A. A. Importing Company #CD/253 Thousand Eyes cobalt cut to crystal cookie jar. 8" high to finial top. Made in Poland. Circa 1978 – 1980. Jar $90.00 – 100.00.

Plate 380. Consolidated Lamp and Glass Company. Known as "Open Heart Arches" to collectors. Circa 1905.
Left to right: (1) Sweet meat jar with hand painted flower decoration. 7⅜" high to finial top. $200.00 – 250.00. (2) Handled cracker jar with hand painted flower decoration. 8" high to finial top. $400.00 – 500.00. (3) Handled sweet meat jar with hand painted flower decoration. 8" high to finial top. $200.00 – 250.00.

Plate 381. Hazel-Atlas Glass Company Royal Lace cookie jar in Ritz blue. 7½" high to finial top. Circa 1936 – 1940s. Jar $250.00 – 300.00.

KITCHEN ITEMS

Plate 382. Hazel-Atlas Glass Company refrigerator jars in Ritz blue. Known as "Crisscross" to collectors. Circa 1936 – 1938.
Left to right: (1) Two #9779 refrigerator jars with covers. 4" x 4" x 3½" high. Each $40.00 – 50.00. (2) #9780 refrigerator jar with cover. 4" x 8" x 3½" high. $90.00 – 120.00. (3) #9783 refrigerator jar with cover. 8" x 8" x 3½" high. $120.00 – 130.00.

Plate 383. Hazel-Atlas Glass Company #9659 egg beater base in Ritz blue. 4⅛" high x 4½" diameter. The base is the same as the ice tub in the "Sportsman" series, with a metal beater by A&J Manufacturing Company, Binghamton, New York, Pat. October 9, 1923. This set circa 1936 – 1940s. Set $90.00 – 100.00.

Plate 384. Imperial Glass Corporation #142 two-piece canape set in fish shape in Ritz blue. 7" long x 5¼" wide. Circa 1932 – 1940s. Set $20.00 – 25.00.

Kitchen Items

Plate 385. Imperial Glass Corporation cheese dish. 5" square plate with 2½" high cover. Sold with wrapped Kraft cheese under the cover. This set has been seen with an original Imperial label on the plate, probably made from a #760 saucer in the "Hazen" pattern (named by Hazel Marie Weatherman). Circa 1940s. Set $15.00 – 20.00.

Plate 386. McKee Glass Company batter jug. 9½" high to top of lid. Circa 1930s. Jug $110.00 – 120.00.

Plate 387. German silver tea bag strainer with cobalt insert. 1½" high x 2½" diameter. Metal and glass are both marked "Germany." Circa 1900? Tea bag holder $35.00 – 40.00.

Kitchen Items

Plate 388. Unattributed handled kerosene warmer with cobalt cased crystal, cut to clear. 4⅝" high x 5" diameter. Circa late 1800s. Warmer $140.00 – 150.00.

Plate 389. United States Glass Company three-section plate with cup ring and cup. 8½" diameter. Unknown gold encrusted acid etching on plate and gold trim on cup. Advertised in *The Pottery, Glass & Brass Salesman*, December 11, 1924. Set $25.00 – 30.00.

Plate 390. Unattributed item in the shape of a rolling pin. 15¼" long. Free blown; unequal diameter indicates that this was probably not a production piece. Most sources consider this to be a whimsey rolling pin, circa 1930s. Other sources however suggest that it was used as a vessel to transport salt in the days of the spice trade in the 1900s. Rolling pin or salt vessel $100.00 – 110.00.

CUPS AND SAUCERS

Plate 391. Cambridge Glass Company #865 Decagon cup and saucer in Ritz blue. Cup: 2½" high x 3¾" diameter. Saucer: 6" diameter. Marked with the Cambridge C in a triangle. Circa 1929 – 1931. Set $25.00 – 30.00.

Plate 392. Cambridge Glass Company #3400/54 cup and saucer in royal blue. Cup: 2½" high x 3¾" diameter. Saucer: 5½" diameter. Marked with the Cambridge C in a triangle. Circa 1931 – 1940s. Set $15.00 – 20.00.

Plate 393. Cambridge Glass Company #494 open stock table service cup and saucer in royal blue. Cup: 2½" high x 3¾" diameter. Saucer: 5⅝" diameter. Circa 1931 – 1940s. Set $20.00 – 25.00.

Cups and Saucers

Plate 394. Cambridge Glass Company #925 round after dinner cups and saucers in royal blue. Cup: 2¼" high x 2¼" diameter. Saucer: 4½" diameter. Set on left with gold trim. Both sets marked with the Cambridge C in a triangle. Circa 1931 – 1940s. Set, each $35.00 – 40.00.

Plate 395. Cambridge Glass Company #7 Mount Vernon cup and saucer in royal blue. Cup: 2¼" high x 3½" diameter. Saucer: 5¾" diameter. Circa 1931 – 1940s. Set $55.00 – 60.00.

Plate 396. Cambridge Glass Company #1402/19 Tally-Ho cup and saucer in royal blue. Cup: 2⅝" high x 3½" diameter. Saucer: 5¾" diameter. Circa 1935 – 1940s. Set $30.00 – 35.00.

Cups and Saucers

Plate 397. Canton Glass Company #836 cup and saucer. Named "Futura" by Hazel Marie Weatherman. Cup: 2¼" high x 3" diameter. Saucer: 6⅛" diameter. Circa 1932. Set $15.00 – 20.00.

Plate 398. Central Glass Works #1450 cup and saucer in royal blue. Cup: 2⅜" high x 3½" diameter. Saucer: 5¼" square. Circa 1920s – 1939. Set $25.00 – 30.00.

Plate 399. Central Glass Works? cup and saucer. Cup: 2⅛" high x 4⅛" diameter. Saucer: 5⅝" diameter. Circa 1930s. Set $10.00 – 15.00.

Cups and Saucers

Plate 400. Diamond Glass-Ware Company Victory cup and saucer. Cup: 2¼" high x 3⅜" diameter. Saucer: 5½" diameter. Circa 1929 – 1931. Set $30.00 – 40.00.

Plate 401. Diamond Glass-Ware Company #99 cup and saucer. Named "Charade" by Hazel Marie Weatherman. Cup: 2⅛" high x 2⅜" diameter. Saucer: 5½" diameter. Circa 1930 – 1931. Set $10.00 – 15.00.

Plate 402. Duncan and Miller Glass Company #111 Terrace cup and saucer. Cup: 2⅜" high x 3⅜" diameter. Saucer: 4¾" square. Circa 1935 – 1937. Set $35.00 – 45.00.

Cups and Saucers

Plate 403. Fenton Art Glass Company #1700 Lincoln Inn cup and saucer in royal blue. Cup: 2⅜" high x 3⅝" diameter. Saucer: 5¾" diameter. Circa 1928 – 1939. Set $15.00 – 20.00.

Plate 404. Fenton Art Glass Company #1639 cup and saucer in royal blue with unknown flower and leaves gray cutting. Cup: 2⅜" high x 3¼" diameter. Saucer: 5⅝" diameter. Circa 1930 – 1933. Set $20.00 – 25.00.

Plate 405. Fenton Art Glass Company #1611 Georgian cup and saucer in royal blue. Introduced as Agua Caliente in 1931. Cup: 2½" high x 3½" diameter. Saucer: 5⅝" diameter. Circa 1931 – 1939. Set $15.00 – 20.00.

Cups and Saucers

Plate 406. Fostoria Glass Company #2440 Lafayette cup and saucer in regal blue. Cup: 2½" high x 3" diameter. Saucer: 6" diameter. Circa 1934 – 1942. Set $25.00 – 35.00.

Plate 407. Fostoria Glass Company #2350 Pioneer after dinner cup and saucer in regal blue. Cup: 2⅛" high x 2¼" diameter. Saucer: 4¼" diameter. Circa 1934 – 1937. Set $15.00 – 20.00.

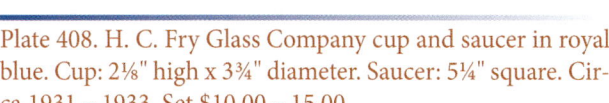

Plate 408. H. C. Fry Glass Company cup and saucer in royal blue. Cup: 2⅛" high x 3¾" diameter. Saucer: 5¼" square. Circa 1931 – 1933. Set $10.00 – 15.00.

Cups and Saucers

Plate 409. H. C. Fry Glass Company #3101 cup and saucer in royal blue. Cup: 3¾" high x 5⅞" diameter. Saucer: 5⅞" diameter. Circa 1931 – 1933. Set $15.00 – 20.00.

Plate 410. Hazel-Atlas Glass Company Moderntone cup and saucer in Ritz blue. Cup: 2⅜" high x 4" diameter. Saucer: 5½" diameter. Circa 1934 – 1937. Set $5.00 – 10.00.

Plate 411. Hazel-Atlas Glass Company Newport cup and saucer in Ritz blue. Also known as "Hairpin" to collectors. Cup: 2¾" high x 3¼" diameter. Saucer: 5⅝" diameter. Circa 1936 – 1940. Set $10.00 – 15.00.

Cups and Saucers

Plate 412. Hazel-Atlas Glass Company Royal Lace cup and saucer in Ritz blue. Cup: 2⅝" high x 3½" diameter. Saucer: 5¾" diameter. Circa 1936 – 1941. Set $20.00 – 25.00.

Plate 413. Hazel-Atlas Glass Company Aurora cup and saucer in Ritz blue. Cup: 2¼" high x 3¾" diameter. Saucer: 5½" diameter. Circa 1937 – 1938. Set $10.00 – 15.00.

Plate 414. Imperial Glass Corporation #160/37 Cape Cod coffee cup and saucer in Ritz blue. Cup: 2⅝" high x 3⅛" diameter. Saucer: 5½" diameter. Circa 1932 – 1937. Set $100.00 – 115.00.

149

Cups and Saucers

Plate 415. Imperial Glass Corporation #242/2 cup and saucer in Ritz blue. Named "Ida" by Hazel Marie Weatherman. Cup: 2¼" high x 3¾" diameter. Saucer: 5⅝" diameter. This pattern was also made by Imperial for the Morgantown Glass Works, who marketed it as #1511. Circa 1930s. Set $10.00 – 15.00.

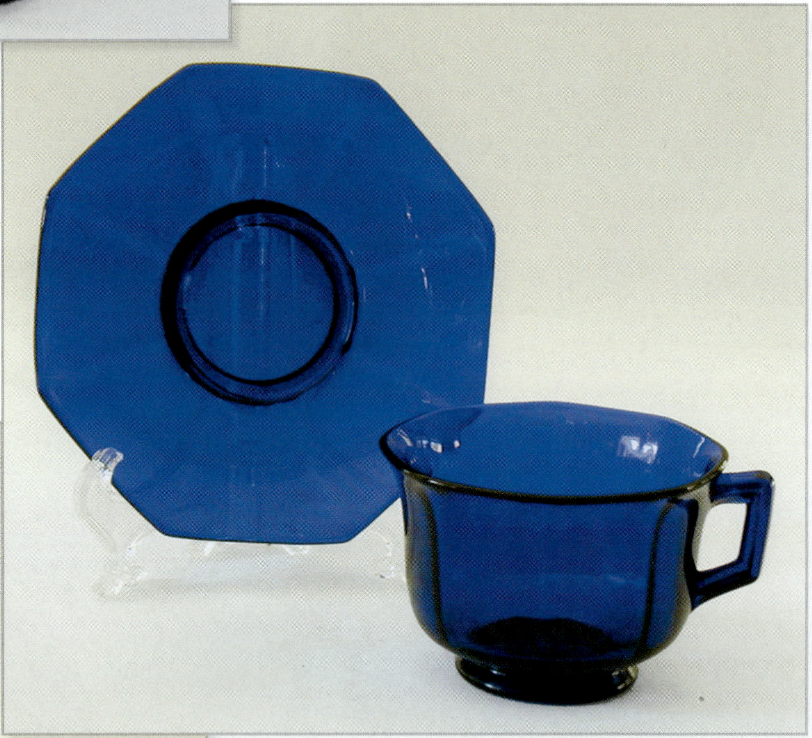

Plate 416. Imperial Glass Corporation #752/2 Octagon cup and saucer in Ritz blue. Also known as "Molly" (named by Hazel Marie Weatherman). Cup: 2½" high x 3½" octagon. Saucer: 5¼" octagon. Luncheon sets were made in this pattern. Circa 1932 – 1940s. Set $10.00 – 15.00.

Plate 417. Imperial Glass Corporation #134 Olive cup and saucer in Ritz blue. Cup: 2¼" high x 3⅝" diameter. Saucer: 5¾" diameter. Circa 1932 – 1940s. Set $15.00 – 20.00.

Cups and Saucers

Plate 418. Imperial Glass Corporation #749 Lace Edge (or Laced Edge) cup and saucer in Ritz blue. Also sometimes listed as #743, 745, and 780. Cup: 2⅜" high x 3⅛" diameter. Saucer: 5⅝" diameter. Circa 1935 – 1940s. Set $100.00 – 120.00.

Plate 419. Imperial Glass Corporation #701 Reeded cup and saucer in Ritz blue. Also called "Spun" by Hazel Marie Weatherman. Cup: 2⅜" high x 3¾" diameter. Saucer: 5½" diameter. Circa 1935 – 1940s. Set $20.00 – 25.00.

Plate 420. MacBeth-Evans Glass Company American Sweetheart #7575-R cup and #7576-R saucer. Cup: 2½" high x 3⅝" diameter. Saucer: 5⅞" diameter. Circa 1934 – 1936. Set $150.00 – 180.00.

Cups and Saucers

Plate 421. Ludwig Moser & Sohne after dinner cup and saucer, both with gold leaf decoration. Cup: 2¼" high x 2¼" diameter. Saucer: 4⅛" diameter. Circa 1889 – 1920. Set $50.00 – 60.00.

Plate 422. Ludwig Moser & Sohne after dinner lobed cup and saucer. Cup: 2½" high x 2¾" diameter. Saucer: 5⅝" diameter. Circa 1890. Set $30.00 – 40.00.

Plate 423. New Martinsville Glass Manufacturing Company #34 cup and saucer in Ritz blue. Named "Addie" by William Heacock, in honor of early researcher, Addie Miller. Cup: 2½" high x 3½" diameter. Saucer: 5½" diameter. Circa 1932 – 1940s. Set $10.00 – 15.00.

Cups and Saucers

Plate 424. New Martinsville Glass Manufacturing Company #34 after dinner cup and saucer in Ritz blue. Named "Addie" by William Heacock, in honor of early researcher, Addie Miller. Cup: 2⅜" high x 2⅜" diameter. Saucer: 4⅛" diameter. Circa 1932 – 1940s. Set $15.00 – 20.00.

Plate 425. New Martinsville Glass Manufacturing Company #35 cup and saucer in Ritz blue. Known as "Fancy Squares" to collectors. Cup: 2½" high x 3½" diameter. Saucer: 5¼" square. Circa 1932 – 1940s. Set $15.00 – 20.00.

Plate 426. New Martinsville Glass Manufacturing Company #36 cup and saucer in Ritz blue. Cup: 3⅝" high (same as New Martinsville #35 cup). Saucer: 3⅜" square. Circa 1932 – 1937. Set $15.00 – 20.00.

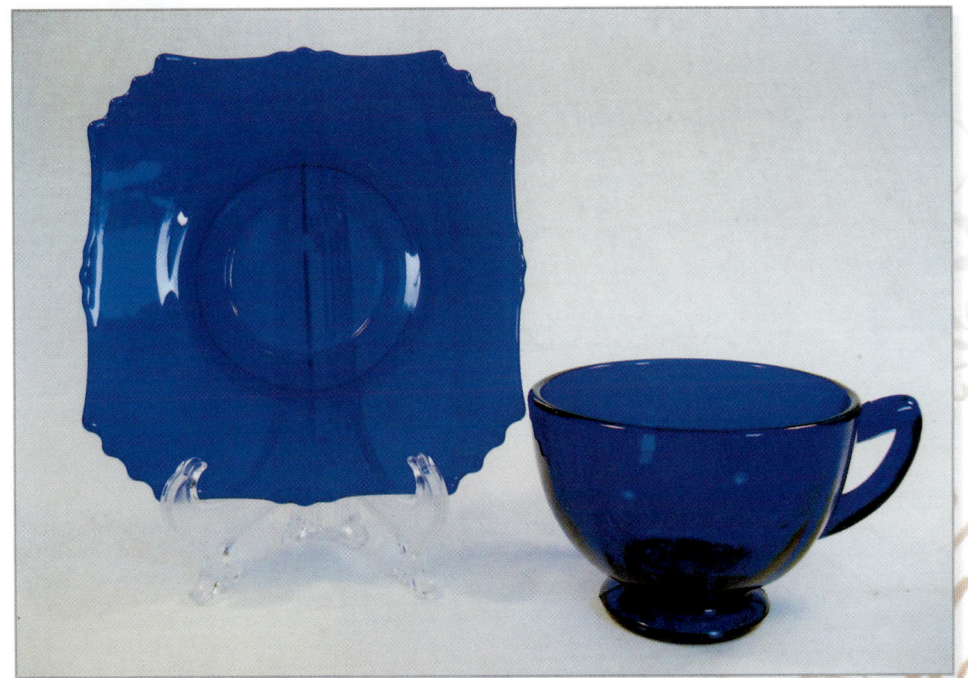

Cups and Saucers

Plate 427. New Martinsville Glass Manufacturing Company #37 Georgian cup and saucer in Ritz blue. Georgian is the original company name for the pattern better known under the name given by Hazel Marie Weatherman, "Moondrops." Cup: 2¾" high x 3¾" diameter. Saucer: 5¾" diameter. Circa 1932 – 1940. Set $15.00 – 20.00.

Plate 428. New Martinsville Glass Manufacturing Company #38 cup and saucer in Ritz blue. Referred to as Hostmaster or Repeal in advertisements, but known to collectors as "Mildred" (name given by Hazel Marie Weatherman). Cup: 2¼" high x 3⅝" diameter. Saucer: 5½" diameter. Circa 1934 – 1940s. Set $15.00 – 20.00.

Plate 429. Paden City Glass Manufacturing Company #890 cup and saucer in royal blue. Named "Crow's Foot Round" by Jerry Barnett. Cup: 2⅛" high x 3⅝" diameter. Saucer: 6½" diameter. Circa 1930s. Set $5.00 – 10.00.

Cups and Saucers

Plate 430. Paden City Glass Manufacturing Company #412 cup and saucer in royal blue. Named "Crow's Foot Square" by Jerry Barnett. Cup: 2⅛" high x 3½" diameter. Saucer: 6" square. Circa 1930s. Set $5.00 – 10.00.

Plate 431. Paden City Glass Manufacturing Company #991 cup and saucer in royal blue. Named "Penny Line" by Hazel Marie Weatherman. Cup: 2¼" high x 3¼" diameter. Saucer: 6" diameter. Circa 1932 – 1940. Set $10.00 – 15.00.

Plate 432. Paden City Glass Manufacturing Company #994 cup and saucer. Named "Popeye & Olive" by Hazel Marie Weatherman. Cup: 2½" high x 3⅛" diameter. Saucer: 5⅞" diameter. Circa 1932 – 1940s. Set $30.00 – 35.00.

Cups and Saucers

Plate 433. Paden City Glass Manufacturing Company #881 Gadroon cup and saucer in royal blue. Also named "Wotta Line" by Hazel Marie Weatherman. Cup: 2⅛" high x 3⅝" diameter. Saucer: 5⅞" diameter. Circa 1932 – 1940s. Set $15.00 – 20.00.

Plate 434. Paden City Glass Manufacturing Company #215 Glades cup and saucer in royal blue. Also named "Hotcha" by Hazel Marie Weatherman. Cup: 2" high x 3½" diameter. Saucer: 6" diameter. Circa 1936 – 1940s. Set $10.00 – 20.00.

Plate 435. Paden City Glass Manufacturing Company #220 cup and saucer in royal blue. Named "Largo" by Jerry Barnett and "Cantina" by Hazel Marie Weatherman. Cup: 2⅛" high x 3½" diameter. Saucer: 6¼" diameter. Circa 1937 – 1940s. Set $15.00 – 20.00.

Cups and Saucers

Plate 436. Pitman-Dreitzer and Company Newport cup and saucer. Cup: 2⅜" high x 3⅞" diameter. Saucer: 5¾" diameter. Pitman-Dreitzer was a manufacturer's representative and distributor. This pattern was probably made by the New Martinsville Glass Manufacturing Company, since most of Pitman-Dreitzer's advertisements from this time period featured New Martinsville glass. Circa 1935. Set $10.00 – 15.00.

Plate 437. L. E. Smith Glass Company #505 cup and saucer. Named "Mount Pleasant" by Hazel Marie Weatherman and also known as "Double Shield." Cup: 2¼" high x 3½" diameter. Saucer: 6¼" diameter. Circa 1935 – 1936. Set $4.00 – 10.00.

Plate 438. Unattributed cup and saucer with silver decoration. Cup: 2½" high x 3½" diameter. Saucer: 5⅜" diameter. Set $20.00 – 25.00.

MUGS

Plate 439. Cambridge Glass Company #3400/107 14-ounce mug in royal blue. 3¾" high x 2⅞" diameter at rim. Circa 1931 – 1940s. Mug $30.00 – 40.00.

Plate 440. New Martinsville Glass Manufacturing Company mug in Ritz blue. 3½" high x 3" diameter top. Introduced in 1932, this mug was described as a reproduction of a Belgian original. (See page 288.) Circa 1930s. Mug $25.00 – 30.00.

GLASSES AND TUMBLERS

Plate 441. Hazel-Atlas Glass Company Royal Lace. Circa 1934 – 1941.
Left to right: (1) 12-ounce ice tea. 5⅜" high. $100.00 – 105.00. (2) 10-ounce water. 4⅞" high. $105.00 – 110.00. (3) 9-ounce water. 4⅛" high. $35.00 – 40.00. (4) 5-ounce juice tumbler. 3½" high. $40.00 – 45.00.

Plate 442. Hazel-Atlas Glass Company "Ships," also known to collectors as "Sailboat" or "Sportsman Series," in Ritz blue. Circa 1936 – 1940.
Left to right: (1) 10½-ounce ice tea tumbler. 4⅞" high. $12.00 – 15.00. (2) 9-ounce straight-side water. 4⅝" high. $10.00 – 12.00. (3) 5-ounce juice. 3¾" high. $10.00 – 12.00. (4) 8-ounce old fashioned. 3⅜" high. $15.00 – 18.00. (5) 6-ounce roly poly. 2¼" high. $10.00 – 12.00. (6) 2-ounce shot glass. 2¼" high. $175.00 – 200.00.

Plate 443. Imperial Glass Corporation Georgian Shape glasses. Called "Shaeffer" by Hazel Marie Weatherman. These were made from molds acquired from the Belmont Tumbler Company. Circa 1932 – 1940s.
Left to right: (1) #451 five-ribbed water glass in Ritz blue. 4" high. Each $6.00 – 10.00. (2) #451 five-ribbed juice glass in Ritz blue. 3" high. Each $5.00 – 8.00.

Plate 444. Imperial Glass Corporation. #701 Reeded tumbler in Ritz blue. Also called "Spun" (by Hazel Marie Weatherman). 3" high. Patented in 1935. Tumbler $25.00 – 30.00.

Pitchers

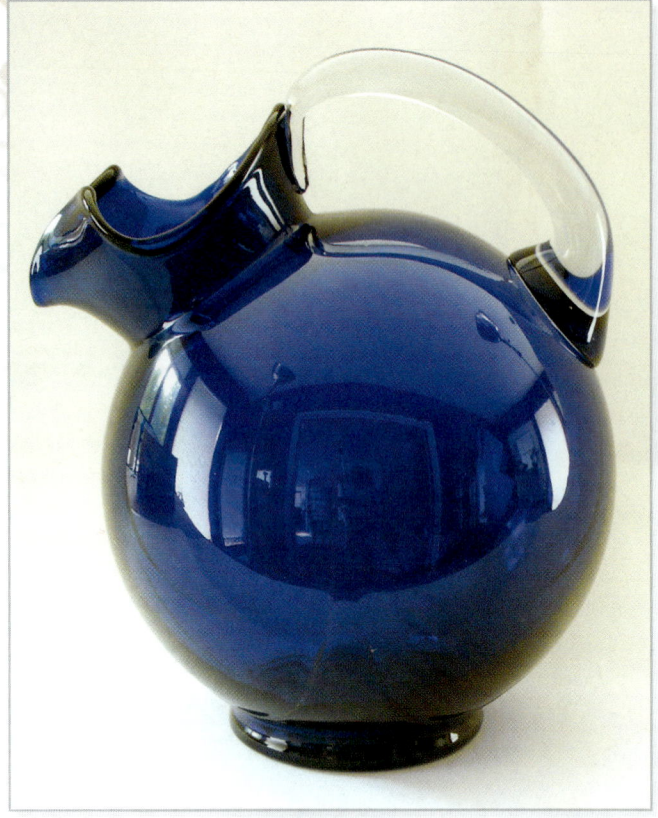

Plate 445. Cambridge Glass Company #3400/38 ball shaped line, 80-ounce jug with ice lip in royal blue. 9" high x 7" diameter. Circa 1931 – 1940s. Jug $100.00 – 125.00.

Plate 446. Co-operative Flint Glass Company #557 pitcher with ice lip. 8¼" high x 5¾" diameter. ½ gallon. Circa late 1920s – 1930s. Pitcher $75.00 – 85.00.

Plate 447. Dugan Glass Company crimped ice lip pitcher with unknown flower decoration. 9⅜" high x 5½" diameter. Circa 1907. Pitcher $65.00 – 75.00.

Pitchers

Plate 448. Dunbar Glass Corporation #5207 82-ounce, reeded handle, ice lip pitcher. 8" high x 5" wide. Circa 1931. Pitcher $65.00 – 75.00.

Plate 449. Dunbar Glass Corporation ice lip pitcher, part of set #132. 9" high x 6⁷⁄₁₆" diameter. Circa 1930s. (See plate 769, page 272.) Pitcher $75.00 – 85.00.

Plate 450. Hazel-Atlas Glass Company New Century 80-ounce pitcher. 4¼" high x 5¾" diameter. Advertised in Butler Brothers' spring 1938 catalog in "true blue" at $2.00 for the dozen. (See plate 772, page 276.) Circa 1930 – 1938. Pitcher $40.00 – 50.00.

Pitchers

Plate 451. Hazel-Atlas Glass Company Royal Lace 96-ounce pitcher. 8½" high x 6⅜" diameter. With 12-ounce tumbler (5⅜" high) and 10-ounce tumbler (4⅞" high). Circa 1934 – 1941. Pitcher $350.00 – 425.00. 12-ounce tumbler $100.00 – 105.00. 10-ounce tumbler $105.00 – 110.00.

Plate 452. Hazel-Atlas Glass Company Royal Lace 48-ounce straight-sided, ice lip pitcher. 6⅞" high x 5⅜" diameter. With two 5-ounce tumblers. 3½" high. Circa 1934 – 1941. Pitcher $100.00 – 120.00. Tumbler, each $40.00 – 45.00.

Plate 453. Hazel-Atlas Glass Company. Circa 1936 – 1939. Left to right: (1) #9937 40-ounce fine ribbed tilt pitcher. 6½" high x 5⅝" diameter. Pitcher $40.00 – 50.00. (2) Fine ribbed juice glass. 3½" high. Glass $6.00 – 8.00. (3) 80-ounce fine ribbed tilt pitcher. 8½" high x 7⅛" diameter. Pitcher $50.00 – 60.00. (4) Fine ribbed tumbler. 4" high. Tumbler $10.00 – 12.00.

Pitchers

Plate 454. Hazel-Atlas Glass Company #9908 panel optic, 80-ounce, blown pitcher with ice lip. 8½" high x 5¾" diameter. Circa 1936 – 1939. Pitcher $75.00 – 85.00.

Plate 455. Hazel-Atlas Glass Company #1816 82-ounce pitcher in the "Sportsman Series." 8½" high x 5⅝" diameter. With two 9-ounce straight water tumblers. 3¾" high. All with "Sailboat" decoration #420. Circa 1936 – 1939. Pitcher $50.00 – 60.00. Tumbler, each $10.00 – 15.00.

Plate 456. Hazel-Atlas Glass Company #1816B 82-ounce ice lip pitcher in the "Sportsman Series" with the #420 "Sailboat" decoration. 8½" high x 5⅝" diameter. With two 9-ounce "Sailboat" water tumblers. 4⅝" high. A set consisting of the pitcher and eight tumblers was offered in Butler Brothers' spring 1938 catalog at 67 cents for all nine pieces. (See plate 772, page 276.) Circa 1936 – 1939. Pitcher $50.00 – 60.00. Tumbler, each $10.00 – 15.00.

Pitchers

Plate 457. Hazel-Atlas Glass Company #1816B 82-ounce interior panel pitcher. 8½" high x 5⅝" diameter. Circa 1936 – 1939. Pitcher $40.00 – 50.00.

Plate 458. Hazel-Atlas Glass Company #G-1488 diamond optic, 54-ounce pitcher with ice lip. 6⅞" high x 5½" diameter. Circa 1936 – 1939. Pitcher $75.00 – 85.00.

Plate 459. Imperial Glass Corporation #451 Georgian Shape 80-ounce ice lip pitcher in Ritz blue. Called "Shaeffer" by Hazel Marie Weatherman. 7¼" high x 6¼" diameter. With two 12½-ounce tumblers. 4⅛" high. All pieces with unknown platinum line decoration. These were made from molds acquired from the Belmont Glass Company. Circa 1932 – 1940s. Pitcher $50.00 – 60.00. Tumbler, each $10.00 – 15.00.

Pitchers

Plate 460. Imperial Glass Corporation #701 Reeded 80-ounce ice lip pitcher in Ritz blue. Also called "Spun" by Hazel Marie Weatherman. 7¼" high x 6½" diameter. Circa 1935. Pitcher $125.00 – 150.00.

Plate 461. Louie Glass Company (?) ribbed, tilted ball, ice lip pitcher. 8" high x 6½" diameter. The glass, reeded handle, ice lip, and top rim finish are all consistent with Louie, but no documentation has been found to date. Circa 1930s. Pitcher $60.00 – 70.00.

Plate 462. Louie Glass Company #25 ice lip pitcher. Named "Chico" by Hazel Marie Weatherman. 8¾" high x 6¼" diameter. Circa 1936. Pitcher $50.00 – 60.00.

Pitchers

Plate 463. Louie Glass Company ice lip pitcher. Named "Harpo" by Hazel Marie Weatherman. 9" high x 6⅜" diameter. With two tumblers. Left to right: 4" high and 5⅛" high. Circa 1936. Pitcher $50.00 – 60.00. Tumbler, each $10.00 – 15.00.

Plate 464. Seneca Glass Company Driftwood Casual 32-ounce pitcher. 7⅝" high x 4" diameter. With 14-ounce double old fashion. 3¾" high. With a paper label reading "Driftwood Casual by Seneca, patent no. 170666. Hand blown." The patent was approved in 1953. Pitcher $50.00 – 60.00. Old fashion $10.00 – 15.00. (Photograph courtesy of Louis Lopilato-Cartagena.)

Plate 465. West Virginia Glass Specialty Company #451 ice lip pitcher. 7¾" high x 6¼" diameter. This pitcher can be distinguished from the Imperial Glass Corporation #451 by the molded flat spot where the top of the handle attaches to the ribs. (See plate 459 on page 164.) Circa 1930s. Pitcher $50.00 – 60.00.

Plate 466. Romanian crystal handled, rough pontil pitcher. 8" high x 4⅛" diameter. Sticker on bottom reads "Made in Romania, LOC-S.A., R. M. Vilcea." Pitcher $20.00 – 25.00.

DECANTERS

Plate 467. Cambridge Glass Company #52 Mount Vernon 40-ounce decanter in royal blue. 11½" high with stopper. With two #1401 Martha Washington 1-ounce cordials. 3⅛" high. Circa 1931 – 1942. Decanter $250.00 – 300.00. Cordial, each $25.00 – 30.00.

Plate 468. Cambridge Glass Company #1070 36-ounce, three pinch decanter in royal blue. 10¾" high with stopper. Both the ball stopper and the decanter have the spires denoting the #3400 line. With two #107 2-ounce pinched tumblers. 2⅜" high. Circa 1931 – 1942. Decanter $175.00 – 200.00. Tumbler, each $15.00 – 20.00.

Plate 469. Cambridge Glass Company #1322 fluted neck and base 26-ounce decanter in royal blue. 10¾" high with stopper. Circa 1931 – 1942. Decanter $200.00 – 225.00.

167

Decanters

Plate 470. Cambridge Glass Company #3400/119 12-ounce ball shaped cordial decanter in royal blue. 4¾" high. With two #1341 1-ounce cordials. 1⅞" high. Circa 1931 – 1942. Decanter $200.00 – 250.00. Cordial, each $15.00 – 20.00.

Plate 471. Cambridge Glass Company #1321 28-ounce crystal footed decanter in royal blue. 10¾" high with stopper. With two #7966 2-ounce sherry glasses. 5½" high. Circa 1931 – 1942. Decanter $200.00 – 250.00. Wine glass, each $25.00 – 30.00.

Plate 472. Cambridge Glass Company #3078 32-ounce decanter in royal blue. 11¾" high with stopper. Circa 1931 – 1942. Decanter $150.00 – 160.00.

Decanters

Plate 473. Cambridge Glass Company #3450 Nautilus in royal blue. Circa 1932 – 1942.
Left to right: (1) 40-ounce crystal handled decanter. 8¾" high with stopper. Decanter $175.00 – 200.00. (2) Two 2-ounce tumblers. 2⅝" high. Tumbler, each $20.00 – 25.00. (3) 14-ounce crystal handled decanter. 6" high with stopper. Decanter $140.00 – 150.00. (4) Two 1-ounce tumblers. 1⅞" high. Tumbler, each $20.00 – 25.00.

Plate 474. Cambridge Glass Company #3400/156 12-ounce decanter in royal blue. 8⅜" high with stopper. With two #3400/127 2½-ounce crystal handled tumblers or mugs. 2¼" high. Circa 1931 – 1942. Decanter $90.00 – 100.00. Tumbler, each $35.00 – 40.00.

Plate 475. Cambridge Glass Company #1385 28-ounce four-footed decanter in royal blue. 8½" high with stopper. Circa 1931 – 1942. Decanter $150.00 – 175.00.

Decanters

Plate 476. Cambridge Glass Company #1375 10-ounce decanter in royal blue. 7½" high with stopper. Circa 1931 – 1942. Decanter $90.00 – 100.00.

Plate 477. Cambridge Glass Company #3400/113 35-ounce crystal handled decanter in royal blue. 8¼" high with stopper. With two #3400/127 2½-ounce crystal handled tumblers. 2¼" high. Circa 1931 – 1942. Decanter $250.00 – 300.00. Tumbler, each $35.00 – 40.00.

Plate 478. Cambridge Glass Company #3400/92 32-ounce ball-shaped line decanter in royal blue. 6¾" high with stopper. With two #3400/92 2½-ounce tumblers. 2¼" high. Circa 1931 – 1942. Decanter $150.00 – 200.00. Tumbler, each $20.00 – 25.00.

Decanters

Plate 479. Cambridge Glass Company Tally-Ho in royal blue. Circa 1935 – 1942.
Left to right: (1) #1402/38 34-ounce decanter with Cambridge paper label. 9¼" high with stopper. Decanter $90.00 – 100.00. (2) #1402/39 34-ounce crystal handled decanter. 9¼" high with stopper. Decanter with handle $150.00 – 160.00.

Plate 480. Cambridge Glass Company #1402/38 Tally-Ho 34-ounce decanter in royal blue. 9¼" high with stopper. With two #1402/12 2½-ounce wine glasses. 3⅞" high. All with gold #D1007 decoration by Cambridge. Circa 1935 – 1942. Decanter $600.00 – 700.00. Wine glass, each $30.00 – 35.00.

Plate 481. Duncan and Miller Glass Company #55 32-ounce decanter. Named "Gordon" by Hazel Marie Weatherman. 9¼" high with stopper. With unknown silver golfer decoration. Circa 1933. Decanter $170.00 – 180.00.

Decanters

Plate 482. Duncan and Miller Glass Company #55 32-ounce decanter. Named "Gordon" by Hazel Marie Weatherman. 9¼" high with stopper. With two #55 1½-ounce whiskey goblets. 2⅛" high. Circa 1933. Decanter $140.00 – 150.00. Goblet, each $30.00 – 35.00.

Plate 483. Fenton Art Glass Company #1611 21-ounce Georgian decanter in royal blue. This pattern was originally marketed by Fenton as Agua Caliente in 1930 and shortly thereafter changed to Georgian. 6¾" high with no stopper. Circa 1930 – 1935. Decanter $85.00 – 95.00 (with stopper).

Plate 484. Fenton Art Glass Company #1934 decanter in royal blue. 9" high with floral stopper. With two whiskey goblets. 2¾" high. Sold as a set with decanter, six goblets, and tray. Platinum line decoration. Circa 1934 – 1938. Decanter $100.00 – 125.00. Whiskey goblet, each $10.00 – 15.00.

Decanters

Plate 485. Fostoria Glass Company in regal blue. Circa 1933 – 1940. Left to right: (1) Two #4024 1-ounce Victorian cordials. 3⅛" high. Cordial, each $40.00 – 50.00. (2) #2494 decanter. 9" high with stopper. Decanter $90.00 – 100.00. (3) #2494 cordial bottle. 7" high with stopper. Bottle $100.00 – 125.00.

Plate 486. A. H. Heisey and Company #3397 Gascony one-pint footed decanter in Stiegel blue. 10⅛" high with #88 stopper. With two #3397 2½-ounce wine glasses. 2⅞" high. Circa 1933 – 1938. Decanter $900.00 – 1,200.00. Wine glass, each $150.00 – 200.00.

Plate 487. Imperial Glass Corporation #451 34-ounce blown Georgian Shape decanter in Ritz blue. Named "Shaeffer" by Hazel Marie Weatherman. 10" high with stopper. The stopper is a 1½-ounce pressed jigger. With two #451 2½-ounce tumblers. 2⅞" high. Circa 1932 – 1940s. Decanter $125.00 – 150.00. Tumbler, each $10.00 – 15.00.

Decanters

Plate 488. Imperial Glass Corporation #451 34-ounce blown Georgian Shape decanter in Ritz blue. 9" high with stopper. Named "Shaeffer" by Hazel Marie Weatherman. In a chrome holder and tray with six #451 2½-ounce tumblers. 2⅞" high. These were made from molds acquired from the Belmont Glass Company. Circa 1932 – 1940s. Decanter in tray holder $150.00 – 175.00. Tumbler, each $10.00 – 15.00.

Plate 489. Imperial Glass Corporation #160/163 30-ounce Cape Cod decanter. 9¾" high with stopper. With #160 2½-ounce Cape Cod whiskey tumbler. 2⅝" high. Circa 1932 – 1940s. Decanter $250.00 – 300.00. Tumbler $35.00 – 40.00.

Plate 490. Indiana Glass Company #298 37-ounce Jolly Mountaineer decanter. 10" high. Made for Tiara Exclusives. Circa 1984 – 1985. Decanter $25.00 – 30.00.

Decanters

Plate 491. Morgantown Glass Works #24 decanters in Ritz blue. Known as "Circlet." Circa 1930s. Left to right: (1) 24-ounce decanter. 9⅝" high without stopper. This is not the correct stopper. Decanter, without stopper $50.00 – 60.00. Tumbler stopper, add $50.00 – 60.00. (2) 24-ounce decanter. 13" high with 3-ounce tumbler stopper (1¾" diameter). Platinum trim. (See plate 786, page 287.) Decanter $300.00 – 350.00.

Plate 492. Morgantown Glass Works #10½-9051 decanter in Ritz blue. Known as "Lynward." 11" high with stopper. Advertised with a platinum Sparta decoration in 1932. (See plate 781, page 283.) Circa 1930s. Decanter $200.00 – 250.00.

Plate 493. Morgantown Glass Works #1-9051 decanter in Ritz blue. Named "Little King" by Hazel Marie Weatherman. 7¾" high with stopper. Advertised with Morgantown's #12 platinum decoration in 1931. (See plate 781, page 283.) Circa 1930s. Decanter $200.00 – 250.00.

Decanters

Plate 494. New Martinsville Glass Manufacturing Company #37 Georgian decanter in Ritz blue. Better known to collectors as "Moondrops." 12¾" high with fan stopper. With #37 rocket-footed wine glass. 3½" high. Circa 1932 – 1937. Decanter $130.00 – 150.00. Wine glass $50.00 – 60.00.

Plate 495. New Martinsville Glass Manufacturing Company #37 Georgian decanter in Ritz blue. Better known to collectors as "Moondrops." 9¼" high with beehive stopper. With two #37 1-ounce stemmed cordials. 3" high. Circa 1932 – 1937. Decanter $100.00 – 110.00. Cordial, each $25.00 – 30.00.

Plate 496. New Martinsville Glass Manufacturing Company #37 Georgian decanter in Ritz blue. Better known to collectors as "Moondrops." 10½" high with beehive stopper. With #37 2-ounce tumbler. 2¾" high. Circa 1932 – 1937. Decanter $110.00 – 120.00. Tumbler $15.00 – 20.00.

Decanters

Plate 497. New Martinsville Glass Manufacturing Company #237 handled decanter. Named "Michael" by Hazel Marie Weatherman. 11½" high with beehive stopper. Circa 1933 – 1937. Decanter $100.00 – 125.00.

Plate 498. New Martinsville Glass Manufacturing Company #606 in Ritz blue. Circa 1930s. Left to right: (1) Tilted handle decanter with unknown sterling silver decoration of a shield and grapes. 6½" high (stopper missing). Decanter $120.00 – 150.00. (2) Two cordials. 3" high. Cordial, each $10.00 – 15.00. (3) Tilted handle decanter. 7½" high with beehive stopper. Decanter $150.00 – 175.00.

Plate 499. New Martinsville Glass Manufacturing Company #42 12-ounce roly poly decanter in Ritz blue. 6⅜" high with beehive stopper. With two #42 1-ounce tumblers. 1⅜" high. Unknown sterling silver hunt scene of dog and horse with rider. Advertised as a "Novelty Rolly Polly whiskey set" in 1933. (See plate 789, page 289.) Circa 1933 – 1937. Decanter $125.00 – 150.00. Tumbler, each $10.00 – 15.00.

Decanters

Plate 500. New Martinsville Glass Manufacturing Company #42 12-ounce roly poly decanter in Ritz blue. 7½" high with feather stopper. With two #42 1-ounce tumblers. 1⅜" high. Circa 1930s. Decanter $100.00 – 125.00. Tumbler, each $10.00 – 15.00.

Plate 501. New Martinsville Glass Manufacturing Company #15 decanter in Ritz blue. 11½" high with fan stopper. Shown with two of the six #15 stemmed wine cordials (4⅜" high) on a 10½" diameter tray that make up the complete wine set. Circa 1935 – 1937. Decanter, tray, and six tumblers sold as a wine set $100.00 – 120.00.

Plate 502. New Martinsville Glass Manufacturing Company Cozy Cordial decanter in Ritz blue. 6½" high with stopper. With two footed and handled 1-ounce mugs. Advertised 1936. Decanter $70.00 – 80.00. Mug, each $10.00 – 15.00.

Decanters

Plate 504. Paden City Glass Manufacturing #901 23-ounce bar bottle in royal blue with unknown sterling silver thistle decoration. 12" high with stopper. Circa 1932 – 1940. Bar bottle $150.00 – 175.00.

Plate 503. Paden City Glass Manufacturing Company #901 23-ounce bar bottle in royal blue. 12" high with stopper. Circa 1932 – 1940. Bar bottle $75.00 – 85.00.

Plate 505. Paden City Glass Manufacturing Company #901 23-ounce bar bottle in royal blue in royal blue with unknown silver "Scotch" decoration. 12" high with cobalt stopper. Circa 1932 – 1940. Bar bottle $150.00 – 175.00.

Decanters

Plate 506. Paden City Glass Manufacturing Company #994 decanters in royal blue. Named "Popeye and Olive" by Hazel Marie Weatherman. 10" high with clear stopper on left, handled with cobalt stopper on right. With two #994 3-ounce tumblers. 3" high. Circa 1932 – 1940. Decanter, each $175.00 – 200.00. Tumbler, each $15.00 – 20.00.

Plate 507. Paden City Glass Manufacturing Company two-pinch decanter in royal blue with unknown silver hunter and dog decoration. 8" high without stopper. This decanter should have a faceted octagon stopper. Circa 1932 – 1940. Decanter $150.00 – 175.00.

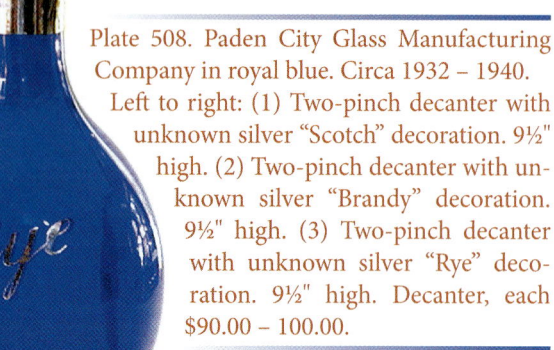

Plate 508. Paden City Glass Manufacturing Company in royal blue. Circa 1932 – 1940. Left to right: (1) Two-pinch decanter with unknown silver "Scotch" decoration. 9½" high. (2) Two-pinch decanter with unknown silver "Brandy" decoration. 9½" high. (3) Two-pinch decanter with unknown silver "Rye" decoration. 9½" high. Decanter, each $90.00 – 100.00.

Decanters

Plate 509. Left to right: (1) Unattributed two-pinch decanter with pewter (?) ring on neck. 9¼" high. Decanter $40.00 – 50.00. (2) Unattributed blown glass decanter with unknown flower decoration. 9" high. Possibly an undocumented Dunbar Glass Corporation product. Decanter $40.00 – 50.00. (3) Paden City Glass Manufacturing Company two-pinch decanter with unknown sterling silver fox hunt scene decoration. 9½" high with stopper. Circa 1932 – 1940. Decanter $100.00 – 150.00.

Plate 510. Paden City Glass Manufacturing Company 29-ounce two-pinch decanter. in royal blue 9½" high with clear stopper. Circa 1932 – 1940. Decanter $90.00 – 100.00.

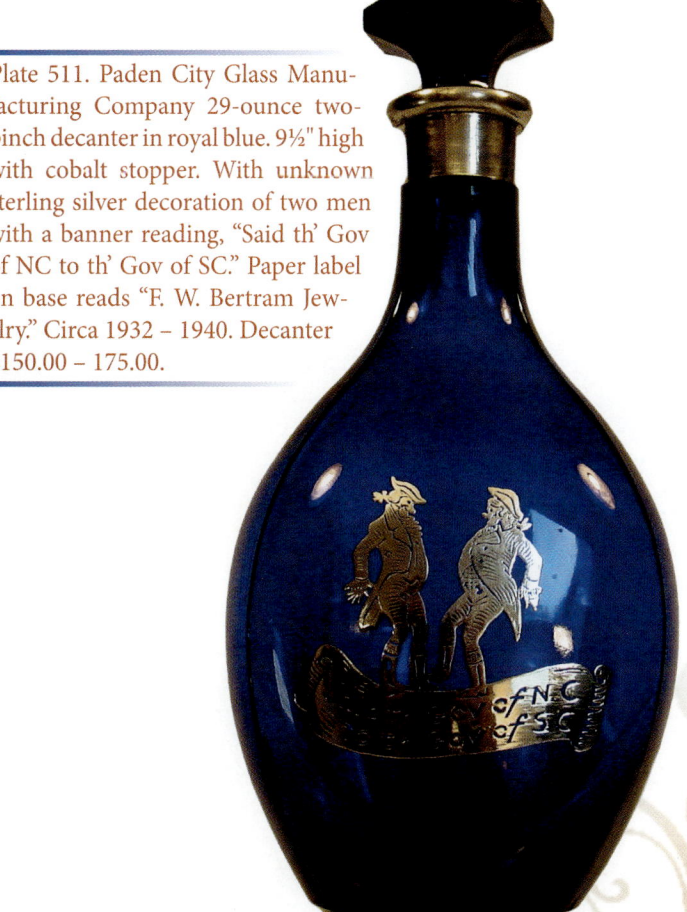

Plate 511. Paden City Glass Manufacturing Company 29-ounce two-pinch decanter in royal blue. 9½" high with cobalt stopper. With unknown sterling silver decoration of two men with a banner reading, "Said th' Gov of NC to th' Gov of SC." Paper label on base reads "F. W. Bertram Jewelry." Circa 1932 – 1940. Decanter $150.00 – 175.00.

Decanters

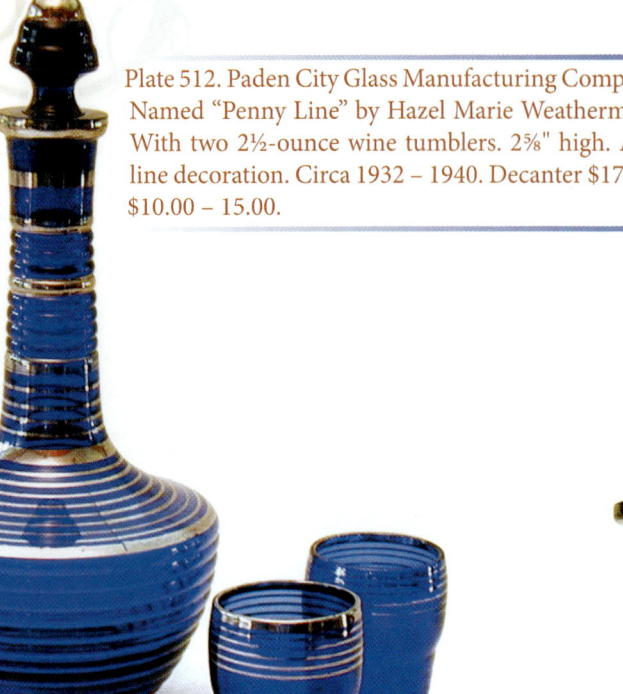

Plate 512. Paden City Glass Manufacturing Company #991 22-ounce decanter. Named "Penny Line" by Hazel Marie Weatherman. 10½" high with stopper. With two 2½-ounce wine tumblers. 2⅝" high. All with unknown platinum line decoration. Circa 1932 – 1940. Decanter $175.00 – 200.00. Tumbler, each $10.00 – 15.00.

Plate 513. Paden City Glass Manufacturing Company #211 four-lobed 29-ounce decanter in royal blue. Known as "Spire" to collectors. 8" high without stopper. With unknown silver lattice and grape decoration. Shown with two #911 high footed wines with platinum line decoration. 4¼" high. The #991 stemware was often combined with decanters and shakers from other lines. Circa 1932 – 1940. Decanter $90.00 – 100.00; add $20.00 for stopper. Wine tumbler, each $20.00 – 25.00.

Plate 514. Paden City Glass Manufacturing Company #215 Glades decanter in royal blue. 8¾" high with crystal stopper. Circa 1937 – 1940. Decanter $135.00 – 150.00.

Decanters

Plate 515. United States Glass Company #055 32-ounce sherry decanter. 10¾" high with stopper. With two #14185 4-ounce optic whiskeys. 3⅛" high. All have unknown silver basket of flowers decoration. Circa 1920s. Decanter $55.00 – 65.00. Whiskey, each $10.00 – 15.00.

Plate 516. Viking Glass Company Mount Vernon decanter. 11¾" high with stopper. Circa 1984 – 1985. Decanter $40.00 – 50.00.

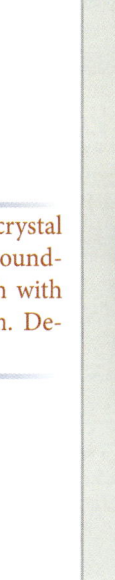

Plate 517. German crystal footed decanter with ground-to-fit stopper. 14½" high with stopper. Dates unknown. Decanter $30.00 – 40.00.

Decanters

Plate 518. Taiwanese falcon decanter. 11" high. Circa 1970s. Decanter $20.00 – 25.00.

Plate 519. Unattributed decanter. Named "Rings of Rings" by Hazel Marie Weatherman. 10" high with stopper. With two tumblers. 3" high. Circa 1930s. Decanter $20.00 – 25.00. Tumbler, each $3.00 – 5.00.

Plate 520. Unattributed cobalt cased crystal bar bottle with cut flutes on neck and bottom. 10⅞" high without stopper. Star pattern cut on base. Bottle $50.00 – 60.00.

BAR ITEMS

Plate 521. Cambridge Glass Company beverage urn in cobalt blue II with plate etching #695. Circa 1925 – 1926. Urn $1,250.00 – 1,300.00.

Plate 522. Cambridge Glass Company #1217 bitters bottle with #3400 spires. 4¾" high. Circa 1931 – 1940s. Bitters bottle $90.00 – 100.00.

Plate 523. Farberware beverage set. Consists of Cambridge Glass Company #3400 pitcher (10" high) in royal blue, four wines glasses (6¾" high) and 11½" x 17" handled tray. Circa 1931 – 1940s. Set $140.00 – 150.00.

Bar Items

Plate 524. Hazel-Atlas Glass Company Royal Lace toddy or cider set in Ritz blue. Consists of cookie jar with metal lid, metal tray, and eight roly poly cups, and ladle. Circa 1936 – 1940s. Set $250.00 – 275.00.

Plate 525. New Martinsville Glass Manufacturing Company #38 Hostmaster (or Repeal) in Ritz blue. Circa 1934 – 1942.
Left to right: (1) Bar bottle. 11" high without stopper. Bar bottle $80.00 – 90.00; add $40.00 for the stopper. (2) Ice tub. 3½" high. Ice tub $100.00 – 125.00. (3) Stemmed tumbler. 4" high. Tumbler $15.00 – 20.00. (4) Shot glass. 2¼" high. Shot glass $10.00 – 20.00. (5) Bitters bottle. 5" high. Bitters bottle $90.00 – 100.00.

Plate 526. Paden City Glass Manufacturing Company #6 percolator or beverage server in royal blue. 11¾" high with lid. Seen here without the glass base that would have originally come with this piece. Silver overlay of peacock sitting on branch with leaves and berries by an unknown decorator. Circa 1930s. Server and lid $150.00 – 160.00.

Bar Items

SHOT GLASS SETS

Plate 527. Unattributed shot glass set. 8½" diameter center handle chrome tray with six 2⅜" high vertical ribbed shot glasses. Was sold at a glass show as Hazel-Atlas Glass Company, but no documentation has been found. Set $30.00 – 40.00.

Plate 528. Unattributed shot glass set. 6" high x 10" diameter chrome, footed center handle tray with six 2¾" high shot glasses. Set $30.00 – 40.00.

187

Bar Items
Pilsners and Flagons

Plate 529. A. H. Heisey and Company #3390 Carcassonne wide optic crystal-footed 12-ounce flagon in Stiegel blue. 9¼" high. Although a drinking vessel, when seen alone, most collectors assume this is a vase. Circa 1933 – 1941. Flagon $75.00 – 85.00.

Plate 530. Seneca Glass Company #903 crystal stem pilsner. 8⅝" high x 2⅜" square base. If purchased individually, one might consider this to be a vase. Advertised in 1932. Pilsner $20.00 – 25.00.

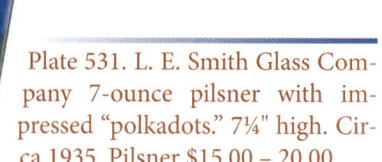

Plate 531. L. E. Smith Glass Company 7-ounce pilsner with impressed "polkadots." 7¼" high. Circa 1935. Pilsner $15.00 – 20.00.

Bar Items

OTHER DRINKING VESSELS

Plate 532. A. H. Heisey and Company #419 Sussex 8-ounce goblet in Stiegel blue. 5¾" high x 3½" diameter top. Circa 1933 – 1941. Goblet $100.00 – 110.00.

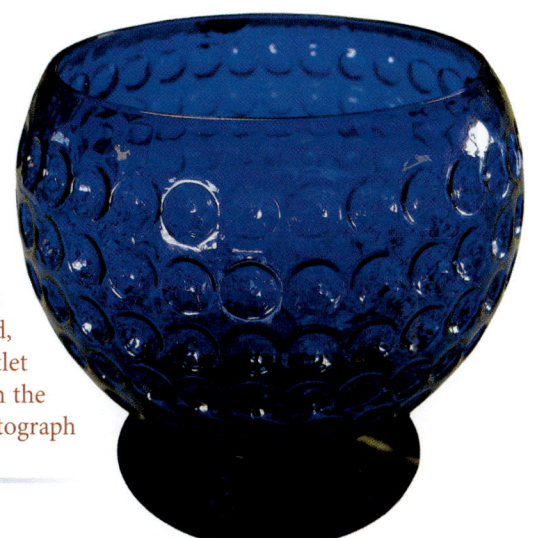

Plate 533. Morgantown Glassware Guild #3055 11-ounce on the rocks tumbler. Known as "19th Hole." 3¾" high. Designed in 1968 when Morgantown was owned by the Fostoria Glass Company. Although listed in a 1969 price list, it is believed this item was never actually retailed, with the few items made sold in the factory outlet in Morgantown. Tumbler $75.00 – 85.00. (From the collection of Helen and Sheldon Chazin. Photograph courtesy of David McInturff.)

LIQUOUR SETS, EGGS, ETC.

Plate 534. Bohemian footed liquor set with ground glass stoppered bottle and six glasses. 14½" high. With beaded glass leaves and flowers decoration. Set $200.00 – 250.00.

Plate 535. Bohemian liquor sets. Left to right: (1) Open egg-shaped liquor set with ground stoppered bottle and six glasses inside. 8¾" high. With beaded glass leaves decoration. Set $120.00 – 130.00. (2) Open liquor set with small ground stoppered bottle and six glasses inside. 10" high. Set $175.00 – 200.00. (3) Egg-shaped liquor set with ground stoppered bottle and six glasses inside. Set $110.00 – 120.00.

189

Bar Items
KEGS

Plate 536. Unattributed American keg in silver plate metal stand marked "A. Schrader's Son. N.Y. Pat. Sept. 27, 1892." 10½" high. Includes six tumblers. 2⅜" high. All have a grey cutting of lines and leaves. Circa 1900. Keg $200.00 – 250.00. Tumbler, each $10.00 – 12.00.

Plate 537. Unattributed, probably American twelve-sided keg with painted flower decoration in silver plated metal stand with six panel optic tumblers (2¼" high). Circa 1920s. Keg $200.00 – 250.00. Tumbler, each $10.00 – 15.00.

Bar Items

Plate 538. Czechoslovakian keg in metal stand. 9½" high. With footed cordial. 3¼" high. Both with silver leaf decoration. Marked "Czecho-slovakia." Circa 1918 – 1930s. Keg $140.00 – 150.00. Cordial $15.00 – 20.00.

Plate 539. Czechoslovakian keg with silver leaf decoration (same as plate 538) on wooden stand. 9½" high. Circa 1918 – 1930s. Keg $140.00 – 150.00.

191

Bar Items

ICE PAILS, ICE TUBS, AND ICE BUCKETS

Plate 540. Cambridge Glass Company #851 Decagon ice pail in royal blue. 5¾" high. Circa 1931 – 1940s. Ice pail $90.00 – 100.00.

Plate 541. Cambridge Glass Company #1121 panel optic ice pail. 6" high. Circa 1931 – 1940s. Ice pail $90.00 – 100.00.

Plate 542. Cambridge Glass Company #1402/52 Tally-Ho ice pail (missing handle) in royal blue. 5½" high. Circa 1935 – 1940s. Ice pail $125.00 – 135.00.

Bar Items

Plate 543. Fenton Art Glass Company #1620 Plymouth ice bucket in royal blue. 6" high x 5" top diameter. This pattern was produced from 1933 to 1939, but is scarce in royal blue. Ice bucket $95.00 – 105.00.

Plate 544. Fostoria Glass Company #2378 ice bucket in regal blue. 6" high. Circa 1933 – 1942. Ice bucket $90.00 – 100.00.

Plate 545. Hazel-Atlas Glass Company "Ships," from the "Sportsman Series," in Ritz blue. Circa 1936 – 1940s. Left to right: (1) Ice tub. 4½" high. $35.00 – 40.00. (2) Cocktail mixer or small ice tub. 4¼" high. $35.00 – 40.00.

Bar Items

Plate 546. Hazel-Atlas Glass Company "Wind Mill" cocktail mixer in Ritz blue, from the "Sportsman Series." 4¼" high. Circa 1936 – 1940s. Cocktail mixer $35.00 – 40.00.

Plate 547. Hazel-Atlas Glass Company ice bowl in Ritz blue in metal holder with tongs. 6⅝" diameter. Bowl marked H.A. Circa 1936 – 1940s. Ice bowl $40.00 – 50.00.

Plate 548. Louie Glass Company #1 ice bucket with platinum trim. 6" high. Circa 1930s. Ice bucket $90.00 – 100.00.

COCKTAIL SHAKERS

Plate 549. Cambridge Glass Company #3400/157 cocktail shaker in royal blue with #4 top. 12" high. With two #3103 3-ounce cocktail tumblers. 3¼" high. Shaker $140.00 – 150.00. Tumbler, each $10.00 – 15.00.

Plate 550. Possible Co-operative Flint Glass Company shaker. 8½" high without top (11¼" high with top) x 3" diameter opening. With two tumblers, 3½" high. All have a signed Rockwell Silver Company decoration. Suspected to be Co-operative Flint because the tumblers with the ring at the base were made by Co-operative Flint. Circa 1920s – 1930s. Shaker $200.00 – 250.00. Tumbler, each $25.00 – 30.00.

Cocktail Shakers

Plate 551. Duncan and Miller Glass Company #11 cocktail shaker. 11¼" high. Circa 1931 – 1940. Shaker $120.00 – 130.00.

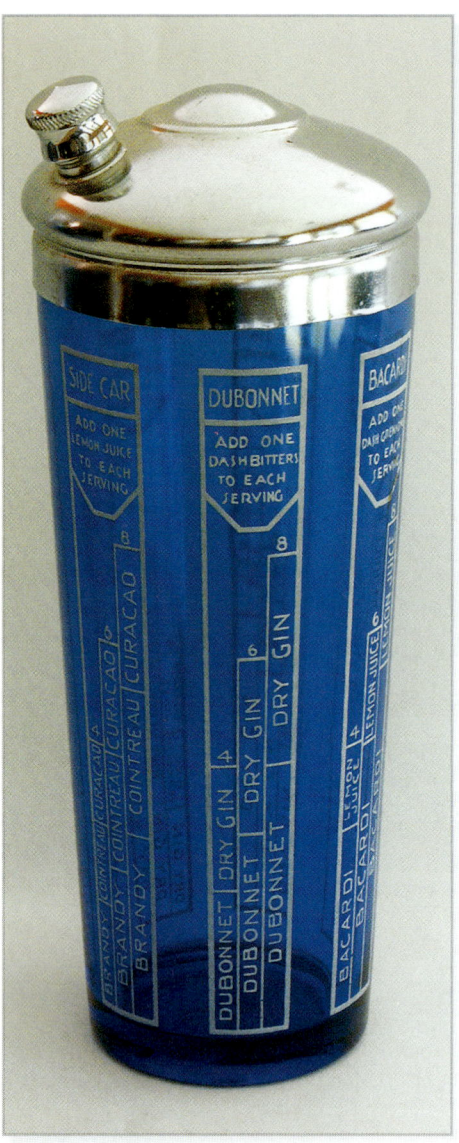

Plate 552. Hazel-Atlas Glass Company 32-ounce cocktail shaker in Ritz blue with recipe measure on the sides. 10" high. This same shaker with a different top was advertised in 1935 as a "Jiggerless cocktail shaker" (see plate 770, page 275). Circa 1934 – 1940s. Shaker $110.00 – 120.00.

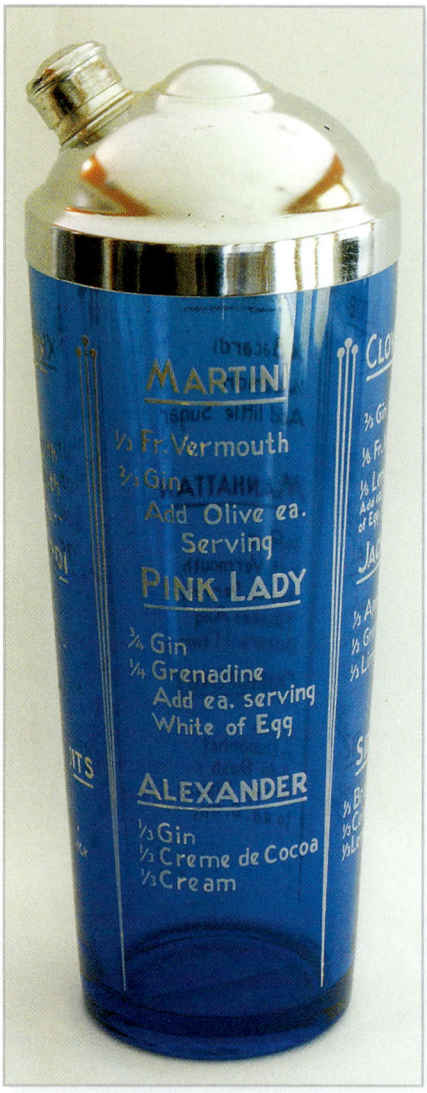

Plate 553. Hazel-Atlas Glass Company 32-ounce cocktail shaker in Ritz blue with recipe measure on the sides. 10" high. Circa 1934 – 1940s. Shaker $110.00 – 120.00.

Cocktail Shakers

Plate 554. Hazel-Atlas Glass Company cocktail shaker with ice crusher in Ritz blue. 11½" high. With drink recipes on the sides. A version of this shaker without the recipes was advertised by Newland, Schneeloch & Piek in 1936 as "The New 1936 Ice Crusher" (see plate 771, page 275). Circa 1936 – 1940s. Shaker $100.00 – 110.00.

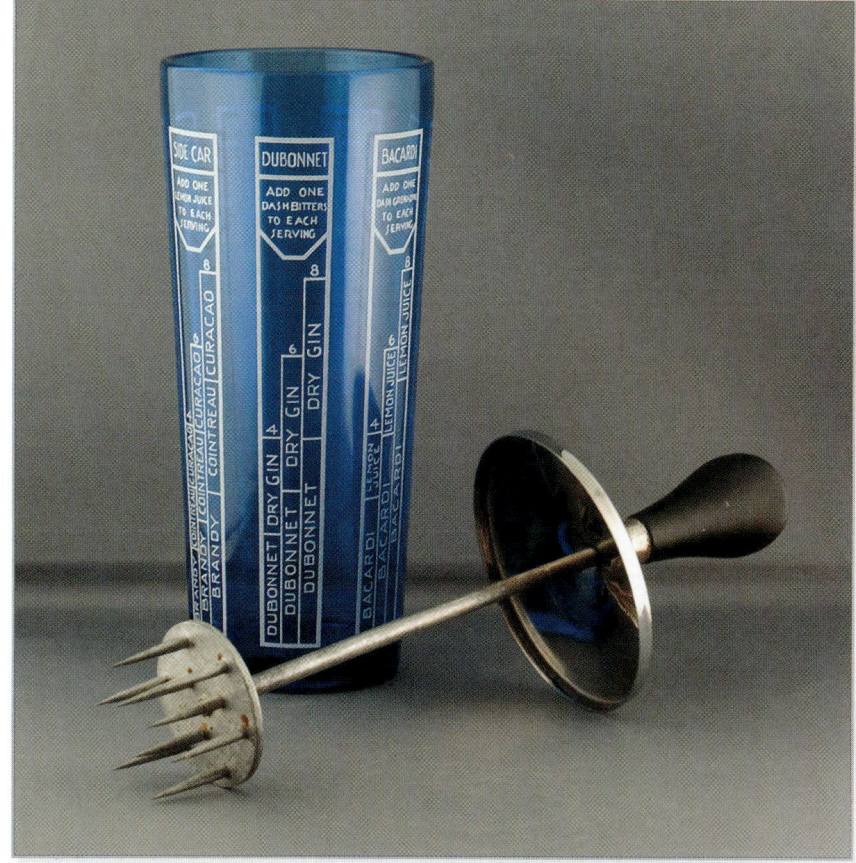

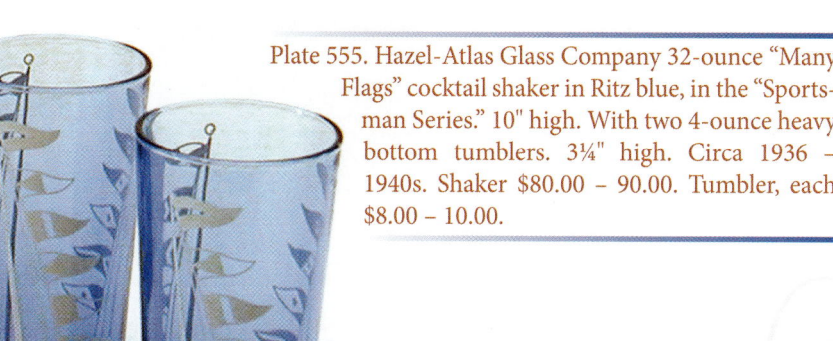

Plate 555. Hazel-Atlas Glass Company 32-ounce "Many Flags" cocktail shaker in Ritz blue, in the "Sportsman Series." 10" high. With two 4-ounce heavy bottom tumblers. 3¼" high. Circa 1936 – 1940s. Shaker $80.00 – 90.00. Tumbler, each $8.00 – 10.00.

Cocktail Shakers

Plate 556. Hazel-Atlas Glass Company 32-ounce "Ships & Stars" cocktail shaker in Ritz blue, in the "Sportsman Series." 10" high. Circa 1936 – 1940s. Shaker $140.00 – 150.00.

Plate 557. Hazel-Atlas Glass Company 32-ounce "Ships" cocktail shaker in Ritz blue, in the "Sportsman Series." 10" high. With 8-ounce old fashion. Circa 1936 – 1940s. Shaker $90.00 – 100.00. Old fashion $10.00 – 12.00.

Plate 558. Hazel-Atlas Glass Company 32-ounce "Wind Mill" cocktail shaker in Ritz blue, in the "Sportsman Series." 10" high. With two 9-ounce tumblers. 4⅝" high. Circa 1936 – 1940s. Shaker $90.00 – 100.00. Tumbler, each $10.00 – 15.00.

Cocktail Shakers

Plate 559. Hazel-Atlas Glass Company 32-ounce "Fish" cocktail shaker in Ritz blue, in the "Sportsman Series." 10" high. With two 5-ounce tumblers. 3¾" high. This shaker was offered in Butler Brothers' spring 1938 catalog as part of a 7-piece cocktail set. (See plate 773, page 276.) The knob on the top is described as red catalin, a form of bakelite. Circa 1936 – 1940s. Shaker $90.00 – 100.00. Tumbler, each $10.00 – 15.00.

Plate 560. Hazel-Atlas Glass Company 32-ounce plain cocktail shaker in Ritz blue. 10" high. With two 4-ounce heavy bottom tumblers. 3¼" high. Circa 1936 – 1940s. Shaker $50.00 – 60.00. Tumbler, each $5.00 – 8.00.

Plate 561. A. H. Heisey and Company #4225 1-quart cocktail shaker in Stiegel blue. Named "Cobel" after the model designer, Ray C. Cobel. 12" high with #1 strainer and #86 stopper. Circa 1933 – 1941. Shaker $1,500.00 to market.

Cocktail Shakers

Plate 562. Imperial Glass Corporation #451 Georgian Shape ribbed base cocktail shaker in Ritz blue. Called "Shaeffer" by Hazel Marie Weatherman. 10¾" high. With tumbler. 3" high. These were made from moulds acquired from the Belmont Glass Company. Circa 1932 – 1940s. Shaker $140.00 – 150.00. Tumbler $8.00 – 10.00.

Plate 563. Louie Glass Company platinum banded, shouldered cocktail shaker. 11" high. With two roly poly tumblers in chromium holders made by the Chase Brass and Copper Company, New York. 3" high. Circa 1936 – 1940. Shaker $140.00 – 150.00. Tumbler, each $15.00 – 20.00.

Plate 564. Louie Glass Company or West Virginia Glass Specialty Company cocktail shaker (missing top). 9" high. Marked "Sterling" silver fox hunt decoration by National Silver Deposit Ware Company, New York. With two martini glasses. 4½" high. Circa 1936 – 1940. Shaker $350.00 – 400.00. Martini glass, each $12.00 – 15.00.

Cocktail Shakers

Plate 565. New Martinsville Glass Manufacturing Company #37 Georgian handled shaker in Ritz blue. Known as "Moondrops" to collectors. 10" high. With two stemmed tumblers. 3½" high. Circa 1932 – 1940. Shaker $175.00 – 185.00. Tumbler, each $10.00 – 12.00.

Plate 566. Paden City Glass Manufacturing Company #449 (?) 30-ounce cocktail shaker in royal blue with platinum line decoration. 11" high. With two glasses. 4⅝" high. Questionable attribution because of the undocumented glasses, which were purchased as part of a set with the shaker. It is possible that they are undocumented pieces from Paden City's #991 "Penny Line." Circa 1930s. Shaker $140.00 – 150.00. Tumbler, each $10.00 – 15.00.

Plate 567. Paden City Glass Manufacturing Company #499 cocktail shakers in royal blue. Circa 1932 – 1940.
Left to right: (1) 30-ounce cocktail shaker with unknown marked "Sterling" fox hunt decoration. 11" high. Shaker $140.00 – 150.00. (2) 30-ounce cocktail shaker with unknown silver tavern scene decoration. 11" high. Shaker $140.00 – 150.00. (3) 30-ounce cocktail shaker with unknown silver sailboat decoration. 11" high. Shaker $140.00 – 150.00. (4) 20-ounce cocktail shaker with marked "Sterling" fox hunt decoration by the National Silver Deposit Ware Company, New York. 8¾" high. Shaker $130.00 – 140.00.

Cocktail Shakers

Plate 568. Paden City Glass Manufacturing Company #69 Georgian cocktail shaker in royal blue. Called "Aristocrat" by Hazel Marie Weatherman. 11½" high. With two #69 2½-ounce tumblers. 2½" high. Circa 1932 – 1940. Shaker $250.00 – 300.00. Tumbler, each $8.00 – 10.00.

Plate 569. Paden City Glass Manufacturing Company #215 Glades cocktail shaker in royal blue with platinum line decoration. 10¼" high. With two Glades tumblers. 3½" high. Circa 1936 – 1940s. Shaker $140.00 – 150.00. Tumbler, each $10.00 – 15.00.

Plate 570. West Virginia Glass Specialty Company #4 30-ounce cocktail shaker with platinum line decoration. 10¾" high. With two #10 3½-ounce tumblers. 4¾" high. Circa 1936 – 1940. Shaker $150.00 – 175.00. Tumbler, each $10.00 – 15.00.

Cocktail Shakers

Plate 571. West Virginia Glass Specialty Company #741 cocktail shaker. Known as "Long Feller." 16" high. With two #10 3½-ounce tumblers. 4¾" high. Circa 1936 – 1940. Shaker $200.00 – 250.00. Tumbler, each $12.00 – 15.00.

Plate 572. West Virginia Glass Specialty Company #742 cocktail shaker with platinum line decoration. Known as "Dumbbell." 13" high. With two #449 3½-ounce tumblers. 2¾" high. Circa 1936 – 1940. Shaker $200.00 – 250.00. Tumbler, each $8.00 – 10.00.

Plate 573. West Virginia Glass Specialty Company #4 cocktail shaker with unknown horizontal gold line decoration. 11" high. With two tumblers. 3½" high. Circa 1936 – 1940. Shaker $150.00 – 175.00. Tumbler, each $8.00 – 10.00.

Cocktail Shakers

Plate 574. West Virginia Glass Specialty Company #4 cocktail shaker. 11" high. With tumbler, 3½" high. Both with silver encrusted acid etched decoration by the Wheeling Decorating Company. Circa 1936 – 1940. Shaker $175.00 – 200.00. Tumbler $12.00 – 15.00.

Plate 575. Left to right: (1) Unattributed ribbed base cocktail shaker with cocktail recipes on the sides. 13½" high. Bottom is stamped "Swank." Shaker $225.00 – 250.00. (2) West Virginia Glass Specialty Company cocktail shaker with platinum trim. Known as "Ribbed Dumbbell." 12¼" high. Circa 1936 – 1940. Shaker $275.00 – 300.00.

Plate 576. Unattributed cocktail shaker. Named "Standing Rib" by Hazel Marie Weatherman. 10½" high. With two tumblers with bases, possibly chrome from Chase Brass and Copper Company, New York. 4½" high. Circa 1930s. Shaker $140.00 – 150.00. Tumbler, each $10.00 – 12.00.

Smoking Items

SMOKING ITEMS

Plate 577. Blenko Glass Company #7017 cigarette lighter. 7" high. Circa 1970 – 1974. Lighter $20.00 – 25.00.

Plate 578. Cambridge Glass Company #3011 Statuesque line cigarette box with cover in royal blue. 7½" high. Circa 1931 – 1940s. Cigarette box $650.00 – 750.00.

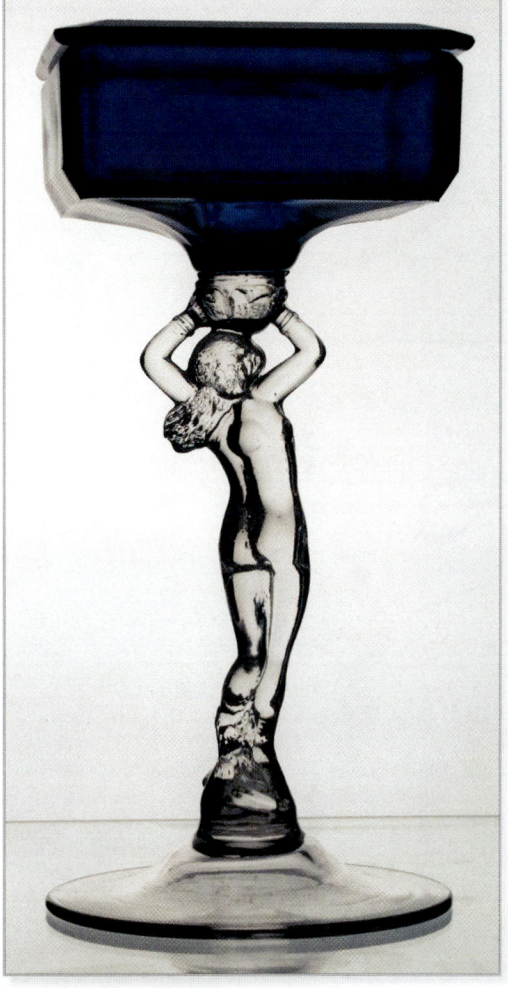

Plate 579. Cambridge Glass Company #3011 Statuesque line ash tray in royal blue. 6⅝" high. Circa 1931 – 1940s. Ash tray $300.00 – 325.00.

Smoking Items

Plate 580. Cambridge Glass Company #3400/144 with cigarette and place card holder in royal blue with a #1066 stem and ashtray base. 3½" high. Circa 1931 – 1940s. Cigarette holder & ash tray $200.00 – 225.00.

Plate 581. Cambridge Glass Company #1312 crystal footed cigarette box and cover in royal blue. 3⅜" high. Circa 1931 – 1940s. Cigarette box $200.00 – 225.00.

Plate 582. Duncan and Miller Glass Company #11 ashtray. 2⅝" high. Circa 1931 – 1940s. Ashtray $60.00 – 65.00.

Plate 583. Fenton Art Glass Company #848 three-leg ashtray in royal blue. 4⅜" diameter. Circa 1932 – 1936. Ash tray $15.00 – 20.00.

Smoking Items

Plate 584. Fostoria Glass Company #2354 cigarette holder with ashtray base in regal blue. 3½" high. Circa 1933 – 1942. Cigarette holder $50.00 – 60.00.

Plate 585. New Martinsville Glass Manufacturing Company/ Viking Glass Company #412-ISJ Janice swan ashtray. 3" high. Circa 1940s – 1950s. Ashtray $20.00 – 25.00.

Plate 586. L. E. Smith Glass Company #1020 three-leg ashtray with silver line decoration. 3½" high x 4½" diameter. Circa 1935 – 1936. Ashtray $15.00 – 20.00.

Plate 587. Unattributed cigar lighter in metal stand. 8" high. Circa 1890. Cigar lighter $90.00 – 100.00.

207

Smoking Items

Plate 588. Unattributed silver plate covered ashtray or silent butler with cobalt insert. 5½" diameter. Circa 1900. Silent butler $60.00 – 70.00.

Plate 589. Unattributed wood smoker stand with cobalt ashtray (4¾" diameter) and two octagon cigarette or tobacco jars (4¼" high) with silver plate covers. Circa 1920s – 1930s. Ashtray $10.00 – 15.00. Cigarette jar, each $20.00 – 25.00.

Plate 590. Unattributed humidor with unknown silver dogwood decoration. 10½" high. Circa 1920s – 1930s. This humidor sits on the bottom shelf of the smoker's stand above. Humidor $175.00 – 200.00.

PERFUMES

Plate 591. Left to right: (1) Unattributed facet cut and polished perfume bottle. 4¼" high. $35.00 – 40.00. (2) Signed A-Jacolima cobalt cased in crystal perfume bottle. 5¼" high. $90.00 – 100.00. (3) Three unattributed silver decorated bottles. 2" high. Each $10.00 – 15.00. (4) Unattributed crystal cased cobalt cut to clear powder. 4¾" high. $40.00 – 50.00. (5) Unattributed crystal cased cobalt diamond hobnail spray perfume bottle. 3¾" high. $40.00 – 50.00. (6) Paden City Glass Manufacturing Company #502-5 one-ounce cologne, with wrong stopper. 5¾" high. $60.00 – 70.00. (7) Signed Daum Nancy cased acid etched perfume bottle. 5⅜" high. $225.00 – 250.00. (8) Unattributed hobnail oval perfume bottle with sprayer. 3⅝" high. $40.00 – 50.00. (9) Murano perfume bottle with round stopper, signed W V M Cappellus Murano. 5¼" high. $120.00 – 130.00. (10) Unattributed bottle with silver base. 3¼" high. $25.00 – 30.00. (11) Avon bottle with gold decoration. 4¾" high. $20.00 – 25.00. (12) Unattributed square cobalt cased in crystal perfume bottle with sprayer. 4¼" high. $30.00 – 40.00. (13) Unattributed hexagon facet cut and polished bottle with stopper perfume bottle. 4¼" high. $35.00 – 40.00.

Plate 592. Boston and Sandwich Glass Company half-pint toilet bottle. 6⅜" high. Circa 1820 – 1840s. Bottle $350.00 – 400.00.

209

BOTTLES

Plate 593. Starting with row one at the top, looking from left to right: Row 1, ink bottles and ink wells. Row 2, three medicine bottles and more ink wells. Row 3, medicine and poison bottles. Row 4, eye lotion and eye wash bottles, with other medicine bottles. Row 5, cologne and perfume bottles. Row 6, Evening in Paris perfume bottles and Vicks containers. Row 7, medicine bottles with labels. Row 8, more medicine bottles with labels, one perfume, two bitters bottles, and seven other medicine bottles, including four old cork top bottles. This is just a sampling of the many hundreds of cobalt blue bottles made over the years.

CHILDREN'S DISHES

Plate 594. Akro Agate Company The Little American Maid Tea Set, called "Large Interior Panel" by collectors. Circa 1930s. 21-piece boxed set $450.00 – 550.00. The set consists of: (1) Four cereal bowls. 3⅛" diameter. Each 30.00 – 35.00. (2) Four plates. 4¼" diameter. Each $15.00 – 20.00. (3) Four cups. 1⅜" high. Each $25.00 – 30.00. (4) Four saucers. 3⅛" diameter. Each $10.00 – 12.00. (5) Sugar and lid. 1⅞" high. $35.00 – 40.00. (6) Creamer. 1⅜" high. $30.00 – 35.00. (7) Teapot and lid. 3¾" high. $65.00 – 75.00.

Plate 595. Alley Agate Company (Alley Glass Company) Toy Dishes or Chiquita 12-piece set. Made for J. Pressman Company, New York. Circa 1930s – 1940s. 12-piece boxed set $100.00 – 120.00. The set consists of: (1) Teapot and lid. 3" high. $20.00 – 25.00. (2) Sugar and creamer. 1½" high. Each $5.00 – 10.00. (3) Four cups. 1½" high. Each $5.00 – 10.00. (4) Four saucers. 3⅛" diameter. Each $3.00 – 5.00.

Children's Dishes

Plate 596. Probably Alley Agate Company (Alley Glass Company) plate and cup. Known as "Vertical Rib." Plate: 4¼" diameter. Cup: 1½" high. Made for J. Pressman Company, New York, with the same handles as the Toy Dishes or Chiquita set in plate 595. Circa 1930s – 1940s. Cup $6.00 – 8.00. Saucer (not shown) $2.00 – 3.00. Plate $6.00 – 8.00.

Plate 597. Mosser Glass #225-3 Lindsey punch bowl set. Punch bowl: 3¼" high x 7½" diameter. With six cups: 1¼" high. Miniature version of the Cambridge Glass Company's Caprice pattern. Circa 1992 – 2003. Punch bowl $10.00 – 12.00. Cup, each $2.00 – 3.00.

Plate 598. Mosser Glass #225-4 Lindsey dinner plates. 4½" diameter. With four #225-2 cup and saucer sets. Cup: 1¼". Saucer: 2½" diameter. Miniature version of the Cambridge Glass Company's Caprice pattern. Circa 1992 – 2003. Plate, each $4.00 – 5.00. Cup, each $2.00 – 3.00. Saucer, each $2.00 – 3.00.

Children's Dishes

Plate 599. Mosser Glass #225-6 Lindsey candlesticks with prisms. 2¾" high. Miniature version of the Cambridge Glass Company's Caprice pattern. Circa 1992 – 2001. Candlestick with prism, each $6.00 – 8.00. With #225-5 Lindsey console set, consisting of fruit bowl (2" high x 5¾" diameter) and small candlesticks (1⅜" high). Circa 1992 – 2003. Bowl: $8.00 – 10.00. Candlestick, each $2.00 – 3.00.

Plate 600. Mosser Glass #225-1 Lindsey water set. Pitcher: 4¼" high. With four tumblers: 2½" high. Miniature version of the Cambridge Glass Company's Caprice pattern. Circa 1992 – 2003. Pitcher $8.00 – 10.00. Tumbler, each $3.00 – 4.00.

213

Children's Dishes

Plate 601. Mosser Glass #225-7 Lindsey relish. 6⅜" long x 3" wide. With four salt dips. 1" square. Miniature version of the Cambridge Glass Company's Caprice pattern. Circa 1995 – 2003. Relish $10.00 – 12.00. Salt dip, each $2.00 – 3.00.

Plate 602. Unattributed "Bead and Dart" pattern glass mugs. 2" high. Circa late 1800s – early 1900s. Mug, each $30.00 – 35.00.

See also plates 107 and 108 on page 44 for additional toy candlesticks.

KEROSENE AND OIL LAMPS

Plate 603. Unattributed hand blown two-part lamp. 12½" high without chimney. Joined with a flattened wafer at oil reservoir and base. Circa mid-to-late 1800s. Lamp $150.00 – 175.00.

Plate 604. Boston and Sandwich Glass Company kerosene banquet lamp with non-original top shade. 18" high. Lamps of the same quality and components are pictured in the 1865 Boston and Sandwich catalog. Banquet lamp $250.00 – 300.00.

Kerosene and Oil Lamps

Plate 606. Unattributed ribbed optic kerosene lamp with brass fittings and marble base. 10" high. Circa 1870s. Lamp $100.00 – 110.00.

Plate 605. Unattributed ribbed optic kerosene lamp with milk glass base. 10" high. Circa 1870 – 1880s. Lamp $90.00 – 100.00.

Plate 607. Unattributed finger lamp. 3½" high. "Pat. October 28, 1873" on bottom. Lamp $55.00 – 65.00.

Kerosene and Oil Lamps

Plate 608. Unattributed alcohol lamp. 3" high. "Pat. June 26, 1883" on base. This patent was granted to Norman Clark of Sterling, Illinois. The flat angles on the base allowed the lamp to be tilted safely when the lamp was being used while soldering. Circa 1883 – 1900. Lamp $100.00 – 110.00.

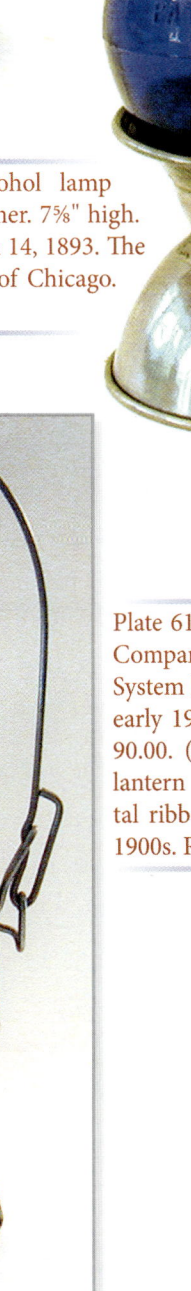

Plate 609. Unattributed alcohol lamp with silver plate base and burner. 7⅜" high. Pat. Sept. 14, 1880, and March 14, 1893. The designer was John H. Purdy of Chicago. Lamp $65.00 – 75.00.

Plate 610. Left to right: (1) R. E. Dietz Company #999 Vesta New York Central System kerosene lantern. 9" high. Circa early 1900s. Railroad lantern $80.00 – 90.00. (2) Western Maryland Railway lantern with unattributed horizontal ribbed glass. 9½" high. Circa early 1900s. Railroad lantern $40.00 – 50.00.

217

Kerosene and Oil Lamps

Plate 611. Unattributed kerosene lamp with metal base and roses molded in the bowl. 11" high. Circa 1900 – 1920s. Lamp $115.00 – 125.00.

Plate 612. Unattributed three-ringed alcohol lamp. 6¾" high. Circa 1900 – 1930s. Lamp $20.00 – 25.00.

Plate 613. Unattributed alcohol lamp. 8" high. Very poor quality glass with mold seams to top of threads. Most likely a reproduction of an old lamp. Lamp $20.00 – 25.00.

Plate 614. Hong Kong. Kerosene lamp with blue shade. 12" high. Circa 1950s – 1970s. Lamp $15.00 – 20.00.

Kerosene and Oil Lamps

Plate 615. Hong Kong. Left to right: (1) Lamp with cobalt chimney and black base. 16¼" high. $20.00 – 25.00. (2) Lamp with clear chimney. 16¾" high. 15.00 – 20.00. (3) Lamp with cobalt chimney and metal base. 14¾" high. $20.00 – 25.00.

Plate 616. Hong Kong. Lamps. Left to right: (1) 11" high. (2) 10" high. (3) 7¼" high. (4) 13¼" high. (5) 8" high. (6) 8" high. (7) 8" high. The last lantern with tall necked chimney is marked "Sailboat" brand, Hong Kong. All lamps, each $10.00 – 15.00.

Kerosene and Oil Lamps

Plate 617. Lamps. Left to right: (1) Hong Kong. 10" high. (2) Hong Kong. 7¾" high. (3) Hong Kong. 5½" high. (4) Hungary. 9½" high. (5) Hong Kong. 8¼" high. (6) Hong Kong. 10" high. Circa 1950s – 1970s. All lamps, each $10.00 – 15.00.

Plate 618. Hong Kong. Miniature lamps. Left to right: (1) 4¾" high. (2) 4½" high. (3) 4¾" high. (4) 4⅛" high. (5) 5" high. (6) 4¾" high. (7) 5" high. (8) 4⅛" high. Circa 1950s – 1970. All lamps, each $8.00 – 10.00.

Plate 619. Aladdin Industries Draped Lincoln lamp. 10" high. Originally made in one piece in the 1940s by the Mantle Lamp Company, this later reproduction was made in two pieces and glued together. Circa 1976. Lamp $150.00 – 160.00.

220

MISCELLANEOUS ITEMS

Plate 620. Central Glass, Company, Oklahoma. Circa 1970s. Many other companies in the Spiro, Oklahoma, area made similar swans. These particular examples could as easliy have been made by The Sunset Glass Company or one of the others. Left to right: (1) 12½" long x 11" wide free form swan bowl. Large swan $35.00 – 40.00. (2) 10" long x 8" wide free form swan bowl. Small swan $25.00 – 30.00.

Plate 621. Mosser Glass Clydesdale horse. 7" high. Made from the original A. H. Heisey and Company mold for the Longaberger Company in cooperation with the National Heisey Museum in 1999. Horse $100.00 – 110.00.

Miscellaneous Items

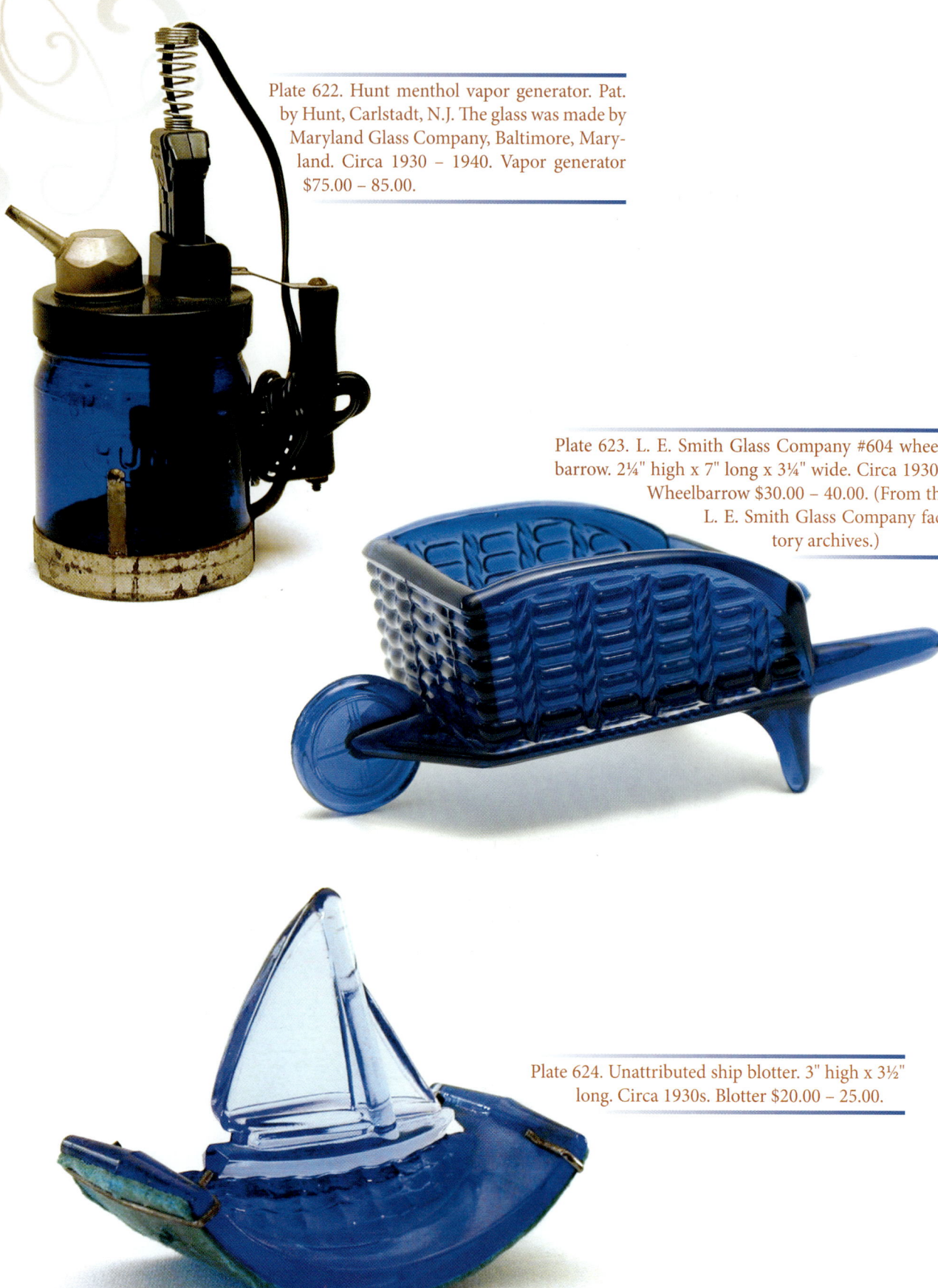

Plate 622. Hunt menthol vapor generator. Pat. by Hunt, Carlstadt, N.J. The glass was made by Maryland Glass Company, Baltimore, Maryland. Circa 1930 – 1940. Vapor generator $75.00 – 85.00.

Plate 623. L. E. Smith Glass Company #604 wheelbarrow. 2¼" high x 7" long x 3¼" wide. Circa 1930s. Wheelbarrow $30.00 – 40.00. (From the L. E. Smith Glass Company factory archives.)

Plate 624. Unattributed ship blotter. 3" high x 3½" long. Circa 1930s. Blotter $20.00 – 25.00.

BASKETS

Plate 625. Fenton Art Glass Company #1615 metal handled diamond optic basket in royal blue. 5½" high flat rim x 4" diameter base x 5" diameter at mouth. Circa 1927 – 1939. Basket $200.00 – 250.00.

Plate 626. Unattributed silver filagree basket with cobalt insert. 5¼" high x 4½" diameter. No markings on silver or glass. Circa early 1900s? Basket $90.00 – 100.00.

Plate 627. Unattributed Chippendale-style glass handled basket. 10" high x 7½" x 4" diameter opening. Although the Central Glass Works or Jefferson Glass Company have been suggested as attribution, no documentation has been found to support this. Circa 1930s. Basket $200.00 – 250.00.

VASES

Plate 628. Beaumont Company three-footed cupped rose bowl with silver overlay by an unknown decorator. 3¼" high x 4¾" diameter. The feet have veins in them like tree bark that continue up to the side of the bowl. This bowl is normally found with a flower frog insert. The same mold was used to make a flared and crimped bowl, or candy dish, to which a glass lid was added. Probably circa 1930s. Rose bowl $175.00 – 200.00.

Plate 629. Beaumont Company bowl vase (5" high) with two 6¼" high vases on 2½" high four-leg black bases. All three with a silver overlay cattails and stork decoration. Probably circa 1930. Six piece set $1,000.00 – 1,200.00.

Plate 630. Cambridge Glass Company #94 special article sweet pea vase in Ritz blue. 7" high x 8¼" diameter. With gold encrusted #708 acid etching by Cambridge. Circa 1929 – 1931. Vase $300.00 – 325.00.

224

Vases

Plate 631. Cambridge Glass Company vases in royal blue. Circa 1931 – 1940s. Left to right: (1) #1447 aero optic cupped vase with #3400 spires. 8" high. Vase $140.00 – 150.00. (2) #3400/102 globe vase. 5" high. Vase $120.00 – 130.00. (3) #1242 flared vase with #3400 spires. 11" high. Vase $150.00 – 160.00.

Plate 632. Cambridge Glass Company #1236 keyhole stem ribbed ivy ball in royal blue. 8" high. Circa 1931 – 1940s. Vase $100.00 – 120.00.

Plate 633. Cambridge Glass Company #1239 keyhole stem flared vase in royal blue. 14" high. Circa 1931 – 1940s. Vase $215.00 – 225.00.

Vases

Plate 634. Cambridge Glass Company vases in royal blue. Circa 1931 – 1940s. Left to right: (1) #1234 keyhole stem bud vase. 12" high. Vase $150.00 – 160.00. (2) #1233 keyhole stem bud vase. 9½" high. Vase $125.00 – 135.00. (3) #1238 keyhole stem flared top vase. 12" high. Vase $155.00 – 165.00. (4) #1237 keyhole stem flared top vase. 10" high. The #1237 is listed in catalogs as 9" high. Vase $155.00 – 165.00.

Plate 635. Cambridge Glass Company #1300 crystal footed bud vase in royal blue. 8" high. Circa 1931 – 1940s. Vase $50.00 – 60.00.

Plate 636. Cambridge Glass Company #1299 crystal footed flared urn vase in royal blue. 11" high. Circa 1931 – 1940s. Vase $250.00 – 275.00.

Vases

Plate 637. Cambridge Glass Company #1410 diamond optic rose bowl in royal blue with original Cambridge sticker. 6" high. Circa 1931 – 1940s. Vase $100.00 – 120.00.

Plate 639. Cambridge Glass Company #306 vase in royal blue. 3⅜" high. Circa 1936 – 1940s. Vase $20.00 – 25.00.

Plate 638. Cambridge Glass Company #3011/25 Statuesque Line ivy ball in royal blue. 9¼" high. Circa 1931 – 1940s. Ivy ball $250.00 – 275.00.

Plate 640. Cambridge Glass Company #44 Sea Shell flower center vase in royal blue with crystal foot and ball stem. 5¾" high x 4¼" diameter. Circa 1935 – 1940s. Vase $495.00 – 500.00.

227

Vases

Plate 641. Cambridge Glass Company Caprice vases in royal blue. Circa 1936 – 1940s.
Left to right: (1) #239 ring neck plain top vase. 8½" high. Vase $350.00 – 375.00. (2) #238 ring neck plain top vase. 6½" high. Vase $200.00 – 225.00. (3) #241 short neck plain top vase. 4" high. This vase was reissued in blue royale in 1989 by the Fenton Art Glass Company as #9753. The Fenton reissue has a ruffled top and is marked with the Fenton logo. Vase $125.00 – 135.00. (4) #242 short neck plain top vase. 6" high. This vase was reissued in blue royale in 1989 by the Fenton Art Glass Company as #9751. The Fenton reissue has a crimped top and is marked with the Fenton logo. Vase $200.00 – 225.00.

Plate 642. Central Glass Company, Oklahoma, vase. 7¾" high with severely crimped top. Circa 1970. Vase $15.00 – 20.00.

Plate 643. Dugan Glass Company (predecessor to Diamond Glass-Ware Company) Filigree Art Ware vase. 8" high x 3" diameter base. Advertised in 1907. Vase $150.00 – 160.00.

Vases

Plate 644. Dunbar Glass Corporation favor vases. Probably circa 1930s.
Left to right: (1) Favor vase with two horizontal bulges. 3" high. Same as the #4230 A. H. Heisey and Company favor vase, but without the diamond or swirl optic found on all Heisey favor vases. Vase $10.00 – 15.00. (2) Favor vase with three horizontal bulges. 3" high. Same as the #4227 A. H. Heisey and Company favor vase, but without the diamond or swirl optic found on all Heisey favor vases. Vase $10.00 – 15.00.

Plate 645. Dunbar Glass Corporation #410, 3350, 3351, 3382, 6209, or 6349 blown vase with three rings on the shoulder and bottom. 8" high. Pictured in the 1931 catalog in crystal with many numbers, depending upon the decoration. Production in cobalt circa 1930s. Vase $10.00 – 20.00.

Plate 646. Dunbar Glass Corporation blown crimped top vase. 8" high. Circa 1930s. Vase $10.00 – 15.00.

Vases

Plate 647. Dunbar Glass Corporation five horizontal ribbed vase. 8⅜" high. This vase has been attributed to Dunbar by various glass writers. Circa 1930s. Vase $25.00 – 30.00.

Plate 648. Dunbar Glass Corporation #753 three horizontal ribbed vase. 8" high x 5" diameter top. Gold and silver decoration on the three ribs and top of vase. Stamped on the bottom with the Rockwell Silver Company mark ("Rockwell" in a shield). This vase was advertised in 1937 and was still listed as late as a 1950 catalog. Vase with Rockwell decoration $50.00 – 60.00. Vase, plain $20.00 – 25.00.

Plate 650. Duncan and Miller Glass Company #12 three-footed rocket-style vase with unknown Art Deco painted flower and gold decoration. 9" high. Circa 1932 – 1937. Vase $200.00 – 225.00.

Plate 649. Duncan and Miller Glass Company #12 three-footed rocket-style vase. 9" high. With Duncan and Miller paper sticker. Circa 1932 – 1937. Vase $175.00 – 200.00.

Vases

Plate 651. Duncan and Miller Glass Company #5 Venetian footed vase. 10½" high. Advertised with the #126 Venetian line in 1932. Circa 1932 – 1937. Vase $250.00 – 275.00.

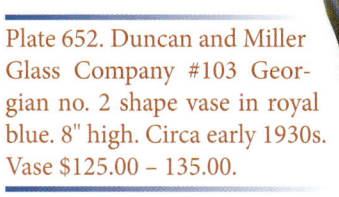

Plate 652. Duncan and Miller Glass Company #103 Georgian no. 2 shape vase in royal blue. 8" high. Circa early 1930s. Vase $125.00 – 135.00.

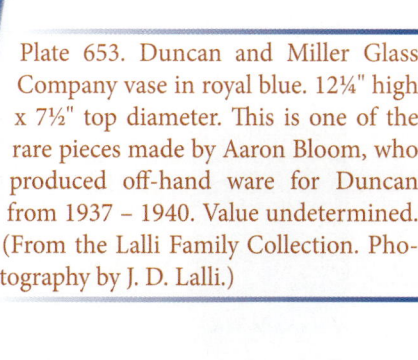

Plate 653. Duncan and Miller Glass Company vase in royal blue. 12¼" high x 7½" top diameter. This is one of the rare pieces made by Aaron Bloom, who produced off-hand ware for Duncan from 1937 – 1940. Value undetermined. (From the Lalli Family Collection. Photography by J. D. Lalli.)

Vases

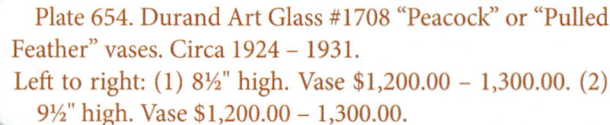

Plate 654. Durand Art Glass #1708 "Peacock" or "Pulled Feather" vases. Circa 1924 – 1931. Left to right: (1) 8½" high. Vase $1,200.00 – 1,300.00. (2) 9½" high. Vase $1,200.00 – 1,300.00.

Plate 655. Fenton Art Glass Company #1611 Georgian footed vase with flared top and nine-sided base in royal blue. 6¾" high. This vase is made from the candy jar mould with its top flared. Introduced in 1930 as Agua Caliente, the pattern name was later changed to Georgian. Circa 1930 – 1938. Vase $85.00 – 95.00.

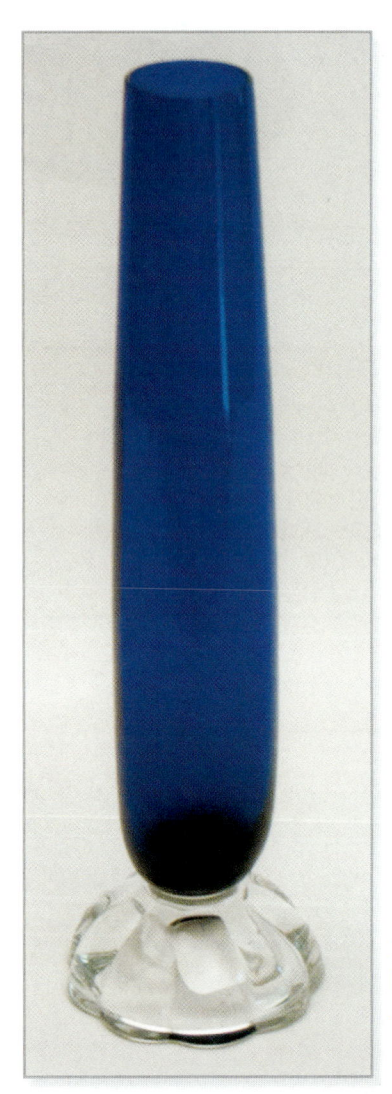

Plate 656. Fostoria Glass Company #5088 crystal footed bud vase in regal blue. 8½" high. The base matches the #4024 line of bowls, candlesticks, and stemware. Circa 1934 – 1940. Vase $35.00 – 40.00.

Vases

Plate 658. Fostoria Glass Company #2404 ground and polished top fish bowl vase in regal blue. 5¾" high. Circa 1934 – 1935. Vase $100.00 – 110.00.

Plate 657. Fostoria Glass Company #2470 crystal footed flared vases in regal blue. Circa 1934 – 1939.
Left to right: 9⅝" high. Vase $175.00 – 185.00. (2) 11⅜" high. Vase $175.00 – 185.00.

Plate 659. H. C. Fry Glass Company ivy ball in royal blue with crystal swirl connector. 6¾" high. Circa 1931 – 1933. Vase $115.00 – 125.00.

Vases

Plate 660. Gillinder Glass Bird vase. 15" high. Originally made in crystal and ruby stained crystal prior to World War II. This vase in cobalt was made circa 1970 – 1980s by a Gillinder glass blower from glass left in a tank prior to vacation in July when the plant shut down. In the 1990s it was reissued by Gillinder in cobalt. Vase $90.00 – 100.00.

Plate 661. Hazel-Atlas Glass Company exterior panel vase. 7¾" high. Marked H superimposed over an A on the bottom. Circa 1936 – 1940s. Vase $15.00 – 20.00.

Plate 663. A. H. Heisey and Company favor vases in Stiegel blue. Circa 1933 – 1941.
Left to right: (1) #4229 diamond optic favor vase. 3" high. Vase $225.00 – 250.00. (2) #4230 diamond optic favor vase. 3" high. Vase $215.00 – 225.00.

Note: Similar vases without optics were made by Dunbar Glass Corporation. See plate 644, page 229.

Plate 662.
A. H. Heisey and Company favor vases in Stiegel blue. Circa 1933 – 1941. Left to right: (1) #4231 diamond optic favor vase. 3" high. Vase $300.00 – 325.00. (2) #4228 diamond optic favor vase. 3¼" high. Vase $300.00 – 325.00.

Vases

Plate 664. A. H. Heisey and Company #1420 footed vase in Stiegel blue. Known as "Tulip" by collectors. 9" high. Circa 1933 – 1937. Vase $475.00 – 500.00.

Plate 665. A. H. Heisey and Company #1421 footed and handled vase in Stiegel blue. Known as "Hi Lo" to collectors. 8" high. Circa 1933 – 1937. Vase $400.00 – 425.00.

Plate 666. A. H. Heisey and Company #1428 Warwick "horn of plenty" vases in Stiegel blue. Circa 1933 – 1941. From left to right: (1) 9" high. Vase $425.00 – 450.00. (2) Two 2¼" high vases. Each $125.00 – 135.00. (3) 7" high. Vase $400.00 – 425.00. (4) 5" high. Vase $250.00 – 275.00.

Vases

Plate 667. A. H. Heisey and Company #1433 flared vase in Stiegel blue. Known as "Thumbprint and Panel" to collectors. 8" high. Circa 1934 – 1937. Vase $800.00 – 900.00.

Plate 668. Imperial Glass Corporation #359 white hearts and trailing vines free hand vase. 6" high. Circa 1923 – 1924. Vase $600.00 – 700.00.

Plate 669. Imperial Glass Corporation #306 white hearts and trailing vines free hand iridized vase. 9" high. Circa 1923 – 1924. Vase $650.00 – 700.00.

Vases

Plate 670. Imperial Glass Corporation #623 white hearts and trailing vines free hand vase. 10" high. Circa 1923 – 1924. Vase $650.00 – 700.00.

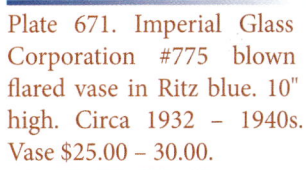

Plate 671. Imperial Glass Corporation #775 blown flared vase in Ritz blue. 10" high. Circa 1932 – 1940s. Vase $25.00 – 30.00.

Plate 672. Left to right: (1) Unattributed bulb base vase with flared top. 7" high. (2) Unattributed sweet potato vase with fired polished top rim. 5⅝" high. (3) Imperial Glass Corporation hyacinth vase in Ritz blue. 7" high. Circa 1932 – 1940. All vases, each $10.00 – 15.00.

Vases

Plate 673. Imperial Glass Corporation Lace Edge (or Laced Edge) pattern in Ritz blue. Circa 1932 – 1940. Left to right: (1) #743 B four-toed diamond hobnail vase. 5½" high. (2) #780 four-toed panel optic vase. 5½" high. Vase, each $25.00 – 35.00.

Plate 674. Imperial Glass Corporation #701/6 Reeded ball vase in Ritz blue. Called "Spun" by Hazel Marie Weatherman. 3⅛" high x 4" diameter. Circa 1935 – 1940. Vase $35.00 – 45.00.

Plate 675. Imperial Glass Corporation #701/2 Reeded rose bowl in Ritz blue. Called "Spun" by Hazel Marie Weatherman. 5⅜" high x 6" diameter. Circa 1935 – 1940. Rose bowl $55.00 – 65.00.

Plate 676. Imperial Glass Corporation #71755 Quilted Diamond flip vase in sapphire blue. 6" high. Made originally for the Metropolitan Museum of Art (marked "MMA") and in 1977 marketed nation-wide by Imperial. Circa 1977 – 1984. Vase $15.00 – 20.00.

Vases

Plate 677. Left to right: (1) Louie Glass Company #93 (?) Spittoon shaped vase with crimped top. 4½" high. Circa 1930s. Vase $5.00 – 10.00. (2) Unattributed footed three-ring stem bud vase with gray cutting of grapes and leaves. 7¼" high. Vase $25.00 – 30.00. (3) Unattributed molded ball vase with flared chimney. 3¾" high. Vase $8.00 – 10.00. (4) West Virginia Glass Specialty Company (?) crimped top vase with three platinum bands. 6" high. Circa 1930s. Vase $10.00 – 15.00. (5) Louie Glass Company #600V6-1/2 C crimped top vase. 6½" high. Line number is from a 1960s catalog page, but this vase is circa 1930s. Vase $10.00 – 15.00. (6) Imperial Glass Corporation #86 high ruffled top vase in Ritz blue with beaded lines up the sides. 7" high. Circa 1960s. Vase $10.00 – 15.00. (7) Imperial Glass Corporation #86 (or #51757) vase in Ritz blue with beaded flared top and beaded lines up the sides. 4¾" high. Circa 1960s. Vase $8.00 – 10.00.

Plate 678. Louie Glass Company crimped top spittoon-shape vase. 6½" high x 7¼" diameter. Circa 1930s. Vase $20.00 – 25.00.

Plate 679. Louie Glass Company crimped top vase with four pair of vertical indentations on the body. 7¼" high x 6½" diameter. Circa 1930s. Vase $20.00 – 25.00.

Vases

Plate 680. Louie Glass Company crimped top vase or urn with two applied reeded handles and six horizontal ribs above the base. 9¾" high. This vase was made from the same mold as the #854 ice tea jug. Circa 1930s. Vase $30.00 – 35.00.

Plate 681. Louie Glass Company (?) ribbed urn-shaped vase with crimped top. 8" high. Circa 1930s. Vase $50.00 – 60.00.

Plate 682. Left to right: (1) European bulb bottom, long neck favor vase with gold ring decoration. 5¾" high. Vase $10.00 – 15.00. (2) Unattributed blown bulb bottom, long neck bud vase with ground top. 9¾" high. Vase $20.00 – 25.00. (3) Louie Glass Company/Weston Glass Company #1818 marmalade jar without the lid. 4¼" high. Circa 1930s. Jar $10.00 – 12.00 (without lid); $20.00 – 25.00 (with lid). (4) Caffco International footed bud vase with unknown light cutting of ovals and lines. 8½" high. Vase $10.00 – 15.00. (5) Unattributed footed bud vase with gray cutting of dots and leaves. 5⅛" high. Vase $10.00 – 15.00. (6) Dunbar Glass Corporation #3321 ivy ball with crimped top (catalog description). 5" high x 4" diameter. This line number may designate a decoration rather than the blank. Circa 1931. Ivy ball $10.00 – 15.00.

Vases

Plate 683. Left to right: (1) Unattributed crystal ball stem and foot high necked bud vase with gray cutting of dots and leaves. 8½" high. Vase $25.00 – 30.00. (2) Dunbar Glass Corporation bud vase. 9" high. Eight horizontal bulging rings with crimped top. Circa 1930s. Vase $15.00 – 20.00. (3) Louie Glass Company crimped top vase. 7¾" high x 2⅞" diameter base. Circa 1930s. Vase $10.00 – 15.00. (4) Louie Glass Company crimped top vase with three horizontal rings above the base. 8¾" high x 3⅛" diameter base. Circa 1930s. Vase $15.00 – 20.00. (5) Duncan and Miller Glass Company #99 crystal footed, fluted bud vase. 10" high. Circa 1931 – 1940s. Vase $35.00 – 40.00. (6) Unattributed crystal ball stem and foot bud vase with gray cutting of dots and leaves. 8" high. Vase $25.00 – 30.00. (7) Louie Glass Company #112V9C crimped top vase with eight horizontal rings. 9" high x 2¼" diameter base. Pictured in a circa 1960s catalog page with the line number above. Cobalt manufactured circa 1930s. Vase $15.00 – 20.00. (8) Louie Glass Company crimped top vase. 7⅜" high x 2¼" diameter base. Circa 1930s. Vase $10.00 – 15.00.

Plate 684. Left to right: (1) Louie Glass Company #112V6C crimped top vase with eight horizontal rings. 6¼" high x 1⅞" diameter base. Line number from the 1960s. Cobalt manufactured circa 1930s. Vase $15.00 – 20.00. (2) Unattributed horizontal ribbed vase with flared neck. 4⅜" high. "USA" molded on bottom. Vase $8.00 – 10.00. (3) Unattributed horizontal ribbed neck ball vase. 3" high. "USA" molded on bottom. Vase $8.00 – 10.00. (4) Louie Glass Company (?) three-bulb flared and crimped top vase. 7" high. Circa 1930s. Vase $10.00 – 12.00. (5) Unattributed molded horizontal ribbed bud vase. 6¾" high. Vase $8.00 – 10.00. (6) Louie Glass Company #42 crimped top vase. 5⅜" high x 1¾" diameter. Circa 1930s. Vase $10.00 – 15.00.

241

Vases

Plate 685. Louie Glass Company four horizontal rib, crystal foot crimped vase. 10" high. This vase appears in the Louie display at the Museum of American Glass in West Virginia, Weston. Circa 1930s. Vase $35.00 – 45.00.

Plate 686. Louie Glass Company #96V2 acorn vase with crimped top, hanging in a black metal holder by an unknown manufacturer. Vase: 2" high. Circa 1930s. Vase & holder $20.00 – 25.00.

Plate 687. Louie Glass Company #96V2 crimped acorn vase in white wire bookends. Vase: 2" high. Circa 1930s. Pair of vase bookends $25.00 – 35.00.

Vases

Plate 688. Louie Glass Company #96V2 acorn vases. Circa 1930s.
Left to right: (1) Three crimped acorn vases in white wire music scale wall hanger. Vase: 2" high. Vases & hanger $35.00 – 45.00. (2) Crimped acorn vase in white wire music note wall hanger. Vase: 2" high. Vase & hanger: $15.00 – 20.00. (3) Crimped acorn vase in white wire bass music note wall hanger. Vase: 2" high. Vase & hanger: $10.00 – 15.00.

Plate 689. Louie Glass Company #96V2 crimped acorn vases with wall hangers. Vase: 2" high. Circa 1930s. Vase & hanger, pair $15.00 – 20.00.

Plate 690. Louie Glass Company #96V2 acorn vases. Circa 1930s.
Left to right: (1) Crimped acorn vase in white wire star of David hanger. Vase: 2" high. Vase & hanger, $10.00 – 15.00. (2) Crimped acorn vase in white wire diamond-shaped wall hanger. Vase: 4" high. Vase & hanger $20.00 – 25.00. (3) Crimped acorn vase in white wire circle wall hanger. Vase: 2" high. Vase & hanger $20.00 – 25.00.

Vases

Plate 691. Louie Glass Company #200V5 crimped wall vases in circular white wire wall hangers. Vase: 2" 5" high. Circa 1930s. Vase & hanger, pair $20.00 – 25.00.

Plate 693. Louie Glass Company (?) flared rim rose bowl in white metal holder. 3½" high. Vase & holder $15.00 – 20.00.

Plate 692. Louie Glass Company. Circa 1930s.
Left to right: (1) Two #96V2 crimped acorn vases in white wire wall hanger. Vases: 2" high. Vases & hanger $25.00 – 30.00. (2) Three #96V2 crimped acorn vases in white wire wall hanger. Vases: 2" high. Vases & hanger $30.00 – 35.00. (3) #123-8 crimped wall vase in white metal wire hanger. Vase: 8" high. Vase & hanger $20.00 – 25.00. (4) Two #96V2 crimped acorn vases and #92V4 crimped ivy ball vase in white metal arch and fence holder by unknown metal company. Acorn vases: 2" high. Ball vase: 4" high. Vases & holder $45.00 – 50.00.

Vases

Plate 694. Louie Glass Company #92V4C crimped top ivy ball vase in white metal stand by unknown manufacturer. 4" high. Line number is from the 1960s. Cobalt manufactured circa 1930s. Vase & stand $25.00 – 30.00.

Plate 695. Louie Glass Company #46 flared vase in white metal stand by unknown manufacturer. 8¼" high. Circa 1930s. Vase & stand $25.00 – 35.00.

Plate 696. Louie Glass Company #123-8 crimped wall vase in white metal stand by unknown manufacturer. 8¼" high. Line number is from the 1960s. Cobalt manufactured circa 1930s. Vase & stand $25.00 – 30.00.

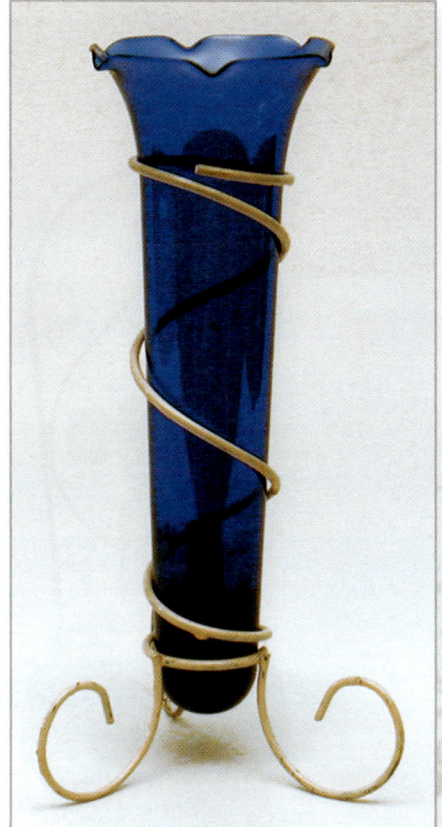

Plate 697. Louie Glass Company #123-8 crimped wall vase in black wire music clef wall hanger. 8¼" high. Line number is from the 1960s. Cobalt manufactured circa 1930s. Vase & hanger $20.00 – 25.00.

Vases

Plate 698. Left to right: (1) Maryland Glass Corporation (or Chattanooga Glass Corporation, Baltimore, Maryland) vase with four vertical panels molded in the glass. 4⅞" high. Marked with M in a circle. Circa 1970s. Vase $10.00 – 15.00. (2) Maryland Glass Corporation (or Chattanooga Glass Corporation, Baltimore, Maryland) vase with free flowing line design molded in the glass. 5⅜" high. Marked with M in a circle. Circa 1970s. Vase $10.00 – 15.00. (3) Unattributed blown long neck, flared bud vase. 7⅛" high. Vase $10.00 – 15.00. (4) Louie Glass Company crimped top vase. 4⅜" high x 3" diameter. Circa 1930s. Vase $10.00 – 15.00. (5) Louie Glass Company crimped top vase with a ring at the base of the neck and three raised tapered panels on the bodies. 6" high x 2¼" diameter base. Circa 1930s. Vase $15.00 – 20.00. (6) Louie Glass Company crimped top vase with a ring at the base of the neck and three raised tapered panels on the bodies. 4½" high x 1⅝" diameter base. Circa 1930s. Vase $10.00 – 15.00. (7) Louie Glass Company #43 crimped top vase. 6" high x 1⅞" diameter base. Circa 1930s. Vase $10.00 – 15.00.

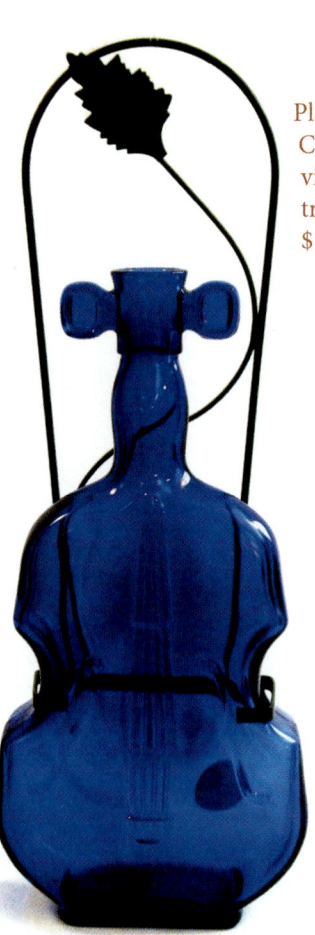

Plate 699. Possibly Maryland Glass Corporation (or Chattanooga Glass Corporation, Baltimore, Maryland) violin-shaped vase in black metal holder. 8" high. Attribution to Maryland has not been documented. Vase $15.00 – 20.00.

Plate 700. McKee Glass Company #1927 diamond hobnail and flower pressed glass car vase. 7½" high. Circa 1910 – 1930. Vase $140.00 – 150.00.

Vases

Plate 701. Morgantown Glass Works #7643 vases in Ritz blue. Circa 1929 – 1940. Left to right: (1) Flared vase with golf ball stem. Known as "Charlotte." 8" high. Vase $175.00 – 185.00. (2) Ivy ball vase with golf ball stem. Known as "Kimball." 6¾" high (with 4" ivy ball). Vase $110.00 – 120.00. (3) Urn vase with golf ball stem. 6½" high. Vase $140.00 – 150.00.

Plate 702. Morgantown Glass Works #65 crystal footed, scalloped edge vase in Ritz blue. Known as "Roxanne." 10" high. Circa 1929 – 1940. Vase $190.00 – 200.00.

Plate 703. Morgantown Glass Works #18 crimped top vase in Ritz blue with unknown silver lilies and butterflies decoration. 10" high. (Also made in 6" and 8" sizes.) Circa 1929 – 1940. Vase $175.00 – 185.00.

Vases

Plate 704. Left to right: (1) Dunbar Glass Corporation (?) footed crimped top bud vase. 8" high. Circa 1930s. Vase $15.00 – 20.00. (2) Morgantown Glass Works #64 crystal foot ivy ball with chimney in Ritz blue. 5" high. Circa 1929 – 1940. Vase $50.00 – 75.00. (3) Morgantown #7662½ crystal foot, flared bud vase in Ritz blue. Known as "Bombay." 9" high. Circa 1929 – 1940. Vase $40.00 – 45.00.

Plate 705. Ludwig Moser und Sohne blown vase with four different gold filled cut flowers. 16½" high. Circa 1880 – 1920. Vase $1,200.00 – 1,500.00.

Plate 706. Ludwig Moser und Sohne. Circa 1918 – 1925.
Left to right: (1) Footed vase with gold encrusted Sovereign acid etching. 5½" high. Vase $175.00 – 200.00. (2) Facet cut vase with gold encrusted acid etching, stamped "Moser #90." 10" high. Vase $600.00 – 650.00. (3) Facet cut vase with gold encrusted acid etching, signed "Moser." 10½" high. Vase $700.00 – 750.00. (4) Facet cut vase with gold encrusted acid etching, signed "Moser." 8¾" high. Vase $700.00 – 750.00.

Vases

Plate 707. New Martinsville Glass Manufacturing Company vases in Ritz blue. Circa 1932 – 1940.
Left to right: (1) & (3) #35/3/25 three-footed rocket-style vases with flared three-crimp top. 7¾" high. This vase is often listed in the #4500 Janice line, which was introduced in 1940, but was actually first made as part of the #35 line, named "Fancy Squares" by Hazel Marie Weatherman, which appeared in 1931. (2) #35 three-footed rocket-style vase with flat top. 7¾" high. Vases, each $140.00 – 150.00.

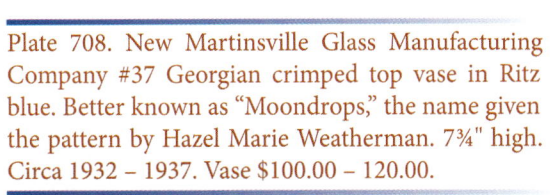

Plate 708. New Martinsville Glass Manufacturing Company #37 Georgian crimped top vase in Ritz blue. Better known as "Moondrops," the name given the pattern by Hazel Marie Weatherman. 7¾" high. Circa 1932 – 1937. Vase $100.00 – 120.00.

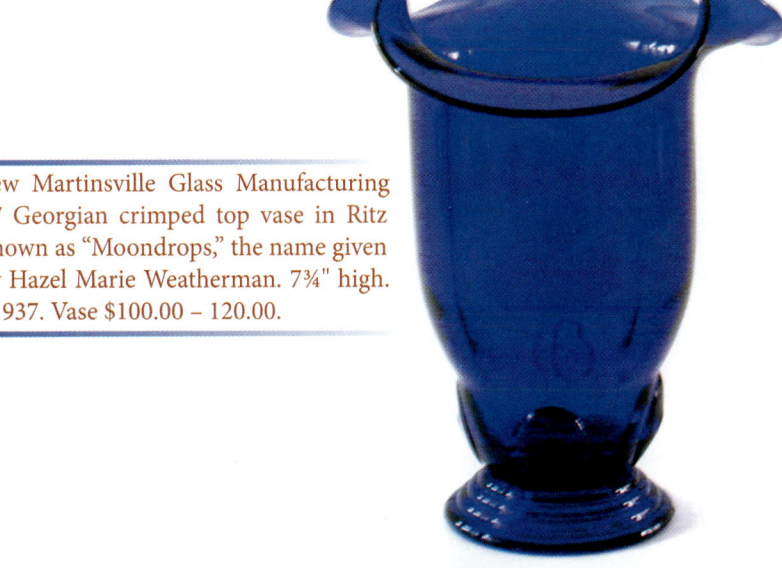

Plate 709. New Martinsville Glass Manufacturing Company Radiance vases in Ritz blue. Circa 1936 – 1940.
Left to right: (1) #4232 crimped top vase. 12" high. Vase $175.00 – 200.00. (2) #42 or #4200 flared top vase. 10" high. The mold for this vase was used to make a pitcher or jug with an applied handle. Vase $110.00 – 125.00. (3) #42 or #4200 flared top vase. 12" high. Vase $175.00 – 200.00.

Vases

Plate 710. Paden City Glass Manufacturing Company #184 flared vase in royal blue with unknown marked "Sterling" silver overlay of flowers, leaves and lines. 12" high x 4¼" diameter base. Circa 1930s. Vase $250.00 – 300.00.

Plate 711. Paden City Glass Manufacturing Company #412 cupped vase in royal blue. Named "Crow's Foot Square" by Jerry Barnett. 8¼" high x 3¾" diameter base. Circa 1930s. Vase $175.00 – 200.00.

Plate 712. Paden City Glass Manufacturing Company flared rim vase with interior panel optic in royal blue. Named "Swanson" by Michael Krumme. 10⅜" high x 3⅜" diameter base. Decorated with marked "Sterling" silver lilies and butterflies overlay by an unknown decorator. Circa 1930s. Vase $250.00 – 300.00.

Vases

Plate 713. Paden City Glass Manufacturing Company flared rim vase with exterior panels in royal blue. Named "Swanson" by Michael Krumme. 10⅛" high x 3⅜" diameter base. Marked "Sterling" silver overlay of berries, cherries, grapes, leaves, and vines by National Silver Deposit Company, 179-181-183 Wooster Street, New York, New York. Circa 1930s. Vase $250.00 – 300.00.

Plate 714. Paden City Glass Manufacturing Company flared rim vase with exterior panels in royal blue. Named "Swanson" by Michael Krumme. 10⅛" high x 3⅜" diameter base. Marked "Sterling" silver overlay by an unknown decorator, named "Pod Flower" by William Walker. Circa 1930s. Vase $250.00 – 300.00.

Plate 715. Paden City Glass Manufacturing Company flared rim vases with exterior panels in royal blue. Named "Swanson" by Michael Krumme. 10⅛" high x 3⅜" diameter base.
Left to right: (1) Decorated with silver overlay of flowers, leaves, and vines by unknown decorator. (2) Decorated with marked "Sterling" silver lilies and butterflies by an unknown decorator. (3) Decorated with marked "Sterling" silver overlay of lattice with grape leaves and clusters of grapes by an unknown decorator. Vases, each $250.00 – 300.00.

Vases

Plate 716. Paden City Glass Manufacturing Company flared rim vase with exterior panels in royal blue. Named "Swanson" by Michael Krumme. 10⅛" high x 3⅜" diameter base. Marked "Sterling" silver overlay of swans, grape leaves, leaves, and clusters. Label reads "Depasse Pearsall." Circa 1930s. Vase $400.00 – 450.00.

Plate 717. Paden City Glass Manufacturing Company flared rim vase with exterior panels in royal blue. Named "Swanson" by Michael Krumme. 10⅛" high x 3⅜" diameter base. With marked "Sterling" silver #65 Springtime decoration by the Lotus Glass Company. Circa 1930s. Vase $250.00 – 300.00.

Plate 718. Pairpoint Corporation #B1107 controlled bubble ball stem vase. 11" high. Circa 1926. Vase $375.00 – 400.00.

Vases

Plate 719. Pairpoint Corporation #B959 controlled bubble ball stem vase. 12" high. Circa 1926. Vase $375.00 – 400.00.

Plate 720. Pilgrim Glass Corporation #1932 Pompeii vase. 12½" high. Circa 1996 – 2002. Vase $25.00 – 30.00.

Plate 721. Pilgrim Glass Corporation flat top vase. 9" high. Circa 2000 – 2002. Vase $25.00 – 30.00.

253

Vases

Plate 722. Pilgrim Glass Corporation vase with vertical ribbed swirl optic inside. 12½" high. With Pilgrim paper label. Circa 2000 – 2002. Vase $40.00 – 50.00.

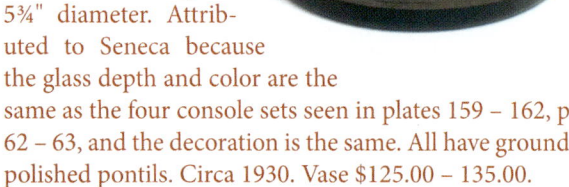

Plate 723. Seneca Glass Company diamond optic vase with silver (white gold) encrusted acid etching by an unknown decorator. 7⅞" high x 5¾" diameter. Attributed to Seneca because the glass depth and color are the same as the four console sets seen in plates 159 – 162, pages 62 – 63, and the decoration is the same. All have ground and polished pontils. Circa 1930. Vase $125.00 – 135.00.

Plate 724. L. E. Smith Glass Company two-handled, footed vase with gold line and dot decoration. 7" high x 3¼" diameter base. This is the same shape as Smith's #1900 vase, but with different handles. Circa 1930s. Vase $20.00 – 25.00.

Vases

Plate 725. L. E. Smith Glass Company three-ringed, flared top vase with hand painted "Leaves and Flowers" silver decoration (also sometimes referred to as "Lily of the Valley"). 9¼" high x 4" diameter base. Circa 1930s. Vase $25.00 – 30.00.

Plate 726. L. E. Smith Glass Company #1000 eight-paneled vases with hand painted "Leaves and Flowers" silver decoration (also sometimes referred to as "Lily of the Valley"). Fan vase: 7½" high x 3¾" octagon base. Cupped vase: 7½" high x 3¾" octagon base. Circa 1930s. Vase, each $25.00 – 30.00.

Plate 727. L. E. Smith Glass Company crimped vase with silver line decoration. 7¼" high x 2¾" square base. This is the same shape as Smith's #432 vase, but lacking handles. Circa 1930s. Vase $15.00 – 20.00.

255

Vases

Plate 728. L. E. Smith Glass Company narrow vertical paneled vase with silver rings at the top. 7" high x 3" diameter base. Circa 1930s. Vase $15.00 – 20.00.

Plate 729. L. E. Smith Glass Company #99 Hobnail crimped vase. 8" high x 2¼" base. Also made in a 6" size. Circa 1934 – 1936. Vase $10.00 – 15.00.

Plate 730. L. E. Smith Glass Company #85 Hobnail ivy bowl. 5" high x 2¾" diameter foot. Circa 1934 – 1936. Ivy bowl $10.00 – 15.00.

Plate 731. L. E. Smith Glass Company #800 urn or vase. 7½" high x 4½" diameter top x 3½" square foot. This vase was available both with and without a lid. Advertised as part of an urn and bowl console set in "Mexican blue" in 1935. (See plate 795, page 292.) Circa 1934 – 1936. Vase without lid $35.00 – 40.00; with lid $45.00 – 50.00.

Vases

Plate 732. L. E. Smith Glass Company #900 trophy vase. 7¾" high x 4¼" square base. This vase also came with a lid, making it a candy jar or covered urn. Circa 1935 – 1936. Vase $25.00 – 30.00.

Plate 733. L. E. Smith Glass Company #2 three-footed fern bowl with Greek key motif molded around the rim. 4¼" high x 4¾" diameter. This bowl is often found with a flower frog insert. Circa 1935 – 1936. Fern bowl $15.00 – 20.00.

Plate 734. L. E. Smith Glass Company #711 flared top vase with oval bumps around the rim and panels around the base. 5⅝" high x 2⅜" diameter base. With silver line decoration. Circa 1936. Vase $10.00 – 15.00.

Plate 735. United States Glass Company #6 vases. 12¾" high. Circa 1930s. Left to right: (1) With an unknown silver peacock decoration. (2) With an unknown silver grapes and grape leaf decoration. This same decoration is on a U.S. Glass bowl and candlesticks shown in plate 168, page 65. Vase, each $60.00 – 70.00.

Vases

Plate 736. United States Glass Company #15319 two-handled, footed vase with unknown gold encrusted acid etching. 10" high. Circa 1930s. Vase $140.00 – 150.00.

Plate 737. West Virginia Glass Specialty Company crimped top vase. 7¼" high. "Souvenier [sic], The Grand Glass Exposition, Sept. 5 – 8, 1938." This was issued in 1938 for a four-day festival held in Weston, West Virginia. Vase $25.00 – 30.00.

Plate 738. West Virginia Glass Specialty Company #105 vase with crystal foot and #57 platinum decoration. 11" high x 4⅜" diameter. This same vase was also made by the Louie Glass Company. A 1937 West Virginia Glass Specialty Company advertisement describes it as "styled by Louie." (See plate 799, page 296.) Circa 1930s. Vase $45.00 – 55.00.

Vases

Plate 739. West Virginia Glass Specialty Company crimped rim vases, one plain and one with platinum ring decoration. 11¾" high. Circa 1930s. Vase, each $65.00 – 75.00.

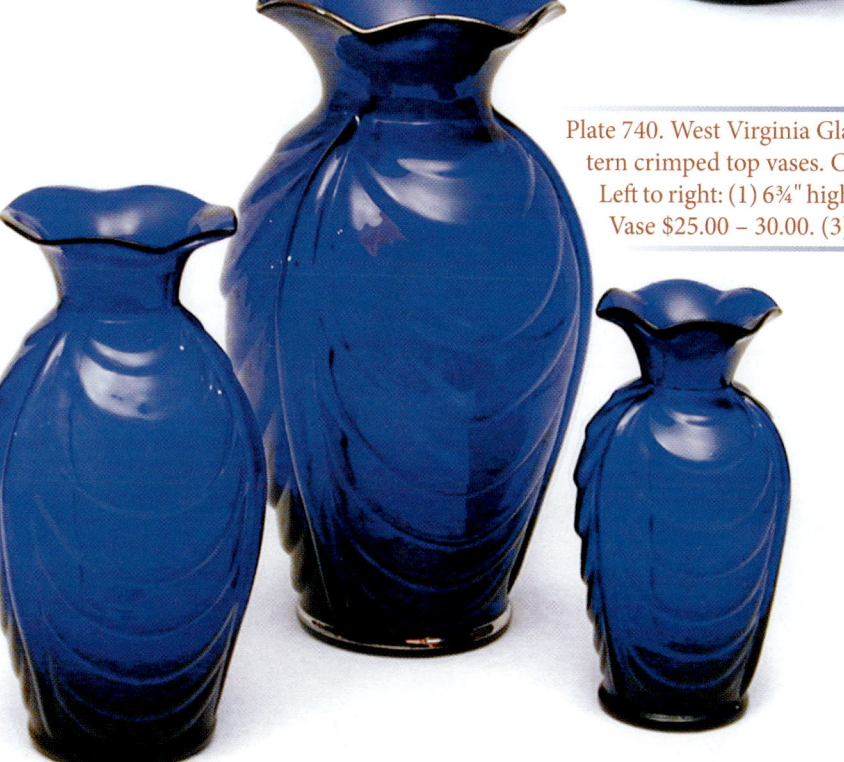

Plate 740. West Virginia Glass Specialty Company draped pattern crimped top vases. Circa 1930s.
Left to right: (1) 6¾" high. Vase $20.00 – 25.00. (2) 8½" high. Vase $25.00 – 30.00. (3) 5½" high. Vase $15.00 – 20.00.

Plate 741. West Virginia Glass Specialty Company bubble ball rose bowl in white wire metal stand. Rose bowl: 3¼" high. Circa 1930s. Rose bowl & stand $25.00 – 30.00.

Vases

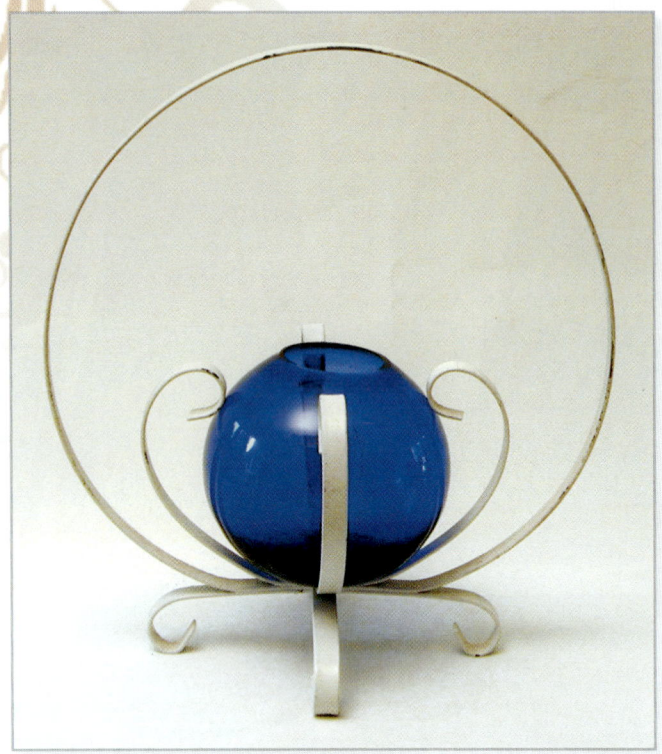

Plate 742. West Virginia Glass Specialty Company bubble ball rose bowl in white wire metal stand. Rose bowl: 3¼" high. Circa 1930s. Rose bowl & stand $25.00 – 30.00.

Plate 743. West Virginia Glass Specialty Company bubble ball rose bowl in white metal stand. Rose bowl: 3¼" high. Circa 1930s. Rose bowl & stand $25.00 – 30.00.

Plate 744. West Virginia Glass Specialty Company bubble ball rose bowl in white metal stand. Rose bowl: 4½" high. Circa 1930s. Rose bowl & stand $25.00 – 30.00.

Plate 745. West Virginia Glass Specialty Company bubble ball rose bowl in black metal stand with maple leaves. Rose bowl: 4½" high. Circa 1930s. Rose bowl & stand $25.00 – 30.00.

Vases

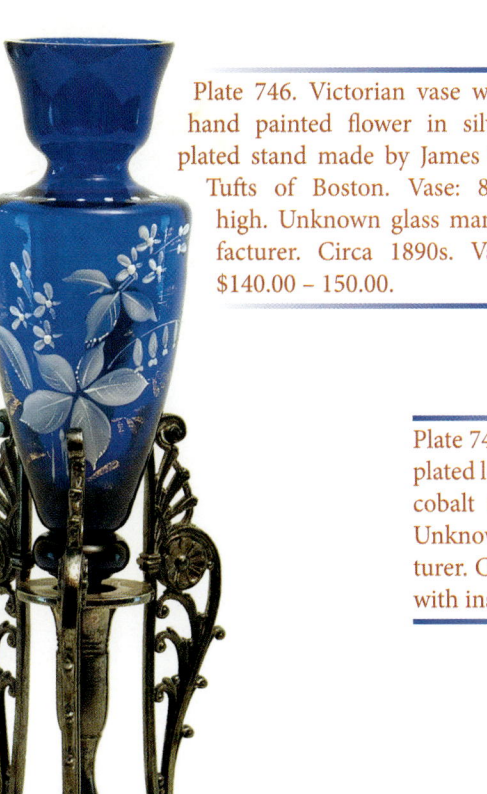

Plate 746. Victorian vase with hand painted flower in silver plated stand made by James W. Tufts of Boston. Vase: 8¾" high. Unknown glass manufacturer. Circa 1890s. Vase $140.00 – 150.00.

Plate 747. Eberle silver plated lotus flower with cobalt insert. 3" high. Unknown glass manufacturer. Circa 1920. Lotus flower with insert $140.00 – 150.00.

Plate 748. Bohemian blown, crimped top Victorian-style vases with rough pontils and hand painted gold and white enamel flowers. 12" high. Circa 1918 – 1930s. Vase, each $40.00 – 50.00.

261

Vases

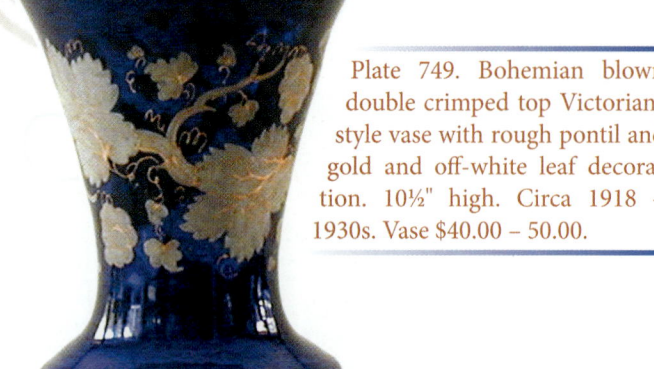

Plate 749. Bohemian blown double crimped top Victorian-style vase with rough pontil and gold and off-white leaf decoration. 10½" high. Circa 1918 – 1930s. Vase $40.00 – 50.00.

Plate 750. Bohemian blown crimped top Victorian-style vase with rough pontil and hand painted gold and white enamel flower decoration. 15" high. Circa 1918 – 1930s. Vase $40.00 – 50.00.

Plate 751. Czechoslovakian or German vases. Circa 1920s – 1930s.

Left to right: (1) Blown footed bud vase with straight tapered sides, decorated with gold lines and leaves. 8½" high. Vase $15.00 – 20.00. (2) Blown, ground top bud vase with unknown silver bird and line decoration. 8¼" high. Base $10.00 – 15.00. (3) Blown vase with rough ground top. 9" high. Stamped "Czecho-Slovakia." Vase $10.00 – 15.00. (4) Blown flared vase with silver decoration. 6¼" high. Vase $20.00 – 25.00.

Vases

Plate 752. Czechoslovakian or German vases with silver birds decoration. Circa 1920s – 1930s.
Left to right: (1) Blown flared vase. 5⅝" high. Vase $20.00 – 25.00. (2) Blown vase with ground top. 7½" high. Vase $10.00 – 15.00. (3) Blown, footed urn-shaped vase. 8" high. Vase $20.00 – 25.00. (4) Blown urn-shaped vase. 6" high. Vase $10.00 – 15.00. (5) Blown urn-shaped vase. 5½" high. Vase $15.00 – 20.00.

Plate 753. German vases. Stamped "Germany" in a circle on the base, with an unknown silver Cupid decoration, also found on Paden City Glass Manufacturing Company glass. Circa 1920 – 1930s.
Left to right: (1) Bulbed straight neck vase. 9¾" high. (2) Flared vase. 8¼" high. (3) Flared, short neck vase. 10½" high. (4) Two-ring, flared vase. 8¾" high. Vase, each $150.00 – 160.00.

Vases

Plate 754. German flared ball stem vase with unknown silver peacock decoration. 8½" high. Stamped "Germany." This is the same peacock decoration as seen on the Paden City Glass Manufacturing Company percolator in bar items (plate 526 on page 186). Circa 1920 – 1930s. Vase $110.00 – 120.00.

Plate 755. Unattributed, possibly German, blown ribbed vase with silver trim. 10" high. Circa 1920 – 1930s. Vase $25.00 – 30.00.

Plate 756. Left to right: (1) Lindshammar blown vase with fire polished rim. 5½" high. With 24 karat gold three-ring decoration Made in Sweden. Circa 1980. Vase $25.00 – 30.00. (2) & (4) Murano blown vases with fire polished rim. 4½" high. With 24 karat gold three-ring decoration by Vecchia Murano Glass Factory. Circa 1980. Vase, each $25.00 – 30.00. (3) Czechoslovakian blown, ground top vase with unknown gold decoration. 6" high. Circa 1920 – 1930s. Vase $10.00 – 15.00.

Vases

Plate 757. Polish Thousand-Eye crimped crystal cased with cobalt cut ball vase. 4" high. Distributed by A. A. Importing Company as #JA/1830. Circa 1976 – 1980s. Vase $45.00 – 50.00.

Plate 758. Unattributed crimped epergne with metal base and vase holder. 18" high x 13" diameter. Circa 1920s. Epergne $400.00 – 500.00.

Plate 759. Unattributed vases. Circa 1930s.
Left to right: (1) Molded ball vase with chimney, possibly Louie Glass Company. 4½" high. Vase $5.00 – 8.00. (2) Horizontal ribbed ivy ball with neck and molded crimped edge. 4⅞" high. "USA" molded on bottom. Vase $10.00 – 15.00. (3) Flared molded vase. 5¾" high. Vase $8.00 – 10.00. (4) Long necked, crimped top vase, possibly Louie Glass Company. 4½" high. Vase $5.00 – 10.00. (5) Molded vase with neck. 4⅝" high. Vase $8.00 – 10.00. (6) Molded vase. 3¾" high. Vase $5.00 – 8.00. (7) Long necked, crimped edge vase, possibly Louie Glass Company. 5½" high. Vase $5.00 – 10.00. (8) Ball vase with crimped top, possibly Louie Glass Company #92. 2½" high. Vase $5.00 – 10.00. (9) Molded ball vase with short chimney. 3¼" high. Vase $5.00 – 8.00.

Vases

Plate 760. Unattributed flared top vase. Called "Ring of Rings" by Hazel Marie Weatherman. 5" high. Vase $10.00 – 15.00.

Plate 761. Unattributed hanging vase with three applied handles. 5" high. Vase $40.00 – 50.00.

Plate 762. Unattributed bulb bottom, long neck, flared top vase with platinum ring decoration. 9" high. Vase $30.00 – 40.00.

APPENDIX: COMPANY INFORMATION

1. **A. A. Importing Company, Inc.**, Saint Louis, Missouri, 1934 to the present. As the name suggests, A. A. Importing does not manufacture glass. They have offered pieces in cobalt since at least the early 1970s. See plates 2 and 379.

2. **Akro Agate Company**, Akron, Ohio, 1911 – 1914; Clarksburg, West Virginia, 1914 – 1951. Primarily known for opaque and slag colors, with cobalt dating to the 1930s. See plate 594.

3. **Aladdin Industries**, Clarksville, Tennessee, 1949 – 1999. Continuation of the Mantle Lamp Company, originator of the famous Aladdin lamps. Currently operated as the Aladdin Mantle Lamp Company. See plate 619.

4. **Alley Agate Company** (later Alley Glass Company and Alley Glass Manufacturing Company), Pennsboro, West Virginia, circa 1934 – 1937; Saint Mary's, West Virginia, 1938 – 1950. Cobalt was probably in production both in the 1930s and 1940s. See plates 595 – 596.

5. **Beaumont Company**, Morgantown, West Virginia, 1918 – 1991. Cobalt was probably made in the 1920s or 1930s. See plates 109 and 628 – 629.

6. **Blenko Glass Company**, Milton, West Virginia 1921 to the present. Sapphire was made 1979 – 1989, then renamed cobalt from 1990 to the present. See plates 3 – 4 and 577.

7. **Boston and Sandwich Glass Company**, Sandwich, Massachusetts, 1825 – 1887. Precise information about cobalt production is unknown, but could have been any time during the history of the factory. See plates 5, 371, 592, and 604.

8. **Caffco International**, Montgomery, Alabama, 1950 to the present. Caffco International offers a wide range of home and garden items to retailers. Initially they imported their goods, but now have their own manufacturing facilities. See plate 682.

9. **Cambridge Glass Company**, Cambridge, Ohio, 1902 – 1958. Cambridge offered several shades of blue over the years. Cobalt blue 1 was probably made around 1924 and only briefly remained in production. Despite the name, this is a medium blue, lighter than most true cobalt. Cobalt blue 2 was introduced January 1925 and continued in production until 1926. It was a little darker than cobalt blue 1, but still not a true cobalt. Ritz blue was offered from 1929 until 1930 or 1931, darker than the earlier colors, but not as dark as royal blue, which was introduced in June 1931 and remained in production until World War II, when the materials required to make this color became scarce.

Crockery & Glass Journal, January 22, 1925: Alex Menzies is rejoicing in some beautiful new lines of glassware recently received from the Cambridge Glass Co., Cambridge, O. at his showrooms of this company at 184 Fifth Ave., New York. Five new lines in gold encrustations include cake plates, sandwich trays, high and low footed comports, cracker and cheese dishes, candy boxes and jars, vases, salad-plates, etc. Colors are amber, cobalt blue, mulberry, besides crystal. One design is a solid encrustation border in conventional pattern broken by medallions in open work effect which makes a charming contrast to the solid border. In another this design is exactly reversed the same border design being worked out in open effect and medallions–the same designs as those described above only in solid gold. These are surprisingly effective numbers. Another line has a gold band about a half inch from the edge. This is simple in character, open through the center and broken by round medallions with six petal flower conventionalized, as a motif.

The Pottery, Glass & Brass Salesman, December 12, 1929: The local office of the Cambridge Glass Company, located in the Shops Building, 17 North Wabash Avenue, is showing for the first time here its newly created "Ritz Blue," which gives promise of becoming one of the season's most outstanding contributions to stemware. The blue, different from any shown during the past year, is yet akin in warmth and depth to the cobalt blue, although it is not nearly as dark.

Appendix: Company Information

Plate 763. Cambridge Glass Company #1206 twist optic beverage set. *Crockery & Glass Journal*, February 1936.

The Pottery, Glass & Brass Salesman, January 8, 1931: Felix Wohlgemuth, Mid-Western representative of the Cambridge Glass Company, Cambridge, Ohio, has received in his Merchandise Mart display rooms samples of several new lines of tableware with which the company is inaugurating the 1931 season.

The new ware includes four new lines of stemware sold under the names "Carmen Krystol" and "Ritz Blue." The names are descriptive of the wares which come in beautiful blendings of deep and clear ruby and a fine shade of blue similar to cobalt, with crystal. These color schemes are used in a tall stemware group with crystal feet and bases and in a low stemware line also with crystal feet and bases. The colors are remarkably clear, with not a bubble or area of unequal diffusion to be seen despite their transparency. The new color is also used in plates and several other pieces of tableware, including sugars and creamers. The latter sets come with crystal foundation dishes.

The Pottery, Glass & Brass Salesman, November 26, 1931: The Cambridge company is also showing in its Chicago salesrooms a new line of stemware manufactured in an especially lovely shape, known as the No. 3122 pattern. The line includes all stemware pieces and comes both in unetched colored glass and in etched crystal. The etching on the crystal glass is known as the "Diane" etching, and is unusually charming, combining a classic grace and simplicity.

The new stem ware is furnished in only one color, a royal blue of unusual depth and consistency. The color, as well as the new etching, is also furnished in a complete line of tableware. Mr. Wohlgemuth reports that the new stemware and the line of novelty pieces have met with gratifying success at the hands of local quality retailers, including the State Street merchants.

Crockery & Glass Journal, November 1932: Heading the list of new items at Cambridge this month is the debut of the Mount Vernon Decanter. This pattern seems to lend itself particularly well to the rather substantial shape they've used .... it's really excellently modelled and boasts of a huge stopper that's very much in keeping with the general feeling of the Mount Vernon pattern. This looks smart as can be in ruby with a crystal stopper, and it is made in Royal blue, Forest green, amber and all crystal as well. There are some more new decanters too . . . both the Imperial Hunt and the Catawba Grape designs in the Tally-Ho range are smart additions to the assortment.

Crockery & Glass Journal, November 1933: All of the drinking glasses, especially liquor, from Cambridge Glass Co., promise to have great interest with the repeal of the Eighteenth Amendment. They have displayed more and more ingenuity in all of their new developments. They have developed a line of Hoch [sic] glass, in various combinations ... all crystal; crystal bowls and colored stems; colored bowls and crystal stems. The colors are truly in the spirit of their line, forest green, gold, Krystal, emerald, and a truly royal blue. See plates 6 – 18, 110 – 115, 182 – 185, 228 – 242, 278 – 282, 303 – 304, 326, 331, 338, 355 – 357, 365, 372, 391 – 396, 439, 445, 467 – 480, 521 – 523, 540 – 542, 549, 578 – 581, 630 – 641, and 763 – 764.

Plate 764. Cambridge Glass Company #6004 vases. *Crockery & Glass Journal*, July 1936.

Appendix: Company Information

10. Canton Glass Company, Marion, Indiana, 1903 – 1958; Hartford City, Indiana, 1958 – 1999. Relatively little is known about Canton. Cobalt was introduced in 1932 and royal blue is mentioned in a 1962 catalog, with other periods of production for cobalt possible. See plate 397.

11. Central Glass Company, Pocola, Oklahoma, circa 1959 – 1990s. One of several inter-related companies in the Spiro, Oklahoma, area. Sometimes used labels reading "Sooner Glass," "Old Hickory Glass," or "Anchorage Glass by Wagon Hill." See plates 620 and 642.

12. Central Glass Works, Wheeling, West Virginia, 1863 – 1939. Cobalt blue was made prior to the 1890s. Royal blue was introduced in 1922.

Crockery & Glass Journal, April 20, 1922: A. P. Doctor, New York manager for the Central Glass Works, whose salesroom is in the Albemarle Building, 24th Street and Broadway, is displaying an assemblage of very charming creations in colored glassware that will be found of more than average interest.... A line of items in a deep rich royal blue and amethyst are equally as attractive. Some of the articles shown are flower and fruit centers, baskets, jugs, candlesticks, comports and plates.

Crockery & Glass Journal, March 22, 1923: Conspicuous for the graceful shapes and charming in color is the new line of glassware manufactured by the Central Glass Works, and displayed by A. P. Doctor, at the sales office of the company, 1107 Broadway.... Another number which is being featured is a line of console sets at unusually attractive prices. The shapes are remarkably good and the color range includes canary, amethyst, and royal blue, with several numbers in satin finish.... Among the late arrivals is a two-toned effect that is very appealing, comprising ice tea sets, with covered optic jug and handled tumblers and stemware to match in contrasting colors of canary and royal blue. See plates 19 – 20, 116 – 119, 186 – 189, 243 – 245, 339, and 398 – 399.

13. Consolidated Lamp and Glass Company, Fostoria, Ohio, 1894 – 1896; Coraopolis, Pennsylvania, 1896 – 1964. Royal blue was mentioned in trade journal reports in 1894. See plates 377, 380

14. Co-operative Flint Glass Company, Beaver Falls, Pennsylvania, 1879 – 1937. Cobalt was made in the early 1900s, then was again made beginning in 1924 and continued into the 1930s.

The Pottery, Glass & Brass Salesman, January 2, 1930: In the well-stocked display rooms of T. M. Schollenberger, located in the Shops Building, 17 North Wabash Avenue, some of the new items for the coming season from the Co-operative Flint Glass Company, Beaver Falls, Pa., are now being shown. Jugs and tumblers have been added to the ribbed-glass stemware line in aquamarine, green, ruby and cobalt. The jugs and tumblers are a welcome addition to the complete stemware line. Square salads and dainty cups and saucers are also to be had this season in all of the above colors, as well as in black for the salad plates. The Co-operative factory is also represented with a new line of pinch bottles and liquor sets. The liquor sets come only in the crackled crystal and the pinch bottles in the blue or amber. See plates 21 – 26, 246, 446, 550, and 765 – 767.

Plate 765. Co-operative Flint Glass Company candy jar and 7" square plate. *Crockery & Glass Journal*, November 1929.

Appendix: Company Information

Plate 766. Co-operative Flint Glass Company #579 cup and saucer and 6" square plate. *Crockery & Glass Journal,* May 1930.

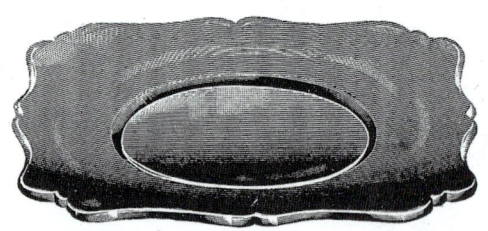

Above is an illustration of a new 6" No. 579 square plate with gracefully scalloped edge, and at the left is one of No. 492 cup, round, on No. 579 square saucer with its scalloped edge matching the outline of the plate. These and additional items in the square 579 pattern, such as 7½" salad plate, 8½" dinner plate, 10" handled tray and sugar and creamer, are the newest offerings of the Co-operative Flint Glass Co., Beaver Falls, Pa., who are making all of these items in rose, green, amber, cobalt blue, ruby and black glass. They are offered in 15-piece luncheon sets, and other compositions of square items may be made up to suit the buyer. The entire line is on display with the firm's New York representatives, Horace C. Gray Co., 200 Fifth Ave.

EARLY AMERICAN GLASSWARE

Refectory items in our Early American Pattern No. 587

This pattern is available in Crystal, Green, Amber, Cobalt-blue, Rose, Topaz and Ruby

CoOperative Flint Glass Co.

Beaver Falls, Pa.

SALES REPRESENTATIVES
NEW YORK—H. C. Gray Co., Fifth Ave Bldg.
PHILADELPHIA—U. S. Crockery & Glass Exchange, 1001 Market St.
CHICAGO—T. M. Schollenberger Co., 1575 Merchandise Mart.
DALLAS, TEX.—Fred Kline, 718 Santa Fe Terminal Bldg.
COLUMBUS, O.—R. L. Hutchison, Chittenden Hotel.
NEW ENGLAND—F. I. McBride, 148 N. Harriet Ave., No. Quincy, Mass.
PACIFIC COAST—Shaw, Newell & Co., 212 Lissner Bldg., Los Angeles.
Shaw, Newell & Co., 220 Post St., San Francisco.
SOUTHERN—John A. Dobson & Co., 110 Hopkins Pl., Baltimore.
Factory Representative—Norton C. Boyer.

When in Pittsburgh we suggest that you visit our factory salesroom at Beaver Falls, located on the Pennsylvania and New York Central Lines, 30 miles from Pittsburgh

15. Dalzell Viking, New Martinsville, West Virginia, 1987 – 1998. This was a continuation of the New Martinsville Glass Manufacturing Company. Cobalt was in production throughout Dalzell Viking's entire existence. See plates 27 – 31 and 283.

16. Daum, Nancy, France, 1878 to the present. See plate 591.

17. Diamond Glass-Ware Company, Indiana, Pennsylvania, 1913 – 1931. Continued from the Dugan Glass Company. Cobalt blue, also known as Ritz blue, was made in the 1920s. In the early years of that decade, it was offered with iridescent and luster finishes.

Crockery & Glass Journal, July 20, 1922: Including a display of three appealing lines in colored and iridescent table glassware the showing of the wares of the Diamond Glass-Ware Co. at the salesroom of Frederick Skelton, Fifth Avenue Building, represents a colorful array of conspicuous beauty. …. In the "Royal Lustre" line a rich, deep blue is most artistically combined with the iridescent tints of gold and silver lustre in the lining which gives a charming vari-tone effect. This ware is obtainable in a good assortment of fancy numbers, including a particularly comprehensive range of bowls in many sizes and shapes, deep and flaring forms of graceful designs, candlesticks, sherbets, salad plates, dinner plate, many with and without black glass bases.

The Pottery, Glass & Brass Salesman, January 25, 1923: A distinct novelty in glassware is a ewer set introduced the first of the year by the Diamond Glass-Ware Company, of Indiana, Pa., and which it is said has made a great hit at the Pittsburgh Exhibition. General Manager H. Wallace Thomas of the concern is naturally very proud of it. A full line of samples are now being displayed by local representative Frederick Skelton at his showrooms in the Fifth Avenue Building.

The sets consist of ewer and basin, toothbrush holder, sponge holder with drainer, and soap dish and drainer, They are made of a high quality iridescent ware for which the concern is famous. The color range includes amethyst, royal blue and green.

The Pottery, Glass & Brass Salesman, February 12, 1931: A fifteen-piece bridge set is shown [by the Diamond Glass-Ware Company] in the No. 99 line in a variety of odd colors, including, aside from the "Wistaria" mentioned, amethyst, royal blue, canary, green and amber, as well as black. It is proving a very popular seller and is mode[r]ately priced. See plates 32 – 34, 120 – 125, 190 – 193, 247, 305, and 400 – 401.

Plate 767. Co-operative Flint Glass Company #587 Early American refectory items. *Crockery & Glass Journal*, January 1932.

Appendix: Company Information

18. **Dugan Glass Company**, Indiana, Pennsylvania, 1904 – 1913. Continued as the Diamond Glass-Ware Company. See plates 447 and 643.

19. **Dunbar Glass Corporation**, Dunbar, West Virginia, 1912 – 1953. Cobalt was made beginning in 1937. See plates 126, 448 – 449, 509, 644 – 648, 682 – 683, 704, and 768 – 769.

Plate 768. Dunbar Glass Corporation vases. Top row, left to right: #702-C, 101-L, 735. Middle row: #666-8, 651-8, 616-C8. Bottom row: #680-C, 673-C, 689-C. 1938 catalog.

Appendix: Company Information

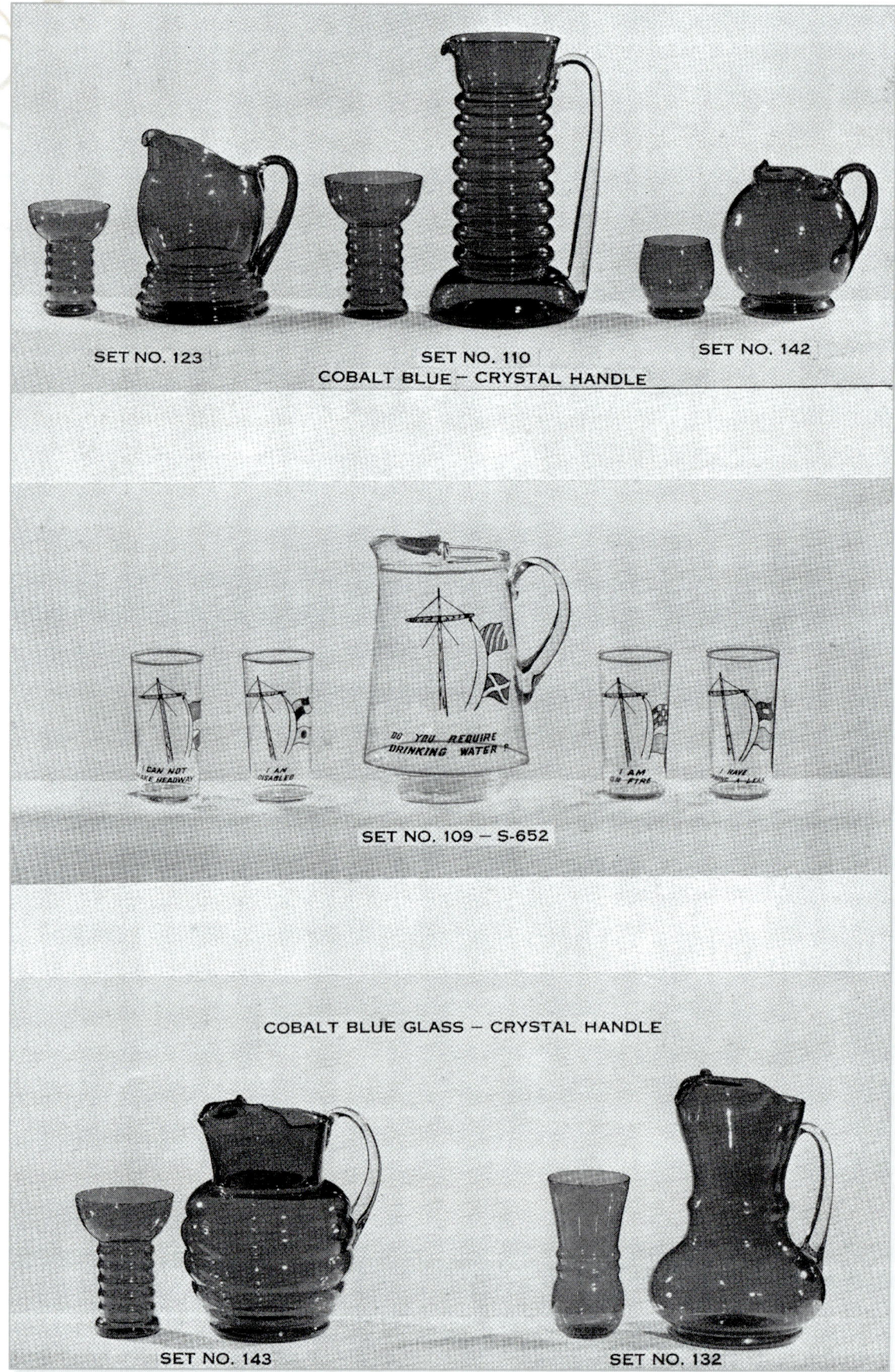

Plate 769. Dunbar Glass Corporation pitcher and tumbler sets. Top row, left to right: #123, 110, 142. Middle row: #109 with decoration #S-652. Bottom row: #143, 132. 1938 catalog.

Appendix: Company Information

20. **Duncan and Miller Glass Company**, Washington, Pennsylvania, 1893 – 1955. Cobalt blue was in production 1931 – 1937.

The Pottery, Glass & Brass Salesman, October 15, 1931: The Duncan & Miller Glass Company, of Washington, Pa., has done some noteworthy things in the matter of colored production, but it is questionable if it has ever surpassed the lovely new blue that the company has just produced and which is suggestive of the blue that is used as a casing on very expensive imported ware. Here is a true cobalt tone and it is interesting to note that it runs remarkably even. The color is certainly a worthy addition to the line and stands up by itself, though it unquestionably looks well adorned with silver, in which form it will probably appear a little later on.

    Samples which so far have been received by local representative Paul Joseph at his showrooms in the Fifth Avenue Building, 200 Fifth Avenue, include eighteen distinct items and number among them berry oval bowls, high flower bowls, covered three-compartment sweetmeat dishes, candlesticks, handled sandwich trays, tumblers in several sizes, ash trays and a new cigarette holder that is given the name of "The Hostess." It is interesting to note that prices are the same as on the other Duncan & Miller colors.

The Pottery, Glass & Brass Salesman, February 1932: The Duncan & Miller Glass Company, of Washington, Pa., has long enjoyed a reputation for the fine quality of its merchandise. The batch is of the best. Only expert workmen are employed, which means that, both in form and in finish, the ware is all but impeccable, and, beyond that, the concern has always been in the forefront in bringing out new shapes and forms galore. In the matter of color, however, Duncan & Miller have tended rather to the conservative. The color, range has been rather limited and up to recently included only, in addition to crystal, green amber and rose. Then, a few months ago, a lovely blue, as fine as any thing could be, either abroad or in this country, was brought out, and now a ruby has been added.

The Pottery, Glass & Brass Salesman, December 15, 1932: New offerings in the way of table and fancy glassware are constantly being made by the Duncan & Miller Glass Company, of Washington, Pa. ….Then, there is the No. 127 vase. This is an absolutely new creation and very much out of the ordinary. The lower part is somewhat on the Georgian order, full bellied and fitted with struts which extend down to form feet or rather feet effect. At the top of this body portion is a series of rings making for a corduroy effect. Above this again the vase flares out in very fanciful form, with four distinct grooves for flowers. The late eighteen century severity of the lower portion and the fancy nature of the upper part are in most striking contrast, and constitute the real outstanding feature of the vase. So, far it is shown in ruby and blue as well as in crystal, giving the Duncan & Miller popular choice of red, white and blue. See plates 35 – 37, 127 – 129, 194, 358, 402, 481 – 482, 551, 582, 649 – 653, and 683.

21. **Durand Art Glass**, division of Vineland Flint Glass Works, Vineland, New Jersey, 1924 – 1931. Produced high quality free-hand wares, similar to Tiffany, Steuben, and Quetzel. See plate 654.

22. **Eales of Sheffield**, England, 1779 – ?. Manufacturer of pewter, silverplate, and other metalware, sometimes with cobalt glass inserts. See plate 373.

23. **Farber Brothers**, New York, 1915 – 1965. Manufacturer of silver hollow-ware and brass goods, best known for their Farberware Krome Kraft (chrome) holders for glass and china inserts. In the 1930s cobalt glass was often used from the Cambridge Glass Company and others. See plate 523.

24. **Farber Shlevin, Inc.**, New York. Manufacturer of chrome ware, sometimes found with cobalt glass inserts. This is presumably an offshoot of Farber Brothers/Farberware, but at present remains elusive. See plate 38.

25. **Fenton Art Glass Company**, Williamstown, West Virginia, 1907 to the present. Cobalt, in various shades and under various names, has been made by this company from the beginning. The earliest use of cobalt was as the base color for carnival glass. 1917 saw the introduction of stretch glass into the company's line. Transparent royal blue dates to as early as 1924 and continued during the 1930s. More recent occurrences, include cobalt: circa 1982 – 1984; blue royal: circa 1988 – 1991; cobalt blue: circa 1995 – 1996, 1999 – present. See plates 39 – 40, 130 – 137, 284, 340, 403 – 405, 483 – 484, 543, 583, 625, and 655.

Appendix: Company Information

26. Fostoria Glass Company, Fostoria, Ohio, 1887 – 1891; Moundsville, West Virginia, 1891 – 1986. Regal blue was made 1933 – 1941. Royal blue was offered from 1961 – 1965. Cobalt blue was made again from 1972 – 1980 and dark blue from 1977 – 1986.

The Pottery, Glass & Brass Salesman, July 20, 1933: The Fostoria Glass Company, Moundsville, W. Va., has many new things to offer the trade for the fall season, many of which are now on display at the local showrooms in the Fifth Avenue Building, 200 Fifth Avenue, in charge of Walter S. Andres. First mention perhaps might be made of the new color range. Fostoria has always been very strong on colored glass, and the new array is particularly beautiful. Three new colors are, respectively, Empire Green, Regal Blue and Burgundy. Perhaps of these the green is the most outstanding. It is called an empire, but it is really very close to the old Sevres green made famous by the master potters of France during the time of Louis XIV..... The Regal Blue is a charming shade rather on the cobalt order, while the Burgundy is just what the name implies; some might describe it as an amethyst. These three colors are brought out in a full range of blown ware with pressed-ware items to match, and it is interesting to note that the color shows up the same both in the blown ware and in the naturally heavier pressed ware.

The Pottery, Glass & Brass Salesman, October 12, 1933: The Fostoria Glass Company, Moundsville, W. Va., has just brought out a new line of highly decorated ware in all kinds of fancy pieces, including bowls, vases and trays. Most of them are in odd shapes, The line is shown in three colors, each with its own special decoration; the decorative work, incidentally, being done in gold. .... The blue shows humming birds floating gracefully over the tops of flowers. Altogether it is a most artistic offering. Samples are now on display at the various sales agencies, including the local showrooms in the Fifth Avenue Building, 200 Fifth Avenue, in charge of Walter S. Andres.

The Gift and Art Buyer, September 1963: "Argus," an early 19th century handpressed flint glass pattern, is being reproduced and adapted by the Fostoria Glass Co. as part of the Henry Ford Museum program to provide homemakers with quality, reasonably-priced Early American reproductions. The pattern is characterized by rows of elongated thumb-prints running between the upper and lower band of deep cut-like facets. Originally created in clear crystal only, "Argus" now comes in crystal, cobalt blue and olive green and is available in nine sizes. Some of the glasses such as the Old Fashioned are authentic reproductions of antique treasures owned and displayed by the Ford museum; others, such as the Goblet, are adaptations. The term "flint glass" has come to mean lead glass of superior quality. In Fostoria's reproductions, mold joint marks are said to be clearly visible and to mark the authenticity of the line, each of the nine pieces will carry a permanent "HFM" identification on the bottom so that it cannot be sold as an original heirloom. See plates 41 – 42, 138 – 139, 248, 285 – 286, 347, 406 – 407, 485, 544, 584, and 656 – 658.

27. Fry (H. C.) Glass Company, Rochester, Pennsylvania, 1902 – 1933. Royal blue was made beginning as early as 1928 and continuing until 1933, when the factory closed.

The Pottery, Glass & Brass Salesman, July 12, 1928: A full line of new modernistic stemware made in a variety of combinations is being shown by the H. C. Fry Glass Company at 308 West Randolph Street, where J. Howard Fry represents the company. The stemware comes in crystal, French blue, rose crystal and royal blue. Other combinations are also being experimented with.
This line is entirely new in shape, with attractive figures blown in the glass The stem, in keeping with the rest of the glass, is built up in four-cornered tiers on the old Egyptian style.

The Pottery, Glass & Brass Salesman, May 9, 1929: In the inviting showrooms of J. Howard Fry, at 308 West Randolph Street, are several attractive stemware lines from the factory of the H. C. Fry Glass Company, Rochester, Pa., which are smart, new and inexpensive. The vogue of colored glassware is easily understood when one views the delightful colors and styles of these pieces. The royal blue, which has proven so popular in stemware of late, tightens its hold on popular favor by the addition of plates to the line. A handsome hexagon plate which may be used instead of the round dinner plate emphasizes the richness of this color. The stemware is available in three different styles. There are the lapidary cut stem, the modernistic cut stem and the tall, slender, slightly cut stem. The gracefully shaped bowls combine beautifully with either of the three stem patterns.

Appendix: Company Information

The Pottery, Glass & Brass Salesman, November 7, 1929: The Fry company's new console set, in ebony, royal blue or the factory's very new amber, is also an important addition to the decorative glassware on the market. The short stem of the bowl and compotes has a crystal spiral optic ball combined with a black, blue or amber foot. Small candle holders to match and flower and bud vases are among the choice articles in this line. A handsome and graceful line of stemware may be used to good effect with the console sets. See plates 43, 140, 249 – 251, 408 – 409, and 659.

28. **Gillinder Glass**, Port Jervis, New York, 1912 to the present. Continuation of Gillinder Brothers. Cobalt has been in production from the 1990s to the present. See plate 660.

29. **Hazel-Atlas Glass Company**, Washington, Pennsylvania, 1902 – 1977. Ritz blue was made from 1926 until the 1940s. A Butler Brothers catalog referred to this color as true blue. See plates 44, 141 – 143, 195 – 197, 252, 287 – 288, 306 – 315, 341, 374, 381 – 383, 410 – 413, 441 – 442, 450 – 458, 524, 545 – 547, 552 – 560, 661, and 770 – 775.

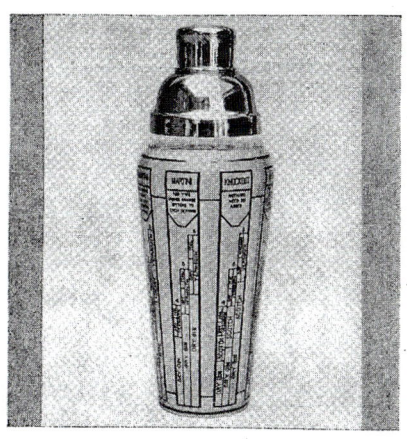

Plate 770. Hazel-Atlas Glass Company cocktail shaker. Advertised by Newland, Schneeloch & Piek in *The Pottery, Glass & Brass Salesman*, January 17, 1935. See plate 552, page 196.

Plate 771. Hazel-Atlas Glass Company Master Senior cocktail shaker. Advertised by Newland, Schneeloch & Piek in *Crockery & Glass Journal*, May 1936. See plate 554, page 197.

Appendix: Company Information

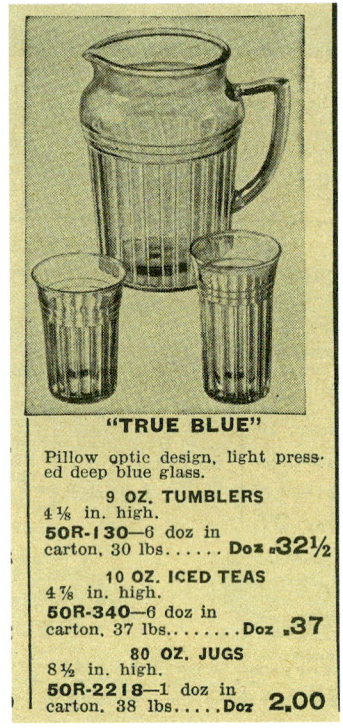

Plate 772. Hazel-Atlas Glass Company beverage sets in "true blue." Top: New Century 80-ounce pitcher, 9-ounce tumbler, and 10-ounce ice tea. (See plate 450, page 161.) Bottom: #1816B 82-ounce ice lip pitcher in the "Sportsman Series" with the #420 "Sailboat" decoration with eight 10-ounce tumblers. (See plate 456, page 163.) Butler Brothers catalog, spring 1938.

Plate 773. Hazel-Atlas Glass Company chrome and glass pieces. Top: Three-piece mayonnaise or salad dressing set; 6-piece table set (salt, pepper, and mayonnaise on tray); preserve or candy dish. Bottom, top row: 32-ounce "Fish" cocktail shaker in Ritz blue, in the "Sportsman Series" with six 5-ounce tumblers. (See plate 559, page 199.) Second row: Three-piece relish (with glass inserts); seven-piece tableware set (consisting of salt, pepper, cream, sugar, and butter dish on tray). Third row: Thirteen-piece beverage set (with six tumblers, six glass stirrers, and tray); four-piece salad set (chrome bowl with insert and wooden spoon and fork). Fourth row: Twelve-piece Royal Lace sherbet set. (See plate 309, page 112.) Butler Brothers catalog, spring 1938.

Appendix: Company Information

Plate 774. Hazel-Atlas Glass Company Moderntone assortment in "true blue." Left to right: cup and saucer, 11" oval platter, 5" nappy, 5-ounce sherbet, 9" dinner plate, 9" vegetable dish, 8" salad plate, salt and pepper, cream and sugar, and 6" pie plate. (See plate 310, page 113.) Butler Brothers catalog, spring 1938.

Plate 775. Hazel-Atlas Glass Company Royal Lace assortment. Top row, left to right: 13" platter, 10" dinner plate, 8½" salad plate, 6" pie plate, 90-ounce jug, 5-ounce tumbler, 9-ounce table tumbler, 12-ounce iced tea, 70-ounce jug. Bottom row: 11" oval vegetable dish, cup and saucer, butter dish (pictured, but not included in items priced below), footed sherbet, covered nappy, cream and sugar. See plate 306, page 111. Butler Brothers catalog, spring 1938.

Appendix: Company Information

30. Heisey (A. H.) and Company, Newark, Ohio, 1896 – 1957. Stiegel blue was made from 1933 – 1941.

Crockery & Glass Journal, January 1933: One of the outstanding lines in Heisey's offerings for 1933 is a Cobalt blue line of stem ware with exceptionally heavy ball stems in crystal, a reproduction of an old Spanish design. In this blue, also, come many odd pieces, vases, candelabra, cocktail shakers and bowls. Four new lines of etched crystal stemware are also shown, one of these in the Spanish design.

The Pottery, Glass & Brass Salesman, January 12, 1933: Mr. Nock has also received from the factory a new complete range of table and stemware in a blue color which is a new Heisey product. Strange[l]y enough, while Heisey has always pioneered in colors, the concern has never before brought out a deep blue. This is a real royal blue. It might even be referred to as a cobalt. Certain it is that it would tie up well with a dinnerware service carrying a rich cobalt band. Possibly the concern had that in mind when the color was produced.

Crockery & Glass Journal, February 1933: They've put a lot of good thought and effort in the new line at Heisey's, and have done a good job indeed by way of achieving new effects–and have added Ritz blue to their color range. ....

The Pottery, Glass & Brass Salesman, March 9, 1933: One of the latest offerings made by A. H. Heisey & Co., of Newark, Ohio, is a short line of fancy glassware consisting of early American legitimate reproductions. These are done in very attractive, if not so familiar, shapes, with the scroll motif featured. Some of the items are entirely in blue, while others are in a combination of blue and crystal. This blue, by the way, is a lovely old Colonial shade and particularly well done by Heisey. The offering takes in vases, candlesticks, compotes, clipper vases, etc. In a few of these a frosted etching is employed. Samples are on display at the local showrooms in the Fifth Avenue Building, 200 Fifth Avenue, which are in charge of E. G. Nock.

Crockery & Glass Journal, October 1933: In keeping with the modern ideas of glassware is the selection over at A. H. Heisey's. ...
They've a swell console set, two horn of plenty vases footed and a correspondingly shaped bowl also footed. This is made up in all of the colors, but the best color to my way of thinking is their simply, grand blue. See plates 45 – 51, 144 – 146, 198, 289, 486, 529, 532, 561, and 662 – 667,

31. Imperial Glass Corporation, Bellaire, Ohio, 1901 – 1984. Originally called the Imperial Glass Company. Ritz blue was offered 1932 – 1943. Royal cobalt blue was made circa 1959. Cobalt was also used as the base for carnival glass over the years, most notably for Aurora jewels, 1970 – 1972, but was also offered without iridescence from 1972 – 1973. Ultra blue (also called sapphire blue) was produced from 1975 – 1984.

The Pottery, Glass & Brass Salesman, March 2, 1933: A brief description of some of the new things from the Imperial factory, and that are now on display at the showrooms of local representatives Newland, Schneeloch & Rhone, 1107 Broadway, would not be amiss. A popular-priced leader is a console set with two-way candlesticks that can be retailed profitably for a dollar, including the cost of the four candles. The bowl in this set is a very good-looking item and carries an attractive pressed design. The candlesticks, as noted, are of the now so popular two-way variety, the holder portion being in the form of a loop set on a base, with one end of the loop slightly higher than the other. The set is obtainable in Ritz blue, Stiegel green, Imperial (light) green, rose and crystal.

Crockery & Glass Journal, May 1935: Glass luncheon sets, in three colors are being offered by the Imperial Glass Co. at Newland, Schneeloch and Piek in New York and by Earl W. Newton & Associates in Chicago. These are pressed glass, in a smart design. The motif is made up of a criss cross patterning with a thumb printed effect about the top and bottom of the hollow ware. The cups have flaring bases and rounded handles to carry out the feeling of roundness, which the set has. The flatware has an added bit, for each piece has a lacy edge. The set is popularly priced at $2.95 for a fifteen-piece set and is being made up in white, green or blue.

Appendix: Company Information

Plate 776. Imperial Glass Corporation #400/228 Candlewick, 1480, and 407 chip & dip plates. The two latter pieces are from Heisey molds. See plate 333, page 122. *China, Glass & Tableware*, March 1959.

Another smart item that is especially appropriate at this time of the year is a reeded type of glassware, that they are offering in water sets. The glass is made in a most interesting fashion, with the inside of each piece smooth and the outside the simple, thin reedy effect–made up in what seems to be a series of glass hairlines, one after the other. The jug is gracefully rounded with a smart easy-to-grip handle, and an ice-lip. These are being offered in green, blue, amber and crystal to date. The water set can be retailed for $1.98 the set, with smartly simple tumblers that greatly enhance the set. In this same type of ware, they are showing some popular priced rose bowls, to retail for about 39 cents each. See plates 52 – 57, 107, 147 – 149, 199 – 202, 253, 327, 332 – 333, 348, 384 – 385, 414 – 419, 443 – 444, 459 – 460, 487 – 489, 562, 668 – 677, and 776.

Appendix: Company Information

32. Indiana Glass Company, Dunkirk, Indiana, 1904 – 2002. Regal blue was made for Tiara Exclusives in 1981, followed by cobalt blue from 1984 – 1986. Cobalt vases were offered from the mid 1990s to the present under the Indiana label, but they are made at the old Bartlett-Collins Company factory in Sapulpa, Oklahoma. See plates 58 – 59 and 490.

33. Louie Glass Company, Weston, West Virginia, 1926 – 2004. Louie Glass was founded by Louie Wohinc, who also owned the Weston Glass Company and the West Virginia Glass Specialty Company, making it very difficult to differentiate between the products of the three factories. Cobalt was made in the 1920s and 1930s and probably discontinued in 1940.

Crockery & Glass Journal, October 1933: The vogue for colors in glassware seems to be holding its own and they have a splendid royal blue over at Hammond's from the Louie Glass Co. These are made up in excellently shaped blanks . . . . one is a positive gem, a bell-shaped blank. This shape has three possibilities (sounds like riddles) either all blue, a crystal stem and base and a blue blank, or blue stem and base and a crystal blank. Not only are these made in a complete stemware line, but this perfectly grand color is carried into shaped tumblers, salad plates, and three types of jugs. But really it's the price that sets it apart in its grandness of value together with the fact that this line is unusually attractive. See plates 461 – 463, 548, 563 – 564, and 677 – 698.

34. MacBeth-Evans Glass Company, Charleroi, Pennsylvania, 1899 – 1936. Also had factories in Marion and Elwood, Indiana. Ritz blue was introduced in 1933.

Crockery & Glass Journal, January 1933: The new idea at Macbeth-Evans is their Monax Glass short line of table ware... very thin in a dainty, fragile effect in two-tone opalescent-white translucent glass... in the Sheffield shape–the plates scalloped and paneled with ribbed flutings... a scroll design is etched in the panelings and on the well of the place... also in ruby and ritz blue... to retail at $3.95 in the 15-piece sets.

Crockery & Glass Journal, December 1933: They have added to their splendid line of Monax glassware at Macbeth Evans Glass Co. tableware that has been tested and found to be in line with the trend. Now they are showing a standard thirty-two piece set, a $3.95 retailer. The new line includes a sherbet dish, footed, a bread and butter plate, an 8½" bowl, an oval platter and baker, and a soup plate. This is the line that they first brought out last year–glass with duotone of delicate bluish translucence. The pattern is a lacy scroll effect, and on this type of ware the impression is one of dainty

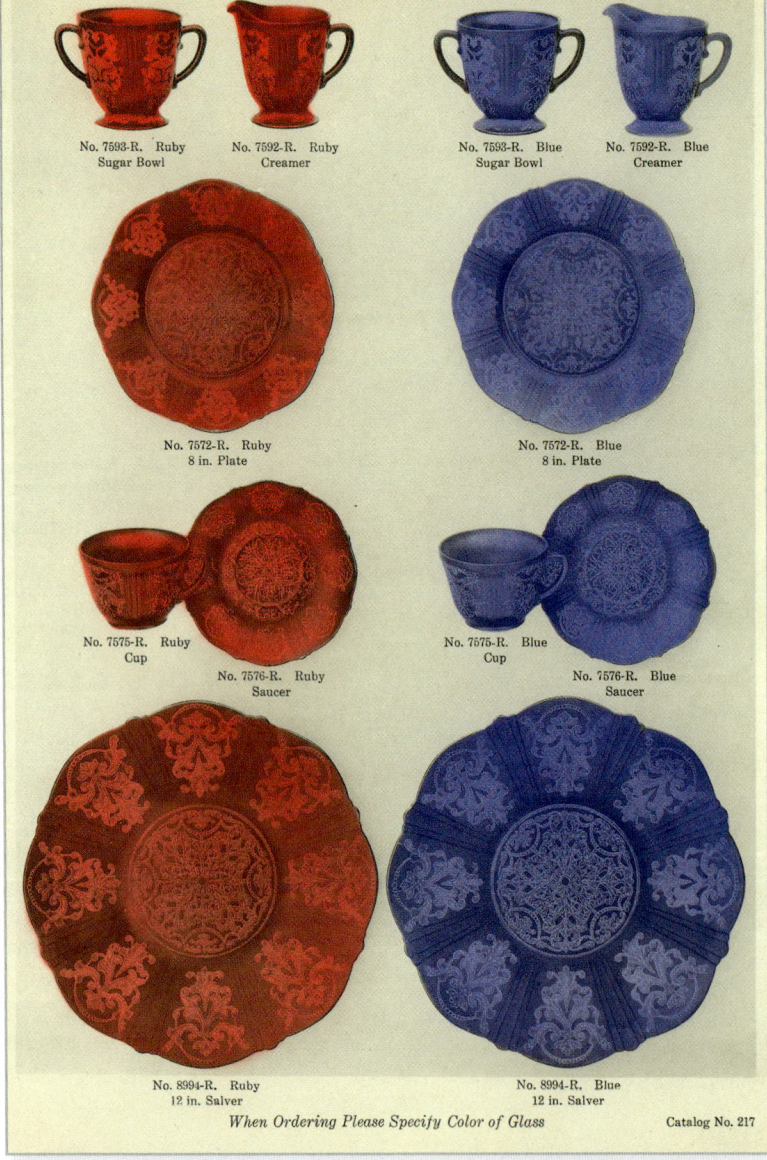

Plate 777. MacBeth-Evans Glass Company American Sweetheart in ruby and cobalt. Catalog 217, circa 1933.

Appendix: Company Information

Plate 778. MacBeth-Evans Glass Company roly poly tumblers and cocktail shaker. The tumblers are made in three sizes so that they can be nested inside one another. *Crockery & Glass Journal*, February 1934.

Appendix: Company Information

lightness, of beauty and style appeal. Here is something to blend with the darker linens that are now being shown. However for the housewife who still believes in white linens, they are showing ruby and blue sets made up in the same type of pieces. For sets a bit more elegant, all of these may be had with coin gold trim, and they are indeed smart looking. See plates 420 and 777 – 778.

35. Maryland Glass Corporation, Baltimore, Maryland, 1907 – 1981. Also known as Chattanooga Glass Corporation. Not to be confused with the Maryland Glass Company of Cumberland, the Maryland Glass Corporation primarily made molded items in cobalt, marked with an M inside a circle. They made many of the bottles for Phillips Milk of Magnesia, Bromo-Seltzer, Vicks, and Noxema. See plates 698 – 699.

36. McKee Glass Company, Jeannette, Pennsylvania, 1904 – 1961. Originally re-organized as the McKee-Jeannette Glass Company, after breaking away from the National Glass Company. Prior to 1904, operated as McKee and Brothers. Ritz blue was brought out in 1929.

Plate 779. McKee Glass Company Lenox 5-ounce low footed sherbet, 5-ounce high footed sundae, 8-ounce high footed goblet, 9-ounce table tumbler, and 3-pint jug. *Crockery & Glass Journal*, December 1929.

Crockery & Glass Journal, November 1932: The McKee Glass people have been doing a lot of practical work in expanding their line in two ways–both decorative and practical–so that in whichever your problem happens to be they may be able to help solve it. ....
In addition to all this they have produced a new line of Sandwich type glass–a full range of tumblers, and stem ware as well as 11" service plates, salad plates and finger bowls–in crystal, ruby and Ritz blue. The pattern used is a smart combination of thumb print and mitre cutting separated by a row of trick dots–raised dots set in punty dots. The stemware is made in both tall and low styles, all with square feet. Goblets may he retailed around $.29. See plates 60 – 61, 150, 386, 700, and 779.

37. Meisenthal, France/Germany, 1794 – 1969. Famed as the location of the factory of Burgun Schverer & Cie (or Verrerie de Meisenthal), where Emile Galle learned to make glass. During its long existence, much pressed glass was also produced. See plate 107.

Appendix: Company Information

38. Morgantown Glass Works, Morgantown, West Virginia, 1899 – 1971. Continuation of the Economy Glass Company. In 1939 the company was reorganized as the Morgantown Glassware Guild. Ritz blue was made circa 1929 to the 1930s and reintroduced as cobalt from 1970 – 1971.

Plate 780. Morgantown Glass Works #64 witchball vase and #35½ vase. *Crockery & Glass Journal*, April 1930.

Plate 781. Morgantown Glass Works. Left: #1-9051 liquor set with #12 platinum decoration. (See plate 493, page 175.) Center: #10½-9051 liquor set with platinum Sparta decoration. (See plate 492, page 175.) Right: #2-9051 liquor set with #12 platinum decoration. *Crockery & Glass Journal*, February 1931.

283

Appendix: Company Information

Crockery & Glass Journal, October 1931: This is the first announcement of the latest Old Morgantown development–Saracenic Art Glassware–a line especially suitable for ornamental uses. Inspiration for Saracenic Art Glassware came from the hand-wrought glass made by Saracen workers of the 13th century. The work of the Saracens compared closely with the patterns of the Byzantines, whose beautiful lamps and vases, used particularly for mosques, survive now only in museums. Their decorations were done in colors, chiefly blue, red and gold.

Old Morgantown's adaptation of Saracenic Art Glassware is made in Black and in Ritz Blue, ornamented with gold applied in a unique veined design. The ware gives a true impression of the fine hand craftsmanship it represents, and, under certain lighting conditions, sometimes appears to be of an unusual metallic composition. This ware, in its initial production, is being featured in a variety of vases, candy jars, compotes and liquor sets, and is manufactured by the Morgantown Glass Works, Morgantown, W. Va. The entire line is on display in New York with D. King Irwin, 200 Fifth Ave.

Crockery & Glass Journal, June 1932: Iced tea sets are already apparent highlights for your summer sales, and you will find some attractive ones at Old Morgantown. A particularly nice set has a rather squat square jug with slightly pinched sides, and the pinched tumblers to match are tall cupped-in affairs ... these are made in ruby, Steigel green and Ritz blue and the pitcher has a crystal handle to add just the right touch of sparkle ... all in all a very sightly set to retail at $2.50 up depending on colors. Their No. 37 jug and 7625 iced tea combine to make a very graceful set. Both the pitcher and the iced teas flare at the top and taper to a crystal foot, while the pitcher has a crystal handle. These you may have in all the standard Old Morgantown colors–Ritz blue, black, ruby and Steigel green, or all crystal if you prefer. This set retails from $5.00 up depending on the colors. See plates 62, 254 – 256, 491 – 493, 533, 701 – 704, and 780 – 787.

Plate 782. Morgantown Glass Works advertisement for Saracenic art glassware. *Crockery & Glass Journal*, October 1931.

Plate 783. Morgantown Glass Works #7924 Bright Old Bristol plate, compote, and goblet. *Crockery & Glass Journal*, November 1931.

Appendix: Company Information

Plate 784. Morgantown Glass Works #606 tumblers and #544 jug. *Crockery & Glass Journal*, June 1932.

Appendix: Company Information

Plate 785. Morgantown Glass Works vases. Top: #78 and 79 vases with golf ball stems. Center: #75 vase with Floret etching and #57 flip vase with Trellis cutting. Bottom: #7688 ivy ball vase with #542 cutting and #7643½ brandy vase. *Crockery & Glass Journal*, July 1932.

Appendix: Company Information

Plate 786. Morgantown Glass Works liquor sets. Top: #24-24 decanter, #9719-3 tumbler, and #9719-12 hi ball. (See plate 491, page 175.) Bottom: #2 decanter, #9051-1½ tumbler, and #8701-14 hi ball with #791 platinum decoration; #10½ bar bottle, #9051-1½ tumbler, and #8071-14 hi ball with Sparta platinum decoration; #10½ bar bottle, #9051-1½ tumbler, and #8071-14 hi ball with Flora platinum decoration; #21-24 decanter, #9051 1½ tumbler, and #8701-14 hi ball with Roses platinum decoration; #10½ bar bottle, #9051-1½ tumbler, and #8701-14 hi ball with Roses platinum decoration. *Crockery & Glass Journal*, November 1932.

Appendix: Company Information

Plate 787. Morgantown Glass Works #7621 tumbler and jug. *Crockery & Glass Journal*, June 1936.

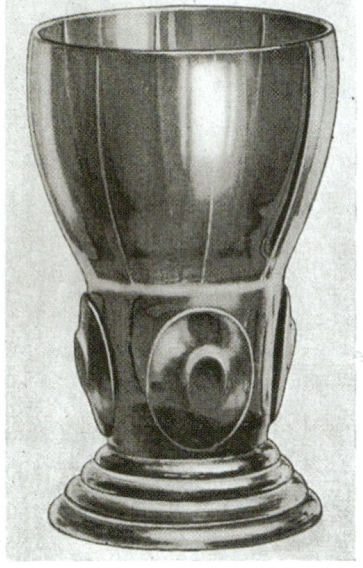

Plate 788. New Martinsville Glass Manufacturing Company #37 "Moondrops" tumbler. *Crockery & Glass Journal*, December 1932.

39. Moser (Ludwig) & Sohne, Karlsbad (later Karlovy Vary), Czechoslovakia, 1857 to the present. See plates 257, 290 – 291, 421 – 422, and 705 – 706.

40. Mosser Glass, Cambridge, Ohio, 1971 to the present. Cobalt has been made throughout the company's existence. See plates 63, 107, 597 – 601, and 621.

41. New Martinsville Glass Manufacturing Company, New Martinsville, West Virginia, 1901 – 1944. Later continued operations as the Viking Glass Company. Ritz blue was made from 1933 until 1942.

The Pottery, Glass & Brass Salesman, October 27, 1932: The New Martinsville Glass Manufacturing Company, of New Martinsville. W. Va., has just revived a high-class type of beer mug that met with considerable, success some years ago. This mug, taken in the first instance from the famous old Belgian original, is of 10-ounce capacity and naturally is rather squat. The employment of punties all over the surface is an outstanding feature. In the original these were, naturally, cut, but in the New Martinsville items they are done right in the mold. The article is well made and excellently finished, with the bottom ground. It is being produced in ruby, crystal and royal blue and put up six to a carton–assorted, if desired. Naturally, the red, white and blue colors attractively decorate any table and make a nice and not too expensive gift. Samples are now on display at the showrooms of local representative Frederick Skelton, in the Fifth Avenue Building, 200 Fifth Avenue. See plates 64 – 70, 151 – 152, 258, 292, 316 – 319, 349, 359, 423 – 428, 440, 494 – 502, 525, 565, 585, 707 – 709, and 788 – 790.

Appendix: Company Information

Plate 789. New Martinsville Glass Manufacturing Company #42 "Rolly Polly" whiskey set. (See plates 499-500, pages 177 – 178.) *Crockery & Glass Journal*, April 1933.

Plate 790. New Martinsville Glass Manufacturing Company #38 pitcher and tumblers. *Crockery & Glass Journal*, March 1934.

42. **Northwood (H.) and Company**, Wheeling, West Virginia, 1902 – 1925. Dark blue was made in the early 1900s. See plates 203 and 259.

43. **Paden City Glass Manufacturing Company**, Paden City, West Virginia, 1916 – 1951. Cobalt blue, also called Ritz blue and royal blue, was made in the 1930s.

The Pottery, Glass & Brass Salesman, December 10, 1931: During recent years ringed lines of tumblers and stemware have made a big hit with the trade. In the foreground of producers in this field–and especially in the pressed end–is the Paden City Glass Manufacturing Company, of Paden City, W. Va. The Paden City line is unique in many respects. The rings are placed rather differently than they are by other factories. There seems to be a certain distinction here that is not to be found elsewhere, and throughout all items the placing of the rings conforms.

The range of items has recently been extended to include stemware, tumblers, plates, candlesticks, bowls, pitchers, etc., all of which are obtainable at a popular price. They may be had in a wide selection of colors, including crystal glass. The colors include a particularly good green, a "Cheriglo," which is rather akin to a pink; an amber, a royal blue, a ruby (and the ruby is one of the outstanding numbers in the array) and the primrose. Samples of all these new things are now on display at the showrooms of local agent D. King Irwin, in the Fifth Avenue Building, 200 Fifth Avenue.

Crockery & Glass Journal, March 1933: Just about as complete as you could want is the No. 881 line of Paden City Glass by this time. Not only is there the complete flatware line, but they also have all sorts of bowls–large and small, salad and console, tall footed comports, candlesticks, vases, sandwich and cake plates–handled or plain, vases and all the rest. As for colors–you may now have crystal, ruby, royal blue, amber, amethyst, pink and green. And then you have your choice in the decorated line of a conventional floral cutting, or etching No. 533 which is done in a wide band effect carrying out the formal and dignified feeling of the embossed-like edge.

Appendix: Company Information

Crockery & Glass Journal, January 1935: Artistry and utility combine to create the moderately priced glass line, Number 895 line of the Paden City Glass Company. This is a complete table line which includes luncheon sets, candy boxes, relish dishes, conosole [sic] sets, salad bowls, and cake plates. The line may be had in ruby, blue, amber, green and crystal. As for the design, it is a simple three part raised motif, repeated three or four times on each piece with plain rim. In the flatware, this motif is used for the shoulder treatment. The bowl of the console set and the candy box have three simple feet, decorated in keeping with the main motif. The candlesticks which complete the console set carry through in the same grand design and offer two simple flip handles which rise right from the body and flare out as does the main part of the candle holder. The cake plate and salad bowl handles also conform in their tri-part decor. See plates 71 – 77, 153 – 158, 204 – 215, 260 – 268, 293 – 298, 320 – 321, 328 – 329, 334 – 335, 342 – 345, 350 – 353, 360, 366 – 367, 369 – 370, 429 – 435, 503 – 514, 526, 566 – 569, 591, 710 – 717, and 791 – 792.

Plate 791. Paden City Glass Manufacturing Company #991 "Penny Line." Top row: 2½-ounce wine tumbler, 9-ounce table tumbler, 12-ounce ice tea, finger bowl, cup and saucer. Bottom row: Low footed grape fruit, low footed sherbet, high footed sherbet, low footed goblet, and high footed goblet. *Crockery & Glass Journal*, March 1932.

Appendix: Company Information

Plate 792. Paden City Glass Manufacturing Company #175 console set. *Crockery & Glass Journal*, January 1935.

44. **Pairpoint Corporation**, New Bedford, Massachusetts, 1894 – 1938. Cobalt was made in the 1920s and 1930s. See plates 78 – 80, 269 – 271, and 718 – 719.

45. **Pairpoint Glass Company**, Sagamore, Massachusetts, 1970 to the present. Cobalt has been made by this indirect reincarnation of the Pairpoint Corporation throughout its existence. See plate 81.

46. **Pilgrim Glass Corporation**, Huntington, West Virginia, 1949 – 1956; Ceredo, West Virginia, 1956 – 2002. Cobalt was made from the 1990s until the factory closed. See plates 720 – 722.

47. **Pitman-Dreitzer and Company**, New York, 1930 – 1962. Established as a representative and distributor of glassware and china, Pitman-Dreitzer sold glass made by a number of companies, including New Martinsville Glass Manufacturing Company and Indiana Glass Company, as well as European imports. See plates 354 and 436.

48. **Plum Glass Company**, Pittsburgh, Pennsylvania, 1984 – 2002. Used molds acquired from the Westmoreland Glass Company after it closed. Cobalt was in production throughout the factory's existence. See plate 82.

49. **Seneca Glass Company**, Fostoria, Ohio, 1891 – 1896; Morgantown, West Virginia, 1896 – 1983. Cobalt blue (also called royal blue) was made beginning in 1931.

Plate 793. Seneca Glass Company #101R tumbler. Named "Streamline" by Hazel Marie Weatherman. *Crockery & Glass Journal*, October 1931.

Appendix: Company Information

Crockery & Glass Journal, February 1931: The Ira A. Jones Co., 308 W. Randolph St., Chicago, are showing the popular new glassware of the Seneca Glass Company, Morgantown, W. Va. The cobalt blue, ruby, and moss, which have been introduced by Seneca, have been attracting a great amount of comment from buyers in the middle west. It is offered in a complete line of table glassware.

Crockery & Glass Journal, May 1931: Ira M. Jones & Co., 308 W. Randolph St., Chicago, are showing the new Cobalt blue of Seneca Glass Co., Morgantown, W. Va. It is available in a complete line of stemware as well as a wide variety of table pieces including vases, console sets, liquor sets. See plates 83, 159 – 163, 464, 530, 723, and 793 – 794.

50. Smith (L. E.) Glass Company, Jeannette, Pennsylvania, 1907 – 1909; Mount Pleasant, Pennsylvania, 1909 to the present. Blue was first made in large quantities from 1934 – 1937. Later production of cobalt extended from 1986 to the present, under various names, including bachelor button blue, country blue, and sapphire blue.

An unusually attractive flower vase is offered by the Seneca Glass Co., and shown by the Chicago representatives of the company, The Ira A. Jones Co. The rippled surface of this Segaco optic produces a rich effect. It may be secured in either a cobalt blue or ruby bowl with a crystal foot.

Plate 794. Seneca Glass Company vase with "Segaco" optic. *Crockery & Glass Journal*, March 1936.

Crockery & Glass Journal, January 1935: A fine simplicity marks the line of the L. E. Smith Glass Company. They are offering a full line of Mexican blue glass with a silver trim which enriches the fine modelling. Many of the shapes are derived from the Empire sources and have been given a new lease of life in the brilliant blue and luxurious silver. As for individual pieces, there is a fine selection–bowls, candlesticks, salad plates, cake plates, cream and sugar sets, cup and saucers, too. Quite a group, yet they are truly popular priced and offer plenty of promotional possibilities. One especially noteworthy group is the urn and bowl console set ... two tall covered urns that have a wide variety of uses and a bowl with wide flaring sides. See plates 84 – 88, 164 – 167, 216 – 220, 299 – 302, 322 – 325, 346, 361 – 363, 368, 437, 531, 586, 623, 724 – 734, and 795.

Plate 795. L. E. Smith Glass Company #800 console set. Described in the accompanying quotation from *Crockery & Glass Journal*, January 1935, as "Mexican blue glass. ... One especially noteworthy group is the urn and bowl console set ... two tall covered urns that have a wide variety of uses and a bowl with wide flaring sides." (See plates 219, page 82, and 731, page 256.)

51. Summit Art Glass Company, Ravenna, Ohio, 1972 – 2005. Cobalt blue was one of the most successful colors made by Summit and was in production during much of their existence. See plates 89 and 107.

Appendix: Company Information

52. United States Glass Company, 1891 – 1963. This was a combination of eighteen factories, which made it the largest single manufacturer of glass in the United States. Factory R, the Tiffin Glass Company, Tiffin, Ohio, continued to operate under its own name until 1980. Along with Factory G in Glassport, Pennsylvania, which operated from 1894 – 1963, these two plants were the ones responsible for production of cobalt blue in the early 1920s, from circa 1935 to the early 1940s, and then again from 1961 – 1962.

Plate 796. United States Glass Company. Top: #319 (or 15319) candlestick. Center: #75 candlesticks with cupped bowl. Bottom: Unidentified plate. *The Pottery Gazette and Glass Trade Review* (London), March 1, 1924.

Appendix: Company Information

Plate 797. United States Glass Company #79 candlesticks and #15179 Touraine compote. The candlesticks can be seen in plate 169, page 65. *The Pottery Gazette and Glass Trade Review* (London), March 1, 1926.

Appendix: Company Information

Crockery & Glass Journal, October 18, 1923: Of more than passing attractiveness is a new line of fancies which the United States Glass Co. has just introduced to the trade and now displayed by Ed. Craig, the New York manager, 1107 Broadway. This appealing line is one of the richest which the company has brought out and the graceful shapes, range of colorings and decorations stamp it as one of the most charming innovations in the market. Particularly attractive is the number of royal blue polished glass, with 1¼" gold incrusted bands in rich and tasteful scroll and floral designs. The items include two new shapes in candlesticks, several shapes in bowls, candy jars, comports, handled trays, etc.

Crockery & Glass Journal, May 1, 1924: Among the novelties in fancy colored glassware, two new numbers of the United States Glass Co.'s line, displayed by E. T. W. Craig, New York representative, 1107 Broadway, are decidedly appealing in both form and color. Designed in the popular modern Colonial period are wall sconces, with a clever and convenient hook on the back by which they may be easily suspended on the wall. Obtainable in a range of the most wanted color and in satin finish, these decorative pieces for the home are most appealing in amber, black, jasper, amethyst, royal blue and canary. Likewise shown in the same range of attractive colors is a graceful wall pocket, with back punched for convenient hanging.

The Pottery, Glass & Brass Salesman, October 9, 1924: At the local showrooms of the United States Glass Company, 30 East Randolph Street, a large display of new items is being made. Among them are new satin-finish bowls, compotes and other tableware pieces in black and royal blue trimmed with bands of matt gold.

Crockery & Glass Journal, March 1933: There is but one dissenting voice [that "the trend is not away from color"] and that is from the U. S. Glass Co. They say the swing, as far as they are concerned is all to crystal and that they are prepared for it. Their showroom looks like a giant icicle, with its profusion of crystal. Though they still feature amber in one line, topaz, pink, and their new Ritz blue, they have pinned their faith to crystal. See plates 90 – 93, 168 – 179, 221 – 222, 272, 330, 336 – 337, 515, 735 – 736, and 796 – 797.

53. Val Saint-Lambert Glassworks Company, Seraing, Belgium, 1826 to the present. See plate 94.

54. Viking Glass Company, New Martinsville, West Virginia, 1944 – 1986. A continuation of the New Martinsville Glass Manufacturing Company. Cobalt was first made in 1949 and then sporadically after that, returned to production from 1974 – 1976 and 1979 – 1986. After Viking closed, many of the same pieces continued in production in cobalt from Dalzell Viking. See plates 95 – 96, 273, 516, and 798.

Plate 798. Viking Glass Company. Top row: #979 bon bon dish and #974-1S swan-neck dish. Bottom row: #951-1S swan-neck oval celery dish and #412-1S swan-neck ash tray. *Crockery & Glass Journal*, December 1949.

Appendix: Company Information

55. West Virginia Glass Specialty Company, Weston, West Virginia, 1930 – 1987. West Virginia Glass Specialty Company was founded by Louie Wohinc, who also owned the Weston Glass Company and the Louie Glass Company, making it very difficult to differentiate between the products of the three factories. Ritz blue (also called royal blue or Louie blue) was made 1936 – 1940. See plates 465, 570 – 575, 677, 737 – 745, and 799.

Plate 799. West Virginia Glass Specialty Company #741 crimped top tropical etched vase, #105 vase with #57 band and line decoration (see plate 738, page 258), and #455/455 seven-piece refreshment set. Note that the text of the ad says that these are "styled by Louie." *The Pottery, Glass & Brass Salesman*, December 1936.

56. Westmoreland Specialty Company, Grapeville, Pennsylvania, 1889 – 1984. Later renamed the Westmoreland Glass Company. Documentation for early cobalt has not been found, but it must have been made in the early 1900s. Cobalt (also called royal blue) was again made in the late 1970s – 1984, primarily for Levay Distributing Company. See plates 97 and 107.

57. Wright (L. G.) Glass Company, New Martinsville, West Virginia, 1937 – 1999. L. G. Wright did not produce any glass, but had glass produced from his collection of original moulds, as well as from many reproduction moulds commissioned by him. Dark blue (cobalt) was offered from at least the late 1960s until the company closed. See plate 98.

REFERENCE AND BIBLIOGRAPHY

Archer, Margaret and Douglas. *Imperial 1904-1938 Catalog Reprints.* Paducah, KY: Collector Books, 1978.
Autenreith, E. Earl and JoAnne S. *The Co-operative Flint Glass Co. of Beaver Falls, Pennsylvania, 1879 – 1934.* Weston, WV: Museum of American glass, 2008.
Baldwin, Gary D. *Moser Artistic Glass.* Ed. 2. Marietta, OH: Glass Press, 1997.
Barnett, Jerry. *Paden City, the Color Company.* Privately printed, 1978.
Bickenheuser, Fred. *Tiffin Glassmasters: bk. II.* Grove City, OH: Glassmaster Publications, 1981.
Bredehoft, Neila. *Collector's Encyclopedia of Heisey Glass, 1925-1938.* Paducah, KY: Collector Books, 1986.
_____. *Heisey Glass, 1896-1957.* Paducah, KY: Collector Books, 2001.
Bredehoft, Neila, editor. *Heisey Glass Formulas--and More.* (The West Virginia Museum of American Glass, Ltd.'s monograph no. 38) Weston, WV: Museum of American Glass in West Virginia, 2004.
Brown, O. O. *Paden City Catalog Reprints from 1920s.* Marietta, OH: Glass Press, 2000.
Bush, David. "Grand Glass Exposition--1938." (In *All About Glass*, vol. 1, no. 3, October 2003, page 19)
Cambridge Glass Company. *Cambridge Glass, 1927-1929.* Springfield, OH: Reprinted by Bill and Phyllis Smith, 1986.
Domitz, Carrie and Jerry. *Encyclopedia of Paden City Glass.* Paducah, KY: Collector Books, 2004.
Felt, Tom, and Elaine and Rich Stoer. *The Glass Candlestick Book: Vol. 1-3.* Paducah, KY: Collector Books, 2003-2005.
Felt, Tom. *L. E. Smith Glass Company: the First One Hundred Years.* Paducah, KY: Collector Books, 2007.
Florence, Gene and Cathy. *Collectors Encyclopedia of Depression Glass.* 17th ed.. Paducah, KY: Collector Books, 2006.
Frost, Sandra and Mario. *The Comprehensive Guide to Pairpoint Glass Shapes and Patterns.* Atglen, PA: Schiffer Publishing, 2006.
Fry (H. C.) Glass Society. *Collector's Encyclopedia of Fry Glassware.* Paducah, KY: Collector Books, 1990.
Gallagher, Jerry. *A Handbook of Old Morgantown Glass*: vol. I. Morgantown, WV: Old Morgantown Glass Collectors Guild, 2001.
Goshe, Ed, Ruth Hemminger, and Leslie Pina. *Depression Era Stems and Tableware: Tiffin.* Atglen, PA: Schiffer Publishing, 1998.
Heacock, William. *Fenton Glass: the First Twenty Five Years.* Marietta, OH: O-Val Advertising Corp., 1978.
_____. *Fenton Glass: the Second Twenty Five Years.* Marietta, OH: O-Val Advertising Corp., 1980.
Heacock, William, James Measell, and Berry Wiggins. *Dugan / Diamond, the Story of Indiana Pennsylvania Glass.* Marietta, OH: Antique Publications, 1993.
Heacock, William, James Measell, and Berry Wiggins. *Harry Northwood: the Wheeling Years, 1901-1925.* Marietta, OH: Antique Publications, 1991.
Krause, Gail. *The Encyclopedia of Duncan Glass.* Tallahassee, FL: Father and Son Associates, 1994.
_____. *The Years of Duncan, 1865-1955.* Hayworth, IL: Heyworth Star, 1980.
Krumme, Michael. *The Paden City Partyline.* Westminster, CA: M. Krumme, 1980s.
Lindbeck, Jenniver A., and Jeffrey B. Snyder. *Elegant Seneca: Victorian, Depression, Modern.* Atglen, PA : Schiffer Publishing, 2000.
Long, Milbra, and Emily Seate. *Fostoria Tableware, 1924-1943: the Crystal for America.* Paducah, KY: Collector Books, 1999.
_____. *Fostoria, Useful and Ornamental: the Crystal for America.* Paducah, KY: Collector Books, 2000.
Martin, Curtis. *Ozark Art Glass: A Collector's Guide.* Gassville, AR: Martin, 2008.
Mauzy, Barbara and Jim. *Mauzy's Depression Glass: a Photographic Reference With Prices.* Rev. & expanded 2nd ed. Atglen, PA: Schiffer Publishing, 2001.
Measell, James, editor. *Imperial Glass Encyclopedia: vol. III.* Marietta, OH: Glass Press, 1999.
_____. *New Martinsville Glass, 1900-1944.* Marietta, OH: Antique Publications, 1994.
Meschi, Edward J. *Durand: the Man and His Glass.* Marietta, OH: Glass Press, 1998.
Miller, Everett R. and Addie R. *The New Martinsville Glass Story.* Marietta, OH: Richardson Publishing Co., 1972.
National Cambridge Collectors, Inc. *The Cambridge Glass Company: Catalog Reprints, 1930-1934.* Paducah, KY: Collector Books, 1991.
_____. *The Cambridge Glass Company: the Decorates.* Cambridge, OH: National Cambridge Collectors, 2002.
_____. *The Cambridge Glass Company: the Non-Cataloged Etchings.* Cambridge, OH: National Cambridge Collectors, 2001.

Reference and Bibliography

_____. *Colors in Cambridge Glass*. Paducah, KY: Collector Books, 1984.
_____. *Fine Handmade Table Glassware by Cambridge: 1940 Catalog Reprint*. Paducah, KY: Collector Books, 1995.
_____. *Fine Handmade Table Glassware by Cambridge, 1949-1953*. Paducah, KY: Collector Books, 1995.
Pina, Leslie. *Blenko: 1962-1971 Catalogs*. Atglen, PA: Schiffer Publishing, 2000.
_____. *1972-1983 Catalogs*. Atglen, PA: Schiffer Publishing, 2001.
_____. *Depression Era Glass by Duncan*. Atglen, PA: Schiffer Publishing, 1999.
Pina, Leslie, and Jerry Gallagher. *Tiffin Glass, 1914-1940*. Atglen, PA: Schiffer Publishing, 1996.
Schmidt, Tom. *Central Glass Works: the Depression Era*. Atglen, PA: Schiffer Publishing, 2004.
Sferrazza, Julie. *Farber Brothers Krome Kraft: a Guide for Collectors*. Marietta, OH: Antique Publications, 1988.
Six, Dean. *Dunbar Glassware in the 1931 Catalog with a Short History*. (*The West Virginia Museum of American Glass, Ltd. monograph no. 61*) Weston, WV : Museum of American Glass in West Virginia, 2007.
_____. *L. E. Alley: a Man and His Marbles ... and Some Other Glass Connections*. (*Monograph No. 2 in the Glass Study Series of the West Virginia Museum of American Glass*) Weston, WV: Museum of American Glass in West Virginia, 1999.
_____. *West Virginia Glass Between the World Wars*. Atglen, PA: Schiffer Publishing, 2002.
_____. *Weston, West Virginia, Glass: Selected Catalog Pages & a Brief History*. (*Monograph no. 4 in the glass study series of the West Virginia Museum of American Glass, Ltd.*) Weston, WV: Museum of American Glass in West Virginia, 1999.
Snyder, Jeffrey B. *Morgantown Glass From Depression Glass Through the 1960s*. Atglen, PA: Schiffer Publishing, 1998.
Stout, Sandra McPhee. *The Complete Book of McKee Glass*. North Kansas City, MO: Trojan Press, 1972.
Torsiello, Paul and Debora, Tom and Arlene Stillman. *Paden City Glassware*. Atglen, PA: Schiffer Publishing, 2002.
Walker, William P., Melissa Bratkovich, and Joan C. Walker. *Paden City Glass Company*. Marietta, OH: Glass Press, 2003.
Weatherman, Hazel Marie. *Colored Glassware of the Depression Era 2*. Ozark, MO: Weatherman Glassbooks, 1974.
_____. *Fostoria, Its First Fifty Years*.Springfield, MO: The Weathermans, , 1972.
_____. *Supplement & Price trends, Colored Glassware of the Depression Era 2*. Ozark, MO: Weatherman Glassbooks, 1982.
West Virginia Museum of American. *The Black Glass Encyclopedia*. Atglen, PA: Schiffer Publishing, 2005.
Whitmyer, Margaret and Ken. *Fenton Art Glass, 1907-1939*. Paducah, KY: Collector Books, 1996.

INDEX

19th Hole (Morgantown pattern) 189
A & J Manufacturing Company 139
A. A. Importing Company.........9, 138, 265, 267
Pattern CD/253 138
Pattern JA/1830 265
Pattern OG1648 9
Addie (New Martinsville pattern) 30, 115, 152-153
Agua Caliente (Fenton pattern) 21, 146, 172, 232
Akro Agate Company............................. 211, 267
Aladdin Industries 220, 267
Aladdin Mantle Lamp Company 267
Alden, Dana K..135
Alley Agate Company............................ 211, 267
Alley Glass Company 211, 267
Amazon Warrior (Moser decoration) 95, 105
American Beauty (Lotus decoration)..........77, 97
American Sweetheart (MacBeth-Evans pattern)................. 151, 280
Anchorage Glass by Wagon Wheel................269
Andres, Walter S...274
Arch (Heisey pattern)......................................75
Argus (Fostoria pattern) 274
Aristocrat (Heisey pattern)............................105
Aristocrat (Paden City pattern) 202
Arrowhead (Smith pattern) 36
Aurora (Hazel-Atlas pattern) 149
Avon..209
Baroque (Fostoria pattern) 22
Bartlett-Collins Company...............................280
Basket Weave (Fenton pattern) 53
Belmont Glass Company 164, 174, 200
Bead and Dart (Unattributed pattern) ...214
Beaumont Company....................29, 45, 224. 267
Pattern 115...45
Bertram (F. W.) Jewelry 181
Bird vase (Gillinder)......................................234
Blenko Glass Company 9, 205, 267
Pattern 7017...205
Pattern 7634...9
Pattern 8810...9
Bloom, Aaron 231
Bombay (Morgantown pattern) 248
Boston and Sandwich Glass Company.... 10, 21, 24, 26-27, 44, 135, 209, 215, 267
Bridal Wreath (etching) 81
Bryce, McKee and Company 38, 65
Burgun Schverer & Cie..................................282
Cabbage Rose (Paden City etching) 77, 97
Caffco International............................. 240, 267
Cambridge Glass Company................7, 10-14, 45-47, 60, 70-71, 86-90, 100, 102-103, 110, 120, 122, 124, 130, 133, 135, 142-143, 158, 160, 167-171, 185, 192, 195, 205-206, 212-214, 224-228, 267-268, 273
Decoration D1007 .... 13, 171
Etching 695 185
Etching 703 88
Etching 708 ....47, 122, 124, 224
Etching 732 86
Pattern 1.......................................110
Pattern 2.......................................110
Pattern 5......................................110
Pattern 7...............................110, 143
Pattern 9......................................102
Pattern 11......................................88
Pattern 29......................................110
Pattern 39..71
Pattern 40......................................110
Pattern 44......................................227
Pattern 52......................................167
Pattern 94......................................224
Pattern 96..88
Pattern 104....................................130
Pattern 107....................................167
Pattern 109......................................10
Pattern 135....................................122
Pattern 142/96..............................133
Pattern 225......................................11
Pattern 238....................................228
Pattern 239....................................228
Pattern 240....................................120
Pattern 241....................................228
Pattern 242....................................228
Pattern 306....................................227
Pattern 389....................................130
Pattern 437................................45-47
Pattern 441......................................45
Pattern 487....................................124
Pattern 494....................................142
Pattern 509......................................70
Pattern 531......................................88
Pattern 627................................13, 46
Pattern 628......................................13
Pattern 646......................................46
Pattern 842......................................46
Pattern 851....................................192
Pattern 865............................110, 142
Pattern 925....................................143
Pattern 993......................................60
Pattern 1066....................................86
Pattern 1070..................................167
Pattern 1090....................................86
Pattern 1111....................................46
Pattern 1121..................................192
Pattern 1206..................................268
Pattern 1217..................................185
Pattern 1233..................................226
Pattern 1234..................................226
Pattern 1236..................................225
Pattern 1237..................................226
Pattern 1238..................................226
Pattern 1239..................................225
Pattern 1242..................................225
Pattern 1273....................................12
Pattern 1299..................................226
Pattern 1300..................................226
Pattern 1304/11..............................102
Pattern 1307....................................47
Pattern 1312..................................206
Pattern 1321..................................168
Pattern 1322..................................167
Pattern 1338....................................14
Pattern 1341..................................168
Pattern 1349....................................47
Pattern 1351....................................71
Pattern 1375..................................170
Pattern 1385..................................169
Pattern 1401..................................167
Pattern 1402/12.............................171
Pattern 1402/19.............................143
Pattern 1402/38.............................171
Pattern 1402/39.............................171
Pattern 1402/52.............................192
Pattern 1402/61...............................90
Pattern 1402/67...............................90
Pattern 1402/80...............................13
Pattern 1410..................................227
Pattern 1447..................................225
Pattern 2862....................................11
Pattern 3011............................89, 205
Pattern 3011/25.............................227
Pattern 3078..................................168
Pattern 3103..................................195
Pattern 3122..................................268
Pattern 3124....................................87
Pattern 3126....................................87
Pattern 3135....................................86
Pattern 3400...............7, 135, 167, 185
Pattern 3400/4.........................46, 86
Pattern 3400/5................................70
Pattern 3400/9..............................102
Pattern 3400/28..............................87
Pattern 3400/38............................160
Pattern 3400/45..............................46
Pattern 3400/54............................142
Pattern 3400/88............................130
Pattern 3400/92............................170
Pattern 3400/102..........................225
Pattern 3400/107..........................158
Pattern 3400/113..........................170
Pattern 3400/119..........................168
Pattern 3400/127....................169-170
Pattern 3400/144..........................206
Pattern 3400/156..........................169
Pattern 3400/157..........................195
Pattern 3400/646............................46
Pattern 3400/1180..........................70
Pattern 3450................................169
Pattern 3500..................................90
Pattern 3500/31..............................12
Pattern 3500/41............................103
Pattern 3500/57............................103
Pattern 3500/74..............................12
Pattern 3500/108............................14
Pattern 7801..................................47
Pattern 7966................................168
Pattern E3400/1185........................70
Candlewick (Imperial pattern).....................279
Cantina (Paden City pattern)............... 117, 156
Canton Glass Company 144, 269
Pattern 836..144
Cape Cod (Imperial pattern).............. 149, 174
Cappellus, W. V. M......................................209
Caprice (Cambridge pattern).....................212-214, 228
Carcassonne (Heisey pattern) 188
Carrie (Smith pattern)..................................109

299

Index

Cascade (Heisey pattern) 24
Catawba Grape (Cambridge decoration) 268
Celeste (Morgantown pattern) 94
Central Glass Company (Oklahoma) 221, 228, 269
Central Glass Works 7, 14-15, 47-48, 71-72, 91, 124, 144, 223, 269
    Pattern 500 71
    Pattern 1435 124
    Pattern 1450 144
    Pattern 2000 .... 14-15, 47-48, 72, 91
Charade (Diamond pattern) 111, 145
Charlotte (Morgantown pattern) 247
Chase Brass and Copper Company 200, 204
Chattanooga Glass Corporation 246, 282
Chico (Louie pattern) 165
Chiquita (Alley Agate pattern) 211
Christmas salt (Sandwich) 135
Circlet (Morgantown pattern) 175
Clark, Norman 217
Clydesdale (Heisey/Mosser figurine) 221
Cobel (Heisey pattern) 199
Cobel, Ray C. 199
Colonial Lace (Smith pattern) 126
Consolidated Lamp & Glass Company 137-138, 269
Co-operative Flint Glass Company 15-17, 64, 92, 126, 160, 195, 269-270
    Pattern 279 15
    Pattern 322 15
    Pattern 448 15
    Pattern 449 .... 15, 92
    Pattern 450 15
    Pattern 492 270
    Pattern 503 16
    Pattern 557 160
    Pattern 579 270
    Pattern 587 270
Cozy Cordial (New Martinsville decanter) .. 178
Craig, Edward T. W. 295
Crisscross (Hazel-Atlas pattern) 75, 139
Crow's Foot Round (Paden City pattern) 7, 33, 78, 98, 107, 117, 129, 154
Crow's Foot Square (Paden City pattern) 33, 60, 77-78, 96-98, 107-108, 121, 123, 125, 128, 134, 155, 250
Crystal Eagle (New Martinsville pattern) 31
Daisy and Button (Wright pattern) 41
Dalzell Viking 17-18, 31, 103, 270, 295
    Pattern 970 18
    Pattern 1911 103
    Pattern 1937 17
    Pattern 1938 18
    Pattern 8566 18
Daum Nancy 209, 270
Decagon (Cambridge pattern) 86, 110, 142, 192
Depasse Pearsall 252
Diamond Glass-ware Company 19, 49-50, 68, 73-74, 92, 111, 145, 228, 270-271
    Pattern 99 .... 19, 50, 111, 145, 270
    Pattern 716 74
Diana Chrome 21
Diana the Huntress (A.A. Importing pattern) 9
Diane (Cambridge etching) 268
Dietz (R. E.) Company 217
Doctor, A. P. 269
Dolphin (Cambridge pattern) 10
Dolphin (Dalzell Viking pattern) 17-18
Dolphin (Fenton pattern) 104
Doric (Westmoreland/Plum pattern) 35
Double Shield (Smith pattern) 118-119, 157
Douglass (Co-operative Flint pattern) 16
Draped Lincoln (Aladdin pattern) 220
Driftwood Casual (Seneca pattern) 166
Dugan Glass Company 160, 228, 270-271
Dumbbell (West Virginia Glass pattern) 203
Dunbar Glass Corporation 51, 161, 181, 229-230, 234, 239-240, 248, 271-272
    Decoration S-652 272
    Pattern 101-L 271
    Pattern 109 272
    Pattern 110 272
    Pattern 123 272
    Pattern 132 .... 161, 272
    Pattern 142 272
    Pattern 143 272
    Pattern 410 229
    Pattern 616-C8 271
    Pattern 651-8 271
    Pattern 666-8 271
    Pattern 673-C 271
    Pattern 680-C 271
    Pattern 689-C 271
    Pattern 702-C 271
    Pattern 735 271
    Pattern 753 230
    Pattern 3321 240
    Pattern 3350 229
    Pattern 3351 229
    Pattern 3382 229
    Pattern 5207 161
    Pattern 6209 229
    Pattern 6349 229
Duncan and Miller Glass Company 20, 51-52, 74, 131, 145, 171-172, 196, 206, 230-231, 241, 273
    Pattern 5 231
    Pattern 11 .... 196, 206
    Pattern 12 .... 52, 230
    Pattern 16 51
    Pattern 28 20
    Pattern 50 51
    Pattern 55 171-172
    Pattern 99 241
    Pattern 103 231
    Pattern 111 .... 20, 131, 145
    Pattern 113 20
    Pattern 126 .... 74, 231
    Pattern 127 273
Durand Art Glass 2, 232, 273
    Pattern 1708 232
Eales of Sheffield 135, 273
Early American (Co-operative Flint pattern) 270
Early American Rock Crystal (McKee pattern) 28, 59
Eberle 261
Economy Glass Company 283
Edna (Heisey pattern) 25
Elizabeth (Fenton pattern) 124
Empress (Heisey pattern) 57
Evangeline (National Silver decoration) 60, 98
Fan Rib (Heisey by Imperial pattern) 122
Fancy Squares (New Martinsville pattern) 30, 128, 153, 249
Farber Brothers 185, 273
Farber-Shlevin, Inc. 21, 273
Farberware Krome Kraft 185, 273
Fenton Art Glass Company .. 12, 21, 52-54, 104, 124, 146, 172, 193, 206, 223, 228, 232, 273
    Pattern 848 .... 54, 206
    Pattern 950 52-53
    Pattern 1092 53
    Pattern 1093 53
    Pattern 1234 54
    Pattern 1502 52
    Pattern 1532 104
    Pattern 1611 .... 21, 146, 172, 232
    Pattern 1615 223
    Pattern 1620 193
    Pattern 1639 .... 124, 146
    Pattern 1700 146
    Pattern 1790 54
    Pattern 1934 172
    Pattern 9751 228
    Pattern 9753 228
    Pattern S5474 21
Filigree Art-Ware (Dugan pattern) 228
Fish (Hazel-Atlas pattern) 199, 276
Flame (New Martinsville/Viking pattern) 18
Flora (Morgantown decoration) 287
Florentine #1 (Hazel-Atlas pattern) 94
Floret (Morgantown etching) 286
Ford (Henry) Museum 274
Fostoria Glass Company 22, 55, 74, 92, 104, 127, 147, 173, 189, 193, 207, 232-233, 274
    Pattern 2219 104
    Pattern 2327 92
    Pattern 2350 147
    Pattern 2354 207
    Pattern 2378 193
    Pattern 2394 .... 55, 74
    Pattern 2404 233
    Pattern 2440 .... 127, 147
    Pattern 2470 233
    Pattern 2494 173
    Pattern 2496 22
    Pattern 4020 104
    Pattern 4024 .... 55, 173
    Pattern 4113 22
    Pattern 5088 232
Fry (H. C.) Glass Company 7, 22, 55, 93, 147-148, 233, 274-275
    Pattern 14 93
    Pattern 2502 93
    Pattern 3101 .... 22, 148
Fry, J. Howard 274
Futura (Canton pattern) 144
Gadroon (Cambridge pattern) 12, 14, 90, 103
Gadroon (Paden City pattern) 61, 79, 106, 128, 156
Galle, Emile 282
Gascony (Heisey pattern) 173
Georgian (Duncan & Miller pattern) 231
Georgian (Fenton pattern) 21, 146, 172, 232
Georgian (New Martinsville pattern) 29-30, 59, 96, 106, 116, 131, 154, 176, 201, 249
Georgian (Paden City pattern) 202
Georgian Shape (Imperial pattern) 164
Gillinder Brothers 275
Gillinder Glass 234, 275
Glades (Paden City pattern) 61, 81, 99, 131, 156, 182, 202
Glenda (Paden City pattern) 81
Gold Line (U.S. Glass decoration) 65, 83, 100

Index

Golf Ball (Morgantown pattern) 29, 94
Gordon (Duncan & Miller pattern)..........171-172
Gothic (Indiana pattern)..................................28
Grand Glass Exposition 258
Grapes (Pairpoint engraving)..........................99
Gray (Horace C.) Co.......................................270
Greensburg Glass Company............................36
Hairpin (Hazel-Atlas pattern) 114, 148
Hanging Garlands and Shields (Wheeling decoration) 91
Harpo (Louie pattern).....................................166
Hazel-Atlas Glass Company 6-8, 23, 56, 74-75, 94, 104-105, 111-114, 125, 136, 138-139, 148-149, 159, 161-164, 186-187, 193-194, 196-199, 234, 275-277
Decoration 420................................. 163, 276
Pattern 1816...163
Pattern 1816B....................................163-164
Pattern 9659...139
Pattern 9779...139
Pattern 9780...139
Pattern 9783...139
Pattern 9908...163
Pattern 9937...162
Pattern G-1488...164
Pattern K976...23
Hazen (Imperial pattern)..............................140
Heisey (A. H.) and Company...............7, 23-25, 44, 57, 75, 105, 122, 173, 188-189, 199, 221, 229, 234-236, 278-279
Pattern 1...199
Pattern 33...44
Pattern 86...199
Pattern 110...24
Pattern 135...57
Pattern 141...25
Pattern 142...24
Pattern 301...23
Pattern 419...189
Pattern 1401...57
Pattern 1404...23
Pattern 1405...24
Pattern 1420...235
Pattern 1421...235
Pattern 1428................................ 25, 57, 235
Pattern 1430...105
Pattern 1433...................................... 57, 236
Pattern 1440...75
Pattern 3390...188
Pattern 3397...173
Pattern 4225...199
Pattern 4227...229
Pattern 4228...234
Pattern 4229...234
Pattern 4230...................................... 229, 234
Pattern 4231...234
Heisey Collectors of America..........................44
Heisey Glass Museum 221
Heron (Cambridge flower frog).......................46
Hi Lo (Heisey pattern) 235
Hobnail (Imperial pattern)..............................27
Hobnail (Smith pattern)................................256
Honesdale Decorating Company . 47, 72, 91, 124
Decoration 905....................... 47, 72, 91, 124
Hostess (Duncan & Miller pattern)..............273
Hostmaster (New Martinsville pattern)........... 116, 154, 186
Hotcha (Paden City pattern)................... 61, 81, 99, 106, 156
Hunt...222
Ida (Imperial pattern)...................................150
Imperial Glass Company 278
Imperial Glass Corporation................. 2, 12, 17, 25-27, 44, 58, 76-77, 94, 120, 122, 127, 139-140, 149-151, 159, 164-166, 173-174, 200, 236-239, 278-279
Pattern 39...58
Pattern 86...239
Pattern 134...150
Pattern 142...139
Pattern 153...58
Pattern 160...174
Pattern 160/37..149
Pattern 160/163...174
Pattern 242/2..150
Pattern 306...236
Pattern 359...236
Pattern 400/228...279
Pattern 407...279
Pattern 451....... 159, 164, 166, 173-174, 200
Pattern 623...237
Pattern 635.. 25, 58
Pattern 643...27
Pattern 701............................. 151, 159, 165
Pattern 701/2..238
Pattern 701/6..238
Pattern 727................................ 76, 94, 122
Pattern 728.. 26, 120
Pattern 743...238
Pattern 745...151
Pattern 749...................................... 127, 151
Pattern 752/2..150
Pattern 753...26
Pattern 760...140
Pattern 775...237
Pattern 780...238
Pattern 1480...................................... 122, 279
Pattern 6567/28...58
Pattern 7286..58
Pattern 7286A...76
Pattern 7497B...76
Pattern 7497/E..76
Pattern 13794 44
Pattern 15783 27
Pattern 51757 239
Pattern 71755 238
Pattern 71762 27
Pattern 71790 26
Imperial Hunt (Cambridge decoration).........268
Indiana Glass Company...........................27-28, 174, 280, 291
Pattern 14...27
Pattern 298...174
Pattern 6222...28
Ipswich (Heisey pattern).................................24
Irwin (Paden City etching).............................61
Irwin, D. King... 284, 289
Jack and the Beanstalk (Diamond decoration) . 50
Jacobi (Morgantown pattern)..........................29
Jacolima, A. 209
Janice (New Martinsville/Viking pattern) 31, 207, 249
Jefferson Glass Company 223
Jolly Mountaineer (Indiana pattern) 174
Jones (Ira A.) Company 292
Joseph, Paul...273
Katy (Imperial pattern) 76
Kimball (Morgantown pattern).....................247
Kobi Basket (Rockwell decoration) 73
Kresge (S. S.) Company..................................54
Lace Edge (Imperial pattern)........................76, 127, 151, 238
Lafayette (Fostoria pattern) 127, 147
Large Interior Panel (Akro Agate pattern)............211
Largo (Paden City pattern)............. 34, 117, 156
Leaf Medallion (Northwood pattern) 77
Leaf Tiers (Fenton pattern).............................54
Leaves and Flowers (Smith decoration) ...64, 255
Lenox (McKee pattern) 282
Levay Distributing Company.......................296
Lily of the Valley (Smith decoration) 64, 255
Lincoln Inn (Fenton pattern) 146
Lindshammar 264
Lindsey (Mosser pattern)........................212-214
Little American Maid Tea Set (Akro Agate)...........211
Little King (Morgantown pattern)................175
Lola (Lotus decoration)...................................86
Long Feller (West Virginia Glass pattern)...........203
Longaberger Company..................................221
Lotus Glass Company.................. 77, 86, 97, 252
Decoration 65 .... 97, 252
Louie Glass Company........... 165-166, 194, 200, 239-246, 258, 265, 280, 296
Pattern 1...194
Pattern 25...165
Pattern 42...241
Pattern 43...246
Pattern 46...245
Pattern 92V4...244
Pattern 92V4C...245
Pattern 93...239
Pattern 96V2...242-244
Pattern 112V6C..241
Pattern 112V9C..241
Pattern 123-8..244-245
Pattern 200V5 244
Pattern 600/V6-1/2.......................................239
Pattern 854..240
Pattern 1818..240
Lucy (Paden City pattern)... 79-80, 98, 121, 123, 126, 129, 133-134
Luxval (Val Saint-Lambert pattern)................39
Lynward (Morgantown pattern) 175
Macbeth-Evans Glass Company .. 6, 151, 280-282
Pattern 7572-R 280
Pattern 7575-R 151, 280
Pattern 7576-R 151, 280
Pattern 7592-R 280
Pattern 7593-R 280
Pattern 8994-R 280
Mae West (Diamond pattern) 19, 49
Mantle Lamp Company 220. 267
Many Flags (Hazel-Atlas pattern).................197
Maryland Glass Company 222, 282
Maryland Glass Corporation................ 246, 282
Massy (Paden City pattern)............................61
Master Senior cocktail shaker (Hazel-Atlas) . 275
Martha Washington (Cambridge pattern)..........167
McKee and Brothers 44, 282
McKee Glass Company 28, 59, 140, 246, 282
Pattern 200...28
Pattern 1927..246
McKee-Jeannette Glass Company 282
Meisenthal... 44, 282
Pattern 2153...44
Menzies, Alex 267
Metropolitan Museum of Art........... 17, 27, 238

Index

Michael (New Martinsville pattern) 177
Mildred (New Martinsville pattern) 116, 154
Minton (Wheeling decoration) 12
Modernistic (Smith pattern) 64
Moderntone (Hazel-Atlas pattern) ... 7, 113-114, 125, 148, 277
Molly (Imperial pattern) 94, 150
Monax (MacBeth-Evans pattern) 280
Montgomery Ward 31
Moon and Star (Smith pattern) 37, 109
Moondrops (New Martinsville pattern) 29-30, 59, 96, 106, 116, 131, 154, 176, 201, 249, 288
Morgantown Glass Works... 29, 94-95, 150, 175, 247-248, 283-288
    Cutting 542 286
    Decoration 12 .... 175, 283
    Decoration 791 287
    Pattern 1-9051 .... 175, 283
    Pattern 2 287
    Pattern 2-9051 283
    Pattern 10 1/2 287
    Pattern 10 1/2-9051 .... 175, 283
    Pattern 18 247
    Pattern 21-24 287
    Pattern 24 175
    Pattern 24-24 287
    Pattern 35 1/2 283
    Pattern 37 284
    Pattern 57 286
    Pattern 64 .... 248, 283
    Pattern 65 247
    Pattern 75 286
    Pattern 78 286
    Pattern 79 286
    Pattern 544 285
    Pattern 606 285
    Pattern 1511 150
    Pattern 7621 288
    Pattern 7625 284
    Pattern 7643 .... 29, 94, 247, 286
    Pattern 7662-1/2 248
    Pattern 7688 286
    Pattern 7924 284
    Pattern 8701-14 287
    Pattern 9051-1 1/2 287
    Pattern 9719-3 287
    Pattern 9719-12 287
Morgantown Glassware Guild 189, 283
    Pattern 3055 189
Moser (Ludwig) und Sohne 6, 95, 105-106, 152, 248, 288
Mosser Glass 29, 44-45, 212-214, 221, 288
    Pattern 154 44
    Pattern 225-1 213
    Pattern 225-2 212
    Pattern 225-3 212
    Pattern 225-4 212
    Pattern 225-5 213
    Pattern 225-6 213
    Pattern 225-7 214
    Pattern 315 29
Mount Pleasant (Smith pattern) 63, 81, 108-109, 118-119, 157
Mount Vernon (Cambridge pattern) . 71, 88, 100, 102, 110, 130, 143, 167, 268
Mount Vernon (Viking/Dalzell Viking pattern) 100, 103, 183
Munsell (Imperial pattern) 26, 94
National Glass Company 282

National Heisey Glass Museum 221
National Silver Deposit Ware Company ... 49, 60, 73, 98, 200-201, 251
National Society United Daughters of 1812 129
Nautilus (Cambridge pattern) 169
New Century (Hazel-Atlas pattern) 276
New England Glass Company 17
New Martinsville Glass Manufacturing Company 18, 29-31, 59, 96, 106, 115-116, 128-129, 131, 152-154, 157-158, 176-178, 186, 201, 207, 249, 288-289, 291, 295
    Pattern 15 178
    Pattern 18 31
    Pattern 34 .... 30, 115, 152-153
    Pattern 35 .... 30, 128, 153, 249
    Pattern 35/3/25 249
    Pattern 36 .... 30, 115, 153
    Pattern 37 ...... 30, 59, 96, 106, 116, 131, 154, 176, 201, 249, 288
    Pattern 37/2 29
    Pattern 37/3 59
    Pattern 38 .... 116, 154, 186, 289
    Pattern 42 .... 177-178, 249, 289
    Pattern 45 31
    Pattern 237 177
    Pattern 412-ISJ 207
    Pattern 451 31
    Pattern 415 18
    Pattern 606 177
    Pattern 970 18
    Pattern 4200 249
    Pattern 4232 249
    Pattern 4500 .... 31, 249
    Pattern 4554 31
Newbound (Imperial pattern) 58
Newland, Schneeloch and Piek 197, 278
Newland, Schneeloch, and Rhone 278
Newport (Hazel-Atlas pattern) 114, 148
Newport (Pitman-Dreitzer pattern) 129, 157
Newton (Earl W.) and Associates 278
Nineteenth Hole (Morgantown pattern) 189
Nock, E. G. 278
Northwood (H.) and Company 77, 96, 289
Octagon (Imperial pattern) 150
Old Hickory Glass 269
Old Sandwich (Heisey pattern) 23
Old Williamsburg (Heisey/Imperial pattern) .. 23, 44
Olive (Imperial pattern) 150
Open Heart Arches (Consolidated pattern) 137-138
Orchid (Paden City etching) 128
Paden City Glass Manufacturing Company 7, 32-34, 45, 60-61, 77-81, 96-99, 106-108, 117, 121, 123, 125-126, 128-129, 131, 133-134, 154-156, 179-182, 186, 201-202, 209, 250-252, 263-264, 289-291
    Etching 533 .... 61, 289
    Pattern 6 186
    Pattern 69 202
    Pattern 115 32
    Pattern 116 32
    Pattern 175 291
    Pattern 184 250
    Pattern 191 .... 32, 290
    Pattern 207 61
    Pattern 211 182
    Pattern 215 .... 61, 81, 99, 131, 156, 182, 202

Pattern 215 ½ 81
Pattern 220 .... 34, 117, 156
Pattern 298 133
Pattern 412 .... 7, 33, 60, 77-78, 96-98, 107-108, 117, 121, 123, 125, 128, 134, 155, 250
Pattern 449 201
Pattern 499 201
Pattern 502-5 209
Pattern 503 108
Pattern 881 .... 61, 79, 106, 128, 156, 289
Pattern 890 .... 7, 33, 78, 98, 107, 117, 129, 154
Pattern 895 .... 79-80, 98, 121, 123, 126, 129, 133-134
Pattern 901 179
Pattern 911 290
Pattern 991 .... 79, 125, 155, 182, 201, 290
Pattern 994 .... 155, 180
Pairpoint Corporation 34-35, 99-100, 252-253, 291
    Pattern 228 99
    Pattern 1600 34
    Pattern A299 99
    Pattern B366 100
    Pattern B372 100
    Pattern B959 253
    Pattern B1107 252
    Pattern B1627 34
Pairpoint Glass Company 21, 35, 291
    Pattern 137 21
    Pattern 202 35
Party Line (Paden City pattern) 32
Peacock (Durand pattern) 232
Penny Line (Paden City pattern) ... 79, 125, 155, 182, 201, 290
Pilgrim Glass Corporation 253-254, 291
    Pattern 1932 253
Pillar Flute (Imperial pattern) 58
Pioneer (Fostoria pattern) 147
Pitman-Dreitzer and Company 129, 157, 291
Plum Glass Company 35, 291
    Pattern 3 35
Plymouth (Fenton pattern) 193
Pod Flower (Paden City decoration) .. 33, 80, 107, 121, 123, 126, 129, 251
Pompeii (Pilgrim pattern) 253
Popeye and Olive (Paden City pattern) 155, 180
Poppy (Hazel-Atlas pattern) 94
Premium (Imperial pattern) 25, 58
Pressman (J.) Company 211-212
Princess Feather (Pairpoint pattern) 35
Pulled Feather (Durand pattern) 232
Purdy, John H. 217
Queen Anne (U.S. Glass pattern) 39
Radiance (Duncan & Miller pattern) 20
Radiance (New Martinsville pattern) 31, 249
Ray (Co-operative Flint pattern) 16
Reeded (Imperial pattern) 151, 159, 165, 238, 279
Regent (Northwood pattern) 77, 96
Repeal (New Martinsville pattern) 116, 154, 186
Ribbed Dumbbell (West Virginia Glass pattern) 204
Ring of Rings (Unattributed pattern) ... 184, 266
Rockwell Silver Company 11, 19, 36, 49, 63, 73, 195, 230
Rose Lady (Cambridge flower frog) 71

Index

Roses (Morgantown decoration) 287
Rosso Wholesaler Glass Dealers, Inc. 38, 44
Roxanne (Morgantown pattern) 247
Royal Lace (Hazel-Atlas pattern) 7-8, 56, 104, 111-112, 138, 149, 159, 162, 186, 276-277
Royal Lustre (Diamond line) 270
Sailboat (Hazel-Atlas pattern) .114, 159, 163, 276
Sailboat (lamp pattern) 219
Saint Regis (Honesdale decoration) 47, 72, 91, 124
Sakier, George 22
Samarkand (Paden City etching) 61, 108, 133
Sandwich Dolphin (Heisey pattern) 24
Sandwich Glass Museum 21
Saracenic Art Glassware (Morgantown pattern) 284
Sawtooth (Co-operative Flint pattern) 15
Schollenberger, T. M. 269
Sea Shell (Cambridge pattern) 227
Seneca Glass Company 36, 62-63, 166, 188, 254, 291-292
    Pattern 12 62
    Pattern 30 62
    Pattern 101R 291
    Pattern 903 188
Shaeffer (Imperial pattern) 159, 164, 173-174, 200
Ships (Hazel-Atlas pattern).....114, 159, 193, 198
Ships and Stars (Hazel-Atlas pattern) 198
Silhouette (silver decoration) 49
Skelton, Frederick 270, 288
Skirted Panel (Heisey pattern) 44
Smith (L. E.) Glass Company 6, 36-37, 63-64, 81-83, 108-109, 118-119, 126, 132-133, 157, 188, 207, 222, 254-257, 292
    Pattern 1 64
    Pattern 2 257
    Pattern 27 37
    Pattern 44 126
    Pattern 50 .... 109, 118
    Pattern 65 132
    Pattern 85 256
    Pattern 93 132
    Pattern 99 256
    Pattern 200 .... 108, 119
    Pattern 309 81
    Pattern 410 119
    Pattern 432 255
    Pattern 505 .... 118, 157
    Pattern 525 118
    Pattern 600 63
    Pattern 604 222
    Pattern 615 37
    Pattern 635 133
    Pattern 711 257
    Pattern 800 .... 256, 292
    Pattern 805 64
    Pattern 870 82
    Pattern 900 257
    Pattern 982 36
    Pattern 1000 255
    Pattern 1020 207
    Pattern 1022 63
    Pattern 1402 36
    Pattern 1900 254
    Pattern 2400 83
    Pattern 4000 64
    Pattern 5204 109

Pattern 5211 37
Smithsonian Institution 26
Sooner Glass 269
Sovereign (Moser etching) 248
Sparta (Morgantown decoration) . 175, 283, 287
Spiral (Westmoreland/Viking pattern) 40
Spire (Paden City pattern) 182
Sportsman Series (Hazel-Atlas pattern) .114, 159, 163, 193-194, 197-199, 276
Springtime (Lotus decoration) 97, 252
Spun (Imperial pattern) 151, 159, 165, 238
Standing Rib (Unattributed pattern) 204
Star (Co-operative Flint pattern) 17
Statuesque Line (Cambridge pattern) 89, 205, 227
Sterling Decorating Company 58
Streamline (Seneca pattern) 291
Summit Art Glass Company 38, 44, 292
    Pattern 1932/2 38
Sunset Glass Company 221
Sussex (Heisey pattern) 189
Swank 204
Swanson (Paden City pattern) 250-252
Tally-Ho (Cambridge pattern) .13, 90, 133, 143, 171, 192, 268
Temple, Shirley 44
Terrace (Duncan & Miller pattern) 20, 131, 145
Thomas, H. Wallace 270
Thousand Eye (A.A. Importing pattern) 138
Thumbprint and Panel (Heisey pattern) . 57, 236
Tiara Exclusives 174, 280
Tiffin Glass Company 39, 68, 293
Touraine (U.S. Glass pattern) 294
Toy Dishes (Alley Agate pattern) 211
Trellis (Morgantown cutting) 286
Tufts, James W. 261
Tulip (Heisey pattern) 235
Twelve Point (New Martinsville pattern) 115
Two Kids (Cambridge flower block) 70
United States Glass Company .19, 38-39, 65-68, 83, 100, 121, 123, 141, 183, 257-258, 293-295
    Decoration 1 .... 65, 83, 100
    Pattern 6 257
    Pattern 055 183
    Pattern 66 67
    Pattern 74 38
    Pattern 75 293
    Pattern 76 .... 39, 68
    Pattern 79 294
    Pattern 151 66
    Pattern 179 66-67
    Pattern 300 38
    Pattern 309 39
    Pattern 319 293
    Pattern 320 65
    Pattern 330 65
    Pattern 8096 65
    Pattern 8105 .... 65-66, 68, 83
    Pattern 8177 100
    Pattern 14185 183
    Pattern 15179 .... 66-68, 83, 294
    Pattern 15319 .... 258, 293
    Pattern 15320 .... 65, 123
    Pattern 15330 65
    Pattern E15179 66
Upper Deck 27
Val Saint-Lambert 39, 295
Vecchia Murano Glass Factory 264

Venetian (Duncan & Miller pattern) 74, 231
Verrerie de Meisenthal 282
Vertical Rib (Alley Agate pattern) 212
Vesta New York Central System 217
Victoria (National Silver Deposit Ware pattern) 49, 73
Victorian (Fostoria pattern) 173
Victory (Diamond pattern) 50, 92, 145
Viking Glass Company 18, 31, 40, 100, 183, 207, 288, 295
    Pattern 412-ISJ 207, 295
    Pattern 415 18
    Pattern 451 31
    Pattern 951-1S 295
    Pattern 970 18
    Pattern 974-1S 295
    Pattern 979 295
    Pattern 1600 100
    Pattern 1827 40
Vilcea, R. M. 166
Warwick (Heisey pattern) 25, 57, 235
West Virginia Glass Specialty Company......166, 200, 202-204, 239, 258-260, 280, 296
    Decoration 57 296
    Pattern 4 202-204
    Pattern 10 202-203
    Pattern 105 .... 258, 296
    Pattern 449 203
    Pattern 451 166
    Pattern 455/455 296
    Pattern 741 .... 203, 296
    Pattern 742 203
Western Maryland Railway 217
Westmoreland Glass Company 17-18, 35, 38, 40, 44, 291, 296
    Pattern 201 35
    Pattern 235 40
    Pattern 1013 44
    Pattern 1049 17-18
    Pattern 1211 44
    Pattern 1933 40
Westmoreland Specialty Company 296
Weston Glass Company 240, 280, 296
    Pattern 1818 240
Wheeling Decorating Company 12, 91, 204
    Etching D-2049 91
Wig Wam (Smith pattern) 64
Wind Mill (Hazel-Atlas pattern) 194, 198
Wohinc, Louie 280, 296
Wohlgemuth, Felix 268
Woolworth (F. W.) Company 54, 63, 81
Wotta Line (Paden City pattern) 61, 79, 128, 156
Wright (L. G.) Glass Company 37, 41, 296
    Pattern 22-15 41
Yesteryear (Viking pattern) 40
Zaricor (Central pattern) 15, 47

Schroeder's ANTIQUES Price Guide

OUR #1 BEST-SELLER!
FULL COLOR!

#1 BESTSELLING ANTIQUES PRICE GUIDE

≈ Almost 40,000 listings in hundreds of categories
≈ Histories and background information
≈ Both common and rare antiques featured

only **$19.95**
608 pages

COLLECTOR BOOKS
P.O. BOX 3009, Paducah KY, 42002-3009

1.800.626.5420

www.collectorbooks.com